BECOMING BETTER MUSLIMS

Princeton Studies in Muslim Politics
Dale F. Eickelman and Augustus Richard Norton,
Series Editors

Becoming Better Muslims

Religious Authority and Ethical Improvement in Aceh, Indonesia

David Kloos

PRINCETON UNIVERSITY PRESS
PRINCETON AND OXFORD

Published by Princeton University Press,
41 William Street, Princeton, New Jersey 08540

In the United Kingdom: Princeton University Press,
6 Oxford Street, Woodstock, Oxfordshire OX20 1TR

press.princeton.edu

Jacket images: 1) Sky background courtesy of Toshiyuki IMAI / Flickr. 2) Entrance
to mosque on the way to Tampeng, Indonesia © Nicole Segers.

Library of Congress Cataloging-in-Publication Data

Names: Kloos, David, author.
Title: Becoming better Muslims : religious authority and ethical improvement
in Aceh, Indonesia / David Kloos.
Description: Princeton, N.J. : Princeton University Press, 2017. | Series: Princeton
studies in Muslim politics | Includes bibliographical references and index.
Identifiers: LCCN 2017037074| ISBN 9780691176642 (hardback) |
ISBN 9780691176659 (paperback)
Subjects: LCSH: Islam—Indonesia—Nanggroe Aceh Darussalam. | Muslims—Indonesia—
Nanggroe Aceh Darussalam—Conduct of life. | Islamic ethics—Indonesia—Nanggroe Aceh
Darussalam. | Islamic law—Indonesia—Nanggroe Aceh Darussalam. | BISAC: SOCIAL SCIENCE /
Anthropology / Cultural. | SOCIAL SCIENCE / Islamic Studies. | SOCIAL SCIENCE /
Sociology of Religion. | RELIGION / Islam / Rituals & Practice. | PHILOSOPHY /
Ethics & Moral Philosophy. | HISTORY / Asia / Southeast Asia.
Classification: LCC BP63.I52 N365 2017 | DDC 297.09598/11—dc23 LC record available at
https://lccn.loc.gov/2017037074

British Library Cataloging-in-Publication Data is available

This book has been composed in Adobe Text Pro and Gotham.

Printed on acid-free paper. ∞

Printed in the United States of America

10 9 8 7 6 5 4 3 2 1

To my parents

CONTENTS

ILLUSTRATIONS

PREFACE AND ACKNOWLEDGMENTS

On December 26, 2004, a massive earthquake and resulting tidal wave, commonly referred to as the "Indian Ocean tsunami," annihilated large parts of the Indonesian province of Aceh, claiming an estimated 170,000 lives across the region. Two years later, I visited Aceh for the first time. It was a spontaneous visit. While I was aware of the fact that the Acehnese, facing "Mecca to the West" rather than "Jakarta to the East," had a reputation for being pious and rebellious, the trip was motivated by a more basic human interest. I was curious to see how people in Aceh had recovered from the tsunami. At the same time, important political developments were taking place. In August 2005, after thirty years of civil war between the separatist Free Aceh Movement (Gerakan Aceh Merdeka, GAM) and the Indonesian military, a peace treaty had been signed. During my visit, the province was preparing for the election of a new governor. Candidates included some former leaders of the (formally disbanded) GAM. It was a significant political experiment, and the campaign was well under way.

A minibus took me from Medan, along the North Coast of Sumatra, to the provincial capital Banda Aceh in roughly eight hours. There I met with two friends, foreigners like me, and Nurdin (not his real name), a shared Acehnese acquaintance and Banda Aceh resident. In the following days, Nurdin showed us around the city and its surroundings. We visited the old Dutch military cemetery—one of the physical reminders of anticolonial resistance—as well as a dusty Aceh Museum. Another historical site was the Gunongan, a sculptured mountain situated in what used to be the gardens of the royal palace, which revealed the blending of Muslim and Hindu-Buddhist symbols, a characteristic feature of many royal courts in early modern Southeast Asia. We visited Banda Aceh's primary landmark, the impressive and beautiful Masjid Raya (Great Mosque) Baiturrahman, which was built by the Dutch colonial government to make up for the destruction of the original mosque, and which has been expanded several times since.

We witnessed the effects of the tsunami. Two years after the disaster, the signs were still everywhere. A large part of the city, which lies stretched out on a lowland plain, had been swept away. In some areas, new neighborhoods had emerged, consisting of houses built by foreign nongovernmental organizations (NGOs). The landscape had changed. Large, formerly inhabited areas had been

FIGURE 1. "Kapal Apung," a floating electricity plant lifted by the tsunami and dropped down in the neighborhood of Punge Blang Cut, Banda Aceh (December 2006). Photo by the author.

transformed into swampy terrain full of debris. Other parts of the city were badly damaged. We visited mass graves, in which only a fraction of the victims lay buried, for most bodies were never found. We visited an enormous ship, a former floating electricity plant, which had been carried several kilometers inland and now stood in the center of a reconstructed neighborhood as an intrusive memorial (figure 1).

One day at noon, we stopped to eat lunch in a makeshift restaurant built of some wooden planks and boards, close to the coast. We were served by a middle-aged woman. She told us that most of her family, her husband and children included, had been swallowed by the waves. She was left alone and had been living in emergency barracks for more than a year. She asked us for help. Nurdin explained to her that, unfortunately, we were not "NGO people." I asked, "Are you not afraid, living so close to the coast?" She shrugged and said, "This is my village." I asked about the restaurant, and she explained that family members had helped her build it. She was thankful, to her family and to God. Her children were in heaven now, but God had decided that it was her task to live. "This is my fate," she said, "so I have to keep making an effort." However brief, I felt confronted in this chance encounter with something I would recognize later as the resilience of the Acehnese people. This woman was speaking defiantly of God and faith, while at the same time taking her fate into her own hands. Her words made a big impression on me, and this was the moment I decided that I would return to Aceh.

Back in the Netherlands, I began to study the literature on the region. I was struck by the fact that, although the Acehnese were known, stereotypically, as orthodox and conservative, there were few ethnographic studies of everyday religious practices and experiences. In contrast, the role of Islam in Acehnese politics and political history had been copiously considered. Moreover, I found troublesome the seemingly easy way in which both the scholarly and the popular literature conflated the Acehnese's religious identity and their region's violent past. There was a need, I decided, for a more grounded approach to Acehnese religiosity and the complex processes through which Islamic norms were being created, contested, and transformed. This book is the result of that decision.

I am deeply grateful to the communities that welcomed me into their midst, and to the individuals who shared their lives and experiences with me. Most of them I cannot mention by name. I hope that I have thanked them sufficiently in other ways. Darwis Soelaiman and Cut Mariani hosted me during my first period of fieldwork in 2008. The scholars attached to Pusat Kajian Pendidikan dan Masyarakat Aceh, Hasnul Arifin Melayu in particular, were very helpful as I set up my research. Erizar M. Zein, Suraiya Kamaruzzaman, and Rika Rahayu gave valuable advice during various stages of the project. Umi Rahimun and Azhar Muhtar graciously welcomed me into their school and their lives.

Muhajir al-Fairusy has been an extraordinary help and friend from the beginning of the project until the end. Our conversations have taught me a lot about Islam and about Aceh. "Nurdin" introduced me to his hometown, Banda Aceh, and stood by me ever since. For some reason, my host family in "Jurong" accepted me, without further ado, as a part of their household, making my stay in the village both pleasant and rewarding. In "Blang Daruet," my landlord and landlady and their neighbors acted as interlocutors, go-to-people for a range of practical issues, and warm hosts.

The research and writing of this book was supported by several institutions. The Faculty of Arts (presently the Faculty of Humanities) of the Vrije Universiteit Amsterdam (VU) funded the research. I am particularly thankful to Joris van Eijnatten, Marco Last, Diederik Oostdijk, and Digna van der Wouden for ensuring a pleasant work environment, and for securing additional funds. Local institutional support was kindly offered by the State Islamic Institute Ar-Raniry in Banda Aceh. I thank Hasbi Amiruddin, Syahrizal Abbas, and Yusny Saby, as well as their staff, for their assistance and advice. The former Aceh Research Training Institute, later merged into the International Centre of Aceh and Indian Ocean Studies, awarded me a travel fellowship and provided an academic community. Leena Avonius, Harold Crouch, Saiful Mahdi, Melizar, Teuku Murdani, Eve Warburton, and Laura Yoder are all gratefully acknowledged. The Islam Research Project, a cooperative venture between the Netherlands Ministry of Foreign Affairs and Leiden University, facilitated two additional field visits in 2012. I thank Marise van Amersfoort, Martin van Bruinessen, Léon Buskens, Kees van Dijk, Nico Kaptein, and my fellow researchers in Indonesia and the Netherlands for their role in this project.

Part of the book was written during a fellowship at the Department of Political and Social Change at the Australian National University, which was generously funded by the Australia-Netherlands Research Cooperation. I thank Edward Aspinall for supporting my application and for hosting me. A fellowship at the International Institute of Asian Studies in Leiden allowed me to continue my work on the book. The Royal Netherlands Institute of Southeast Asian and Caribbean Studies (Koninklijk Instituut voor Taal-, Land- en Volkenkunde, KITLV) granted me a position as a researcher. I thank the management, Rosemarijn Hoefte, Gert Oostindie, and Henk Schulte Nordholt, for giving me the time and the freedom to see the project to a conclusion, and the supporting staff, Christian Klein, Jeannette Poestkoke, Yayah Siegers, Ellen Sitinjak, and Vanessa Hage, for creating excellent work conditions.

This book would not have been possible without the knowledge, expertise, and assistance of the staff of the Royal Library in The Hague, the National Archive in The Hague, the National Archive in Jakarta, the Provincial Archive in Banda Aceh, and the former Library and Special Collections Department of KITLV. I joined KITLV at a difficult time, when the institute was forced, as a result of government cuts, to transfer its renowned collection to Leiden University Library. While the subsequent reinvention of the institute released new energy, I became very conscious in this period of the irreparable damage that had been done to the institute itself, to individual careers, and to the fields of Southeast Asian and Caribbean Studies in the Netherlands.

I am deeply indebted to my PhD advisers, Heather Sutherland and Henk Schulte Nordholt. They have played a crucial role both in the making of this book and in my personal development as a researcher. Heather and Henk introduced me to the field, stimulated me to explore, and helped me to negotiate the tension between scholarly ambition and getting things done. I hope that, in the future, I will be able to show the same kind of commitment to the work of my students.

My former colleagues at the VU and my present colleagues at KITLV are warmly acknowledged for countless inspiring meetings and conversations. Special thanks go to Susan Legêne and Pál Nyiri for their advice and support, and to Sadiah Boonstra, Matthias van Rossum, and Fenneke Sysling for their comradeship and humor. Beyond the walls of these institutions I have benefited enormously from my collaborations with Daan Beekers, Michael Feener, and Annemarie Samuels. I thank all three of them for the important role they have played in sharpening my thinking. Our joint projects are echoed clearly in the central argument of this book. Michael Peletz and Robert Hefner were extremely generous with their advice as I went about preparing the manuscript for publication.

I thank my colleagues around the world. In Jakarta, Ward Berenschot and Suzanne Kroger gave me a place to stay and an opportunity for sharing thoughts and observations. The same goes for Dominic Berger, whose path crossed mine in Penang, Aceh, Canberra, Jakarta, and Kuala Lumpur, and who became a great friend along the way. Agus Wandi let me and my wife stay in his house in Banda Aceh during short visits in 2012. Kathryn Robinson was the driving force behind (and drew my attention to) the digitized field notes of the late Chandra Jayawardena, which proved to be an enormously valuable resource. In addition, this book has benefited from my conversations with, and comments and suggestions provided by, Ahmad Nuril Huda, Michelle Ahmad, Edward Aspinall, Bart Barendregt, the late Gerd Baumann, John Bowen, Robert Cribb, Petra van Dam, Michele Ford, Chiara Formichi, Jesse Grayman, Bram Hendrawan, James Hoesterey, Virginia Hooker, Stijn van Huis, Reza Idria, Irwan Abdullah, Peter Keppy, John Klein Nagelvoort, Gerry van Klinken, Jeroen de Kloet, Martijn de Koning, Mahmood Kooria, Mirjam Künkler, Michael Laffan, Amrita Malhi, Maaike Matelski, Marcus Mietzner, Julian Millie, Willem van der Molen, Moch Nur Ichwan, Mattijs van de Port, Anthony Reid, Kathryn Robinson, Arskal Salim, Samuli Schielke, Sehat Ihsan Shadiqin, Catherine Smith, Eka Srimulyani, Gunnar Stange, Fridus Steijlen, Carolien Stolte, Anton Stolwijk, Andrew Walker, and the audiences of numerous research seminars.

Freek Colombijn, Susan Legêne, Pál Nyiri, Michael Peletz, Patricia Spyer, and Thijl Sunier sat on my defense committee. I thank them for their careful reading and sharp questions. Daan Beekers, Daniel Birchok, Marieke Bloembergen, Sadiah Boonstra, Martin van Bruinessen, Greg Fealy, Michael Feener, Joshua Gedacht, Tom Hoogervorst, and Jessica Roitman all read and commented on draft chapters or parts of the manuscript. Henk Schulte Nordholt, Annemarie Samuels, and two anonymous reviewers read the entire manuscript and gave generous and perspicacious comments. Their efforts have resulted in a much better book. Annemarie shares my fascination for Aceh. No one has read and commented on more drafts and half-finished texts than she has. What started out as a useful exchange of ideas and information developed, in the course of years, into a precious friendship. For this, I feel very grateful.

At Princeton University Press, I thank my editor, Fred Appel, and the series editors, Richard Norton and Dale Eickelman, for their trust in the book. Natalie Baan, Thalia Leaf, Theresa Liu, and Stephanie Rojas guided me through the publication process. I am very grateful, finally, to Natalie Baan and Terry Kornak for their thorough copy-editing of the manuscript. Part of the material in chapter 5 has previously appeared in "Sinning and Ethical Improvement in

Contemporary Aceh," in *Islam and the Limits of the State: Reconfigurations of Practice, Community and Authority in Contemporary Aceh*, edited by R. Michael Feener, David Kloos, and Annemarie Samuels, 56–86 (Leiden: Brill, 2015). I thank the publisher for the permission to use this copyrighted material. The map of Aceh printed here was redrawn by the PUP art department, based on the work of Jaap Fokkema of the Vrije Universiteit Amsterdam. Leiden University Library and John Klein Nagelvoort are gratefully acknowledged for their kind permission to use an image from their collections.

My family and friends are my foundation. I thank my sister and brothers, Esther, Bart, Maurik, Tijmen, and Jonatan, as well as my father-in-law, Hans, and my late mother-in-law, Els, for their support throughout the years. Els witnessed the beginning of this project but not the end. I wish she could have been here with us to see the final result. I thank my parents, Joke and Peter, for their unconditional love and trust. This book will always remind me of my mother's visit to the field, her sharp observations, and our conversations as we camped under the stars in the jungle. My father passed away several years ago, and I can only imagine what a joy it would have been to talk to him about this book and about my gradual entry into anthropology, as father and son, and as scholars. This book is dedicated to them.

This is a study of life trajectories and personal development. Eliza went to Indonesia with me and came to know the country in her own way, dealing with dusty manuscripts and old men adorned with sarongs and ceremonial daggers. She enriches my life, and this book, with her wisdom and love. Vera and Oscar, *cahaya mata kami*, lights of our eyes, remind us every day of the challenges and beauty of growing up.

NOTE ON SPELLING, TRANSLITERATION, AND ITALICIZATION

This book frequently refers to Indonesian words and terms, which I have spelled according to standard Indonesian orthography (see *Kamus Besar Bahasa Indonesia*; http://kbbi.web.id). This includes a substantial number of words and terms that are derived from the Arabic language. In some cases I have decided to privilege a more commonly used transliteration of the Arabic over the standard Indonesian (e.g., *hadith* instead of *hadis*; *fiqh* instead of *fikih*). I have not used diacritics and other symbols, with the exception of the Arabic letters ʿ*ayn* (as in shariʿa) and—when occurring in word-medial position—*hamzah* (as in Qur'an). All non-English terms are italicized, with the exception of some terms that occur (relatively) frequently in the English language (such as shariʿa and ulama).

MAP OF ACEH

Sabang
KOTA SABANG
Strait of Malacca
KOTA BANDA ACEH
Banda Aceh
Sibreh
Indrapuri
Seulimeum
Sigli
ACEH BESAR
Jantho
Meureudu
Tiro
PIDIE JAYA
Samalanga
Bireuen
Lhokseumawe
PIDIE
BIREUEN
KOTA LHOKSEUMAWE
Lhoksukon
ACEH UTARA
Idi Rayeuk
ACEH JAYA
BENER MERIAH
Simpang Tiga Redelong
ACEH TIMUR
Calang
Takengon
ACEH BARAT
ACEH TENGAH
KOTA LANGSA
Langsa
NAGAN RAYA
ACEH TAMIANG
Karang Baru
Meulaboh
Suka Makmue
Blang Kejeren
GAYO LUES
ACEH BARAT DAYA
Blangpidie
INDIAN OCEAN
Lubuhan Haji
Kutacane
ACEH TENGGARA
Tapak Tuan
ACEH SELATAN
SIMEULUE
KOTA SUBULUSSALAM
Sinabang
ACEH SINGKIL
Singkil
ACEH SINGKIL

INDONESIA
Aceh

N
W E
S

0   25   50   75   100 km
0   20   40   60 miles

BECOMING BETTER MUSLIMS

Introduction

INNER ISLAM AND THE PROBLEM
OF ACEHNESE EXCEPTIONALISM

People in Aceh are often uncertain of how to be, or become, good Muslims. Developing a concept of religious agency, this book analyzes how Acehnese Muslims have interacted, on an everyday basis, with the universalizing norms and structural constraints posited by the state and organized religion. As such, it counters a common view that has conflated Acehnese religiosity with an essentialized image of piety and fanaticism. At the same time, the case of Aceh serves to address an urgent and more general problem. During the twentieth and early twenty-first centuries, state and religious authorities throughout the world increased their influence on the religious lives of local communities and individual Muslims. This book examines how ordinary Muslims have dealt with this development. It argues that individual believers exercise considerable agency as they navigate, negotiate, and (re-)appropriate official religious norms. This agency, I contend, is not external to religion. It is a *religious* agency, contingent on the continuous interaction between ordinary Muslims and the forces of normative Islam, and grounded in a widely shared conception of religious life as a conscious, reflective, and highly personal project of ethical improvement.

Drawing on a combination of historical and ethnographic research, this book analyzes the dynamic and shifting interactions among state actors, religious authorities, and ordinary Muslims. To this end, it discusses a range of different, concrete case studies, processes, and situations, bearing on issues such as the gradual interference of the colonial and postcolonial

1

state in religious practices, rituals, and sites; changing relations between local communities and religious institutions; village conflicts and perceived crises of moral authority; shifting commitments to community and family; processes of religious revitalization in the wake of civil war and natural disaster; changing religious routines and practices; and extended trajectories of individual religiosity. What follows, then, is both a detailed analysis of Acehnese religious life and an investigation of the salience in today's world of personal processes of ethical formation.

My argument resonates with a broader trend in the anthropology of Islam that has emphasized personal piety and religious experience. However, in contrast to the recent academic (and political) interest in religious movements and organizations, I am not concerned primarily with pursuits of pious perfection, or modes of self-discipline associated with Islamic activism and the contemporary resurgence of political Islam. Doubt, ambivalence, indifference, and self-perceived religious negligence, I contend, are equally and inextricably part of ethical formation. People in Aceh consciously reflect and act on these perceptions of failure and imperfection as they link them to, and interpret them in conjunction with their lives' unfolding. Indeed, I argue that it is the very sense of a life trajectory, one that consists of a past, a present, and a future, that makes perceptions of failure ethically productive rather than devastating. A central theme, then, concerns the ways in which experiences of age; generation; life phase and life stage transition; and closely related concepts of moral responsibility, disappointment, and intention feed into the making of religious subjectivities.

A Narrative of Violence and Piety

In most constructions of Acehnese ethnic identity, Islam takes center stage. It is commonly considered that to be Acehnese, apart from speaking any dialect of the Acehnese language, following local customs (*adat*), and identifying with the Acehnese past, means to be Muslim. Indeed, the Acehnese are known as a pious people, who famously refer to their homeland as the "Veranda of Mecca" (*Serambi Mekkah*). The latter notion also has another, more political meaning, however. Firmly attached to the claim that Aceh upholds a special relationship with the Islamic heartland is the (politically malleable) assertion that Acehnese Muslims, by simple virtue of being Acehnese Muslims, have a particular responsibility to advance their religion and to engage in "proper" Muslim conduct.

Much has been written about political Islam and religious disciplining in Aceh, from the establishment of religious courts by the pre- and early modern sultanate state to the implementation of Islamic law today (Aspinall 2009; Feener 2013; Hadi 2004; Ito 1984; Lindsey et al. 2007; Lombard 1967;

McGibbon 2006; Miller and Feener 2012; Nur Ichwan 2007, 2011; Riddell 2006; Sjamsuddin 1985; van Dijk 1981). These studies, while analyzing important aspects of Aceh's history and society, have also contributed to the stereotype of Acehnese specialness and pious self-awareness. Relatively little is known, in contrast, about the question of how "ordinary" Acehnese Muslims, without much power, influence, or advanced religious knowledge (Peletz 1997), have shaped and adjusted their own behavior in relation to these processes. How do ordinary Acehnese shape and experience their daily lives? What old or newly formed religious routines and practices do they engage in? How do they deal with the increasing range and intensity of moral admonitions, purist pressures, and knowledge regimes advanced by the state, religious authorities, and other public actors? Formulating an answer to these questions is the main goal of this book.

The idea that the Acehnese are an exceptionally pious people is partly rooted in the contention that Pasai (near present-day Lhokseumawe, on the North Coast) was the first kingdom in the archipelago to convert to Islam. In the sixteenth century, the Sultanate of Aceh incorporated Pasai, as well as a number of other ports in the Strait of Malacca, after which it developed into the most powerful kingdom in the western part of the Malay world. The epitome of this power was the legendary Sultan Iskandar Muda (r. 1607–37). His rule is remembered as Aceh's "golden age" (*zaman mas*), a time in which the kingdom was powerful and Islamic law was properly enforced.[1] The image of a long-standing piety is further fueled by the memory of the colonial period (1873–1942). The armed struggle against the Dutch was led by ulama—religious teachers—and perceived by Acehnese fighters as a "holy war" (*perang sabil*).[2] A war literature emerged, which presented the resistance as a religious duty. In the eyes of colonial administrators, such expressions attested to the Acehnese's deeply rooted religious fanaticism.

In 1945, Aceh became a province of the newly independent Indonesian nation. While the idea of Indonesia was embraced by a majority of Acehnese, the first governor of Aceh, the reformist Islamic teacher and activist Teungku Daud Beureueh, was straightforward about his aspiration to create an Islamic polity. His government prepared for the establishment of a system of Islamic courts (Mahkamah Syariah), to be placed under the control of religious scholars and to function autonomously from the central government. This move was contested, however, and ultimately the attempt to transform the political and legal system failed, partly because of a lack of support from conservative Islamic leaders. Disappointment among reformist ulama, together with a range of social and economic factors, culminated in 1953 in the outbreak of an armed rebellion under the banner of Darul Islam (The Abode of Islam). The goal of this revolt, which had started in West Java in 1949, was to establish an "Islamic State of Indonesia" (Negara Islam Indonesia, NII). In Aceh, the conflict ended in 1962, when the central government granted the Acehnese provincial government special autonomy in the domains of religion, education, and local customs.

The promise of autonomy remained unfulfilled. Under President Suharto's dictatorial "New Order" regime (1965–98), power was concentrated in Jakarta. When, in the early 1970s, enormous reserves of oil and natural gas were discovered near the city of Lhokseumawe (North Aceh), Jakarta's policy of appropriating local resources sowed the seeds for a new conflict. In 1976, Hasan di Tiro, a former Darul Islam supporter and the grandson of a famous Islamic scholar and leader in the war against the Dutch, founded Gerakan Aceh Merdeka (GAM). Although GAM came forth, at least partly, from Darul Islam, this was a very different kind of revolt. Its leaders did not aspire to make the Indonesian state more Islamic. Instead, they developed a secular, ethno-nationalist discourse, aimed at separating Aceh from Indonesia altogether and at restoring the region's precolonial status as an independent polity. The conflict caused massive disruptions, particularly in the 1990s and early 2000s, claiming twelve to twenty thousand lives, perhaps even more (Aspinall 2009, 2).

During the conflict, the Indonesian government and military actively cultivated the stereotype of Acehnese religious fanaticism in order to frame the rebellion as being "Islamic" in character, a rather skewed image that echoes in some scholarly works as well (see, e.g., Geertz 2004, 579; Vickers 2005, 179–80; Voll 1994, 344). In 1999, one year after the collapse of the New Order, Aceh was allowed by the central government to implement a regional formulation of shari'a (a term that literally means "the way" or "the path," but is often translated as "Islamic law"). This initiative was part of a new autonomy package meant to take away some of the long-standing grievances against the state, to diminish the rebellion's popular support, and, ultimately, to end the conflict. It was rejected by the leaders of GAM, who saw in Jakarta's turn to Islam a move to deflect attention from the roots of the conflict and delegitimize the separatists in the eyes of the Acehnese people and international actors.

The establishment of a shari'a legal system was initiated in 2002–2003, when Governor Abdullah Puteh issued a series of bylaws (qanun) regulating creed (aqida), worship (ibadah), and religious symbolism (syiar), as well as the criminal persecution of individuals engaging in the use of intoxicants (khamr), gambling (maisir), and illicit relations between men and women (khalwat). A new set of institutions, including a shari'a police force (Wilayatul Hisbah, WH), was created to enforce and socialize these regulations. After the December 2004 tsunami had ravaged Banda Aceh and the Acehnese West Coast, large numbers of humanitarian workers flocked into the province. They acted as informal observers of the conflict. In August 2005, a peace agreement was signed. GAM was disarmed and turned into a political party, the "Aceh Party" (Partai Aceh, PA), which has been in power at the provincial level and in most districts ever since. The stance of PA toward the implementation of shari'a has been ambiguous. While some of Aceh's new leaders became vocal advocates of the new laws, others made clear that they prioritized different issues.

Unsurprisingly, perhaps, given these developments, the dominant narrative of Acehnese history and society merges together a strong regional attachment, a fraught relationship with Jakarta, a perceived primacy of Islamic law, and a pious outlook that sets the Acehnese apart from other peoples in Indonesia. Besides being prevalent in written work and everyday speech, these stereotypes inform the ways in which the people of Aceh and Acehnese culture are represented in books, films, street names, and tourist attractions (see Drexler 2008, 49–67). This narrative is problematic. In most studies of Aceh, Islam is presented as a factor of change only when it reveals itself as an ideology that legitimizes political action (see, e.g., Aspinall 2009; Kell 1995; McGibbon 2006; Morris 1983; Reid 1979, 2006a; G. Robinson 1998; Sjamsuddin 1985; Sulaiman 1997; van Dijk 1981). The consequence is a conflation of Islam and violence, based on a dubious connection between Aceh's reputation as a place from which the Islamic faith spread into Southeast Asia and its history of struggle. At the same time, the self-explanatory status of Acehnese piety has rendered the study of the region almost immune to the analysis of deep social and religious change, including, ironically, the increasing prominence of Islam in the public sphere, the increasing pervasiveness of formalized Islamic authority, and the impact of these developments on everyday lives.

The people I came to know during my research were generally not fanatical, rebellious, inflexible, or dogmatic. They did, however, take their faith seriously and often wished or hoped for others to do the same. I was surprised, moreover, by the confidence, patience, and eloquence of many of my interlocutors, as they explained to me that faith (*iman*) and worship (*ibadah*) should be understood not as a given, but instead as a lifelong process, part of a personal project of ethical improvement. This book conceives of this mentality as a particular ethical mode, which is based on a habit of continuous, critical reflection on morally defined choices, decisions, and dilemmas, and that indicates, in turn, a particular form of agency (defined as a "socio-culturally mediated capacity to act"; Ahearn 2001, 112). This religious agency, and the dynamic interactions through which it is shaped, is the central focus of this study.

To take religious agency seriously entails a nuanced approach that places Islam in the context of multiple moral-intellectual frameworks, or to borrow from Alasdair MacIntyre (1988), multiple "traditions of moral inquiry." It entails focusing less on the question of what shape, or shapes, Islam takes in any given place (radical, moderate, scripturalist, mystical, syncretistic), and more on the question of how people of different backgrounds try to make the best of their lives while they ask themselves, simultaneously, "How can I be, or become, a good human being?" (Schielke 2009a, 165). It entails, as Magnus Marsden has argued in his work on lived Islam in Pakistan, posing the question of how ordinary Muslims actively engage with the forces of normative Islam (including the pressures of globally salient Islamist movements and their call for religious purification), and how they "think, reflect, and debate the circumstances of the world around them, and make active and varying decisions about what kind of Muslim life to lead" (M. Marsden 2005, 10). This book shows how people in Aceh, over a very long period of time, have learned to be conscious of, and articulate about, their existence as individual Muslims living in a world of moral uncertainty, ambiguity, contradiction, and doubt. Their religious agency should be seen as neither isolated from, nor a form of resistance against, state and religious authorities. Instead, it is the product of dynamic interactions, contingent on the contested meaning of Aceh as a social and geographic space and the place of Islam in historically shaped political visions.

There is, as the case of Aceh shows, a paradoxical side to the rise of normative Islam. While the prescription of "correct" Islamic behavior places particular constraints on the lives of Muslims, the establishment of official norms is, at the same time, perceived by many ordinary believers as enabling in nature because it entails and invites conscious reflection on their own religious lives. By encouraging and forcing individuals to engage consciously, probingly, and reflexively with their own faith, the forces of normative Islam produce space for action as much as they restrict individuals in their personal and collective moral endeavors. As I demonstrate in the chapters to follow, people in Aceh are deeply aware of this tension. The next section elaborates my approach and the contribution of my argument to the history and anthropology of Islam more broadly.

Religious Agency and Ethical Improvement: An Interactive Approach

The state and organized religion are comparable forces in the sense that they constitute relatively coherent (albeit changing) sets of norms and values, relatively coherent sets of standardizing institutions, and distinct hierarchies and networks of individuals. They have also become increasingly intertwined as the modern state has tried to regulate religion while religious actors, in turn, have sought to Islamize the state. Individuals, meanwhile, exert religious agency as they negotiate, select, reject, ignore, redefine, or appropriate these norms to address their own particular goals and desires. This dynamic, tripartite relationship is at the core of this book. I start this section, therefore, by briefly explaining my approach to the concepts of state, religious authority, and the individual.

The state is regarded in this study both as an actor (or a set of actors) and as an arena of contestations (see Barker and van Klinken 2009; Feener, Kloos, and Samuels 2015). The state seeks (among its other roles) to enforce norms. At the same time, groups or individuals address or solicit the state to a variety of ends. Using the state may mean deploying laws or institutions (for example, to coerce people into changing their behavior or to gain access to particular resources) or a particular language or idiom (for example, about the "correct" interpretation of Islam) to realize strategic positions; to mobilize, persuade, or intimidate; or to provide a person or institution with legitimacy. A similar view applies, albeit in a somewhat different way, to religious institutions. While religious experts may use their authority to formulate or prescribe religious norms, the social, political, and pedagogical spaces over which they preside constitute important sites of negotiation and moral contestation. With regard to the historical, sociological, and philosophical qualities of the individual and the "self," finally, I follow Charles Taylor's (1989) thesis that questions of identity cannot be viewed separately from the historical formation of moral subjectivity, and that the remaking of both "self" and "morality" is a key trait of what we call modernity. I agree, in addition, with Craig Calhoun (1991), who argues that, although Taylor's work is based primarily on the ideas of "Great Men," his discursive approach of viewing the self as a moral subject offers a particularly good starting point for enriching our understanding of identity and agency.

In reality, of course, there is a continuous overlap between these different spheres. Lay Muslims may, at any point in their lives, be regarded by their peers as religious authorities. Ulama may become agents of the state. And agents of the state are always also individuals, that is, moral beings who, like everyone else, reflect (often or occasionally) on their "moral selves." My main interest, then, lies not so much in these spheres as such but in the interactions that define their relationships. Religious norms are altered under the influence of shifting political and economic configurations, new religious ideas, and changing physical environments or technological circumstances. This process is accelerated or enforced through violence or coercion (or the threat of such) but more often by law. This relates to the role of the ulama as legal experts but also to that of the state, which, contrary to the Weberian idea regarding its monopoly on violence, derives its power primarily from the administration of law (Cribb 2011, 31). Just like state and religious authorities, ordinary Muslims respond to changing circumstances. Their responses involve a complex of choices and strategies; social, political, and intellectual engagements; and emotions. Let me proceed by working out, in a more concrete form, the nature and implications of these interactions.

As Islam lacks a strong institutional framework for centralizing authority, this study concentrates on the role of religious scholars as the main bearers of normative traditions (Zaman 2002). In the premodern period, the ulama acquired near total control over the canonization and distribution of religious texts, creating "a growing uniformity of Islamic belief and practice throughout the vast area in which Muslims lived" (Bulliet 1994, 21). At the same time, the question of religious authority was always also a question of political authority.

Western imperialism was a particularly challenging condition. Around the turn of the twentieth century, reform-minded ulama throughout the world urged Muslims to modernize themselves, their institutions, and their societies by enhancing their mastery over both secular knowledge (such as natural sciences or language) and religious knowledge, calling for educational institutions to be equipped to offer both. Particularly salient for these reformists was the perceived neglect of the law of God and the perception that Islamic societies indulged in superstitions and detrimental "innovations" (*bidah*), such as the mystical ideas and practices that implied the possibility of intercession by the deceased between humans and God.[3]

Religious standardization was seen by Islamic reformists as a key element of the advent of a global modernity.[4] The role of an increasingly centralized, uniform, and bureaucratic state was, in this respect, regarded as equally crucial (Bayly 2004, 336–43). In fact, the important shift was not the call for standardization as such, for Islam had been going through a process of homogenization for a much longer period, but the conviction, held by reformist ulama and state agents alike, that religious education should be regarded as an instrument of change (Berkey 2007, 41–49). Through the politics of education, Islam was "objectified" (Eickelman and Piscatori 1996, 37–45), a process defined by Gregory Starrett (1998, 89) as "the growing consciousness on the part of Muslims that Islam is a coherent system of practices and beliefs, rather than merely an unexamined and unexaminable way of life." Modern states, by privileging standardized systems of religious or secular education over traditional forms of religious learning, accelerated rather than curbed this process.

The reformist movements that emerged around the turn of the twentieth century are often regarded as the root of many contemporary Islamist organizations (see, e.g., Bubalo and Fealy 2005). It is important, however, not to reduce the spirit of reform to political expressions alone and to consider in conjunction changing ideas about the Muslim "self." Concepts of self and individuality are historically contingent and interlinked with religious change (Shulman and Stroumsa 2002). In Islam, mystical concepts and practices in particular have served to investigate inner selves and the relationship between individual Muslims and God (Sviri 2002). The reformist challenge of particular mystical texts and practices involved—besides the struggle over correct interpretations—a fundamental debate about, and reconfiguration of, the Muslim subject. Francis Robinson (1997, 2004, 2008), in his writings on South Asia, argues that the political domination of the Muslim world by non-Muslim forces led to a period of deep reflection among scholars and intellectuals about the meaning of their faith and their place as Muslims in the world at large. As a result, the nineteenth and twentieth centuries were marked not only by political upheavals, but also by an "inward turn," contingent on a fundamental shift from an "other-worldly" to a "this-worldly" piety. "While in the past, the reflective believer, the mystic, might have meditated on the signs of God, the new type of reflective believer reflected on the self and the shortcomings of the self. Now the inner landscape became a crucial site where the battle of the pious for the good took place" (F. Robinson 2008, 273). At the same time, the followers of mystical traditions reinvented themselves and their organizations, in Indonesia and Aceh as much as in other places (Birchok 2015; Hoesterey 2015; Howell 2010; Nur Ichwan 2015; Soeyatno 1977; van Bruinessen and Howell 2007).

Reformist movements—while inspiring the "inward turn"—have incited new discourses of discipline and constraint, often (but not always) by advancing the need to adhere to shari'a. They have done so in distinct manners. In Indonesia, Muhammadiyah has approached the need to reform Muslim societies by emphasizing (among other things) the "public interest" (*maslahah*) vested in the ability of individual Muslims to interpret the Qur'an and the Sunna. Other groups have emphasized, rather, the primacy of Islamic law over human reason (see, e.g., Khoiruddin Nasution 1996). In Southeast Asia, these competing discourses have been adopted in various ways by the secular state (Bowen 2003; Feener 2007, 2013; Liow 2009; Nurlaelawati 2010; Peletz 2002; Salim 2008; Salim and Azra 2003). There is a marked continuity, nonetheless, in the way in which states, from the colonial era up to the present, have come to regard religion as an ordering principle—that is, as a system organizing "the population into manageable and mobilizable units" (Spyer 1996, 192).

Although these observations help us understand how states function and affect human lives, it is important to note that state power (whether discursive, legal, or physical) is never all pervasive (Barker and van Klinken 2009). Refraining from reducing the analysis to the management of Islam by the state alone, in this book I ask how individual Muslims have tried and succeeded in setting limits to this process, either by resisting it or by becoming part of it. In my view, this requires placing the relations among the state, religious authority, and individual agency, explicitly and consistently, within the contours of practice theory.

Islam, I believe, needs to be studied less as a fixed set of ideas and practices and more as a historically contingent process, driven by historically shaped interactions and shifting conceptions of the self. I am inspired, in this regard, by Joel Robbins's (2004) call, based on his work on Christianity in Papua New Guinea, to combine historical and anthropological methods in order to understand the complex relationship between changing religious ideas and sociopolitical configurations on the one hand, and the shaping of inner religious lives on the other. More generally, I build on what Sherry Ortner (2006, 9) called the historic turn in practice theory, or the observation (based on the work of Pierre Bourdieu and Marshall Sahlins) that "the playing out of the effects of culturally organized practices is essentially processual and often very slow." More specifically, I follow Fredrik Barth (1993, 173), who argued that, to discover patterns of action, it is necessary to "unravel whatever connections and constraints direct the interpretations people make [of events], and thereby give shape to the lives and meanings we are trying to understand." This book takes Barth's (1993, 159) conception of an intermediary realm of conscious and reflexive action, located between particular premises (or one's "cultural stock," including knowledge, concepts, values, and concerns) and routinized behavior, as a point of departure. Moving beyond Barth, however, I see this realm of action as a space of contestations, revealing itself both through the controlling mechanisms of state and religious authorities and through the intentions, interpretations, and expressions of individuals.

Ordinary Ethics, Moral Failure, and the Sense of a Life Unfolding

In his view of orthodoxy, and his influential call to view religion as a "discursive tradition," Talal Asad (1986) placed the study of religious practice squarely in the domain of power. In my view, this approach holds a risk of overemphasizing practices of (bodily) discipline. I am sympathetic, therefore, to Michael Lambek's (2000, 312–13) argument that the anthropology of religion cannot simply "rest with power." As a source and motivation for the shaping of social relations, morality, as the "striving for human good," represents a "significant third domain alongside power and desire." These domains are inextricably connected, but not mutually reducible. They may be, to some extent at least, analytically separated. I find useful in particular Lambek's (2000, 309) contention that morality implies agency, for "contemporary discussions remain merely cynical if they do not delineate the capacity and means for virtuous action as well as the limitations placed upon it." By this I do not mean to say that power relations are somehow less relevant when it comes to studying religious practices and the formation of religious norms. The relationships at the center of this book are almost always also relationships of power, and the historical and ethnographic material presented in the text that follows contains several examples of the ways in which power works to expand or contract religious agency.

At a more general level, my approach to the concept of ethics draws from Lambek's (2010b, 1, 10) later work on "ordinary ethics," which perceives the ethical as both a fundamental "part of the human condition" and a "modality of social action or of being in the world" (see also Das 2012; Lambek 2015). I focus on the second part of this definition. According to Lambek, (ethical) practice must not be conflated with (ethical) action. Whereas practice refers to an ongoing (though continuously changing) process, acts are necessarily "singular" and "irreversible" instances. Acts are performative. They build on "practical judgment" and, as such, "percolate from or disrupt the stream of practice" (Lambek 2010b, 19). I take inspiration from Lambek's argument that ethical judgment can be a source of individual agency, while it is always also based—one way or the other—on the application of particular "shared criteria." This book is a study of the everyday interactions between, on the one hand, the normative forces that claim the authority to formulate criteria for judging "good" and "bad" behavior (and everything in between) and, on the other hand, the individual agency of ordinary Muslims as they act on, respond to, and adapt the religious norms that are based on these criteria.

As I will explain, moreover, in relation to my conceptualization of religious agency, it makes sense to speak not so much of action generally but rather of a particular mode of ethical action, one that is both conscious and reflexive in nature. As Jarrett Zigon (2008) has argued, morality may be viewed as a largely unconscious, habitual domain. Thus he makes an analytical distinction between morality, as denoting a combination of different social-intellectual "spheres," and ethics, as denoting the reflexive acts through which people "*consciously* work on themselves" and cultivate the capacity to be moral beings (Zigon 2008, 43; italics in the original). This book builds on Zigon's work as it investigates the contexts in which ethical reflection takes place and the consequences these reflective engagements have for the religious lives of individuals and the communities of which they are part (see, in particular, Zigon 2009a, b). It analyzes the interactions, processes, and relations through which ordinary Muslims consider, actively and creatively, their social environments and the development of their moral selves. Most importantly, it argues that it is a conscious, reflexive ethical mode that allows individual believers to frame their religious practices and experiences in terms of a personal process of ethical improvement and, on this basis, to engage actively and effectively with the religious norms established by state and religious authorities.

This book is not intended to offer yet another theory of what an "anthropology of ethics" should look like (see, e.g., Faubion 2011; Keane 2015; Laidlaw 2014; Lambek 2010a, 2015; Zigon 2008). It does, however, take a position in a more specific debate about ethics that has arisen, in recent years, within the anthropology of Islam. My observations in Aceh echo a general trend to study personal piety and religious experiences as a mode of agency. Employing an Asadian framework, which views practices of (self-)discipline as a defining aspect of the formation of religious subjects (Asad 1993), scholars such as Lara Deeb (2006), Charles Hirschkind (2006), Humeira Iqtidar (2011), and Saba Mahmood (2005) have foregrounded pious practices and Islamic "revivalist" organizations and lifestyles as a locus of agency. In recent years, this body of literature has become the subject of critical scrutiny. The emphasis placed on pursuits of pious perfection, it has been argued, wrongly assumes that ethical formation is a coherent and straightforward process. Instead, scholars such as Magnus Marsden (2005), Samuli Schielke (2010, 2015), and Gregory Simon (2014) have highlighted the ambivalent and unpredictable ways in which ordinary Muslims navigate between religious considerations, on the one hand, and nonreligious concerns, aspirations, and passions, on the other.

Although I share this critical view, I oppose the implicit suggestion that "everyday life" or "lived Islam," including all possible or associated ambivalences, contradictions, and inconsistencies, precludes a steady and cumulative religious engagement (cf. Fadil and Fernando 2015). One of the main problems is that terms such as tension, contradiction, or moral ambivalence—and, at the level of the individual, the "incoherent" nature of religious selves—have come to function, increasingly, as a kind of final statement when it comes to analyzing the nature of contemporary religion. For example, according to Simon (2014, 15), it is "through grappling with and reflectively attempting to manage tensions—and not simply within the singular lines of discursive logic—that Islamic subjectivity, or moral subjectivity of any kind, emerges in people's lives." The moral subjectivities of Egyptian Muslims, writes Samuli Schielke (2015, 23), are contingent on the contradictions and ambivalences caused by the "perfectionist premises" of normative Islam, romantic love, and economic gain, each contributing to the experience of "a life in the future tense where the state that one has reached is never sufficient, where one must always reach for more than one has, a sensibility that is essentially dependent on its being dynamic and growing." I agree that processes of ethical formation are essentially contingent, fragmented, personal, future-oriented, and inter-subjectively constituted. I take issue, however, with the analytical bromide of "unstable selves" (Marsden and Retsikas 2013b, 8) locked in or struck by a condition of insoluble moral tensions and unattainable futures. What I found most striking about the narratives of my interlocutors in Aceh is that, although they were often uncertain, doubtful, or—indeed—ambivalent about the best way to meet a variety of moral and social demands, they also framed their religious lives in terms of a progressive effort, rocky and unpredictable, but seldom in a deadlock.

An important way forward, I propose, is to recognize perceptions of moral failure as a central aspect of ethical formation. As Daan Beekers and I argue in more detail in the introduction of a volume on senses of failure and ethical formation in lived Islam and Christianity (Kloos and Beekers 2018), the tensions between religious and nonreligious concerns, or between pursuits of pious perfection and the ambivalences of everyday life, can best be approached as a dialectic. By this, we mean the possibility that the struggles inherent in everyday life contribute in productive ways to processes of ethical formation. The perceptions of moral failure inherent in these tensions are, in many cases, consciously acted on by individual believers and, as such, can play a central role in these individuals' attempts to become "good" or "better" Muslims and

Christians. A comprehensive approach toward the religious subject should therefore include both questions about religious commitment and related notions of piety, success, social mobility, transformation, and progress, and questions about its drawbacks, including feelings of shortcoming and stagnation, doubt, religious negligence and sinfulness, and concomitant experiences of stress and disillusion.

Emerging from the ethnography presented in this book is a strong conjunction among failure, ordinary ethics, and life phase. As I will show, the possibility that things might change—even if this is not clearly evident in, or indicated by, the present—can be perceived of as constitutive (and thus not merely a result) of the development of inner religiosities. For my interlocutors in Aceh, perceptions of moral failure depended on "objectified" norms, but also, crucially and simultaneously, on a widely shared conviction that the process of becoming a better Muslim is lifelong, often unpredictable, and full of obstacles and challenges. This conviction turns the sense of a "life long lived"—the awareness that one has (already) changed and that future change is not only possible but also desirable or necessary—into a moral faculty. By focusing on life phase, I do not mean to argue that particular forms and articulations of moral failure—religious negligence, sinning, sudden or prolonged lapses in religious commitment or certainty—are deemed more "acceptable" for people of a particular age or social status (young, old, newlywed, widowed, community leader, socially marginalized figure, and so forth), even if this is also, to some extent at least, the case (cf. Debevec 2012). Rather, my ethnographic material reveals the salience of a specific and widely shared reflexive ethical mode, one that is tied to the sense of a developing life, and that enabled my interlocutors to see their moral shortcomings, under certain conditions, as conducive rather than detrimental to their personal religious development. These connections among failure, life phase, and ethical formation have received very little attention in the anthropology of Islam and religious ethics more generally (cf. Kloos 2018). Explored throughout this book, they inform my understanding of religious agency in crucial ways.

In the past decades, the study of Islam has become increasingly dominated by an emphasis on politics, religious activism, and pietistic movements, and groups and networks engaged in religiously motivated violence or terrorism. In the wake of the global religious resurgence, the acknowledgment that public religion is "here to stay," and rebuttals of theories about the "failure" of political Islam (see, e.g., Ricklefs 2012, 467–79), a tenacious but also misleading conviction has emerged that Muslim societies and political systems around the world are in the grip of a process of "Islamization" as an all-powerful, pervasive, and coherent force (cf. Peletz 2013 for an important critique). Historians and anthropologists have complicated this view by investigating the varieties among Islamic "currents," "orientations," or "world-views," and by analyzing the ways in which these differences may be explained by taking into account nonreligious factors such as gender, class, or locality. Although I agree that it makes little sense to study religious expressions without taking into account these different modes of identification, I resist the implication that religious identities somehow develop independently from inner religiosities (that is, as a product of politics, economic relations, or long-standing cultural traditions). This book takes inner Islam seriously as a driver of religious change, a perspective that is at the forefront as I position the project within the existing study of Islam in Aceh and Southeast Asia.

Islam in Aceh as a Subject of Study

A question that has long occupied scholars of Southeast Asia is the relationship between Islam and "indigenous" culture. Islamic conversion in the eastern parts of the Muslim world has often been understood in primarily political and economic terms. The grand narrative is that the religion was able to spread because pre- and early modern states encouraged and facilitated contacts and alliances with the "great" Muslim empires to the west and because Muslim traders dominated the Indian Ocean economic and cultural zone. Until the 1970s, many anthropologists working in Southeast Asia sought to uncover what they regarded to be the "true" cultures underneath the presupposed "veneer" of Islamic practices (Gibson 2000).[5] Interestingly, it seems that Aceh in this scholarly tradition always functioned as a kind of exception that proves the rule. The region has long been presented as a cradle of Islam in the Indonesian archipelago. Emphasizing the essential place of Islam in its history and culture, scholars of Aceh have typically asked how religious leaders have tried to make the state more Islamic and how their lay (or "secular") counterparts have solicited or tried to manage the religious factor as a part of local struggles for power.

A central question, in this regard, concerns the place and significance of the local, partly pre-Islamic customs, traditions, and values that are commonly glossed as *adat*. This term refers to many things. It lays down the rituals that mark important events, such as birth, death, marriage, or the harvest. One of the most commonly practiced rituals is *peusijeuk*, the practice of "cooling down" things that are new and therefore "hot" (such as newborn children, but also, for instance, a new motorcycle). The ways in which rituals like *peusijeuk* are performed (including dress and the use of objects) are place specific. Thus, people might claim that they are unable to say "what is *adat*" in another district, or even a neighboring village. Local leadership is organized, at least partly, on the basis of *adat* institutions, some of which have an Islamic root. *Geuchik*, the address of the village headman (or headwoman), is an *adat* title, just like the village imam (*teungku meunasah*) and the village "council of elders" (*teuha peut*, lit. the "four elders"). *Adat* governs the ways in which conflicts are solved within communities. Thus, people may argue that it is not necessary to involve state institutions (such as the police or the court) as long as it is possible to deal with a local conflict "by means of *adat*."

The few monographs that have taken Acehnese religiosity seriously as a research subject are all concerned, one way or another, with the durability of *adat* and the transformative power of Islam (Bowen 1993, 2003; Siapno 2002; Siegel 1969; Snouck Hurgronje 1893–94). As I discuss in more detail in the text that follows, particular emphasis is placed in these studies on the gendered aspects of this relationship. While Acehnese society incorporated forms of institutionalized, male-centered Islamic law as early as the sixteenth century, Acehnese conceptions of kinship have a strong matrilocal component. The practice of women inheriting the family house, and of men moving into the houses of their wives after marriage, is still common today. Girls and women remain members of the family core structure. Boys, in contrast, move out of their family home on reaching puberty, after which they develop avoidance relationships with their fathers and their fathers-in-law. Traditionally, they continue their lives by traveling away from their place of birth to look for work, knowledge, and experience. This rite of passage, known as *merantau*, is crucial in the process of achieving manhood and is dependent on the capacity of women to provide for their own subsistence.[6]

Closely related to the practice of *merantau* is the position in Acehnese society of the ulama. When people in Aceh use this term, they may refer to religious teachers generally, the leaders of Islamic boarding schools (*dayah* or *pesantren*), professors at the Islamic University in Banda Aceh, or members of the state ulama council (Majelis Permusyawaratan Ulama, MPU). Dependent on the context, they may refer to a more narrow category of *ulama dayah*, the leaders of traditional Islamic boarding schools, who represent a distinct religious space in Acehnese society, especially in rural areas. A distinction is commonly made between *dayah salafiyah*, the schools that operate a primarily religious curriculum based on the study of *kitab kuning* (classical texts, lit. "yellow books"), and *dayah modern* (modern *dayah*) or *dayah terpadu* (mixed *dayah*), the schools that are based on a partly religious, partly secular or "state" curriculum.[7] The *ulama dayah* are the leaders of *dayah salafiyah*. Although specialists in Islamic law and jurisprudence, they are also commonly recognized as *adat* leaders—that is, as community leaders with extensive knowledge of local customs and traditions.

According to the Dutch orientalist and government adviser Christiaan Snouck Hurgronje, the author of the first major ethnographic study of Aceh, the Acehnese saw Islam and *adat* as inseparable normative systems. In practice, however, *adat* often turned out to be the "mistress" and Islamic law "her submissive slave" (Snouck Hurgronje 1893–94, 1:157). According to Snouck Hurgronje, this was due to the fact that, if push came to shove, orthodox Islam and local traditions constituted opposing and mutually exclusive frameworks of moral and social action. Twentieth-century anthropology treated the subject of Acehnese religiosity in similarly dichotomous terms. More than seventy years after Snouck Hurgronje, James Siegel (1969) focused on the attempts by reformist ulama to modernize religious education and guide Muslims back to the true teachings of Islam. The appeal of this movement, he argued, lay in local perceptions of masculinity. Acehnese men were essentially "guests in their own house" (Siegel 1969, 55; citing Snouck Hurgronje 1893–94, 1:370n1). The scripturalist message of Islamic reformists provided them with a means of escape from their inferior position in society. Jacqueline Siapno, writing in the early 2000s, continued this line of reasoning as she argued that normative Islam represented a male tradition, which, through its "strong attempts at purification," was fundamentally opposed to the strong position of women in traditional Acehnese society (Siapno 2002, 36–37). Less concerned with gender but equally relevant in this context is John Bowen's (1993) work on religious practices and traditions in the Gayo highlands. This area, which had maintained complex relations with coastal Acehnese-speaking communities for centuries, was administratively incorporated into Aceh province by the Dutch. Like Siegel, Bowen traced local contestations about proper Islamic ideas and practices back to the historical formation of dichotomous "modernist" and "traditionalist" dispositions.

In line with Snouck Hurgronje's observations more than a century ago, most Acehnese today reject a sharp division between Islam and *adat*. They state, for example, that Islam and *adat* cannot be separated or that *adat* is in harmony with Islam. Religious teachers are commonly regarded as Islamic leaders (*tokoh Islam*) and *adat* leaders (*tokoh adat*) at the same time. A distinction is made, however, between Islam and *adat* as sources of legal action. Thus, "*adat* law" (*hukum adat*) is seen as something very different from "Islamic law" (*hukum syariah*) and "state law" (*hukum negara*)—the first referring to mediation by village leaders and the second and third to formal court procedures—even though there is a certain level of overlap among these domains. It is certainly not my intention, then, to discard these contrasts, which mean something very concrete to the Acehnese. My critique of the literature cited earlier applies to the extent to which it advances a set of relatively static, often stacked dichotomies (Islam–*adat*, male–female, public–private) as a dominant framework for analyzing the formation of religious subjectivities (cf. Kloos 2016).

To move beyond these dichotomies, I draw from recent developments in the study of Islam in Southeast Asia. It has been forcefully argued, for instance, that processes of religious change and revitalization have been driven by women as much as by men (Aryanti 2013; Blackburn 2008; Künkler and Kloos 2016; Srimulyani 2012; van Doorn-Harder 2006). More generally, the dichotomy between male-centered engagements with Islamic reform and female-centered engagements with local customs and mystical or syncretic traditions has become increasingly untenable (Birchok 2016; Kloos 2016). Earlier, Michael Peletz (1996), in his work on gender representations in Negeri Sembilan (Malaysia), drew attention to the ambivalences inherent in local (Malay) perceptions of masculinity and femininity. Johan Fischer (2008) likewise pointed to the importance of ambivalence, arguing that suburban middle class Malays (both men and women), for the most part unaffiliated with any particular religious or political current or movement, actively select from the discourses of "state" and "public" Islam as they construct opinions; face moral dilemmas; and discard, preserve, or change religious practices. This study elaborates further on the need to transcend the static binaries of tradition versus reform, women versus men, rural versus urban, and *adat* versus Islam, and to move the study of Islam in Aceh beyond the primacy of the "legal," the "political," and the "economic" without negating or underestimating any of these domains (cf. Hoesterey 2015).

Fieldwork

For this book I carried out fieldwork in Aceh for three months in 2008, twelve months in 2009–2010, and during two brief visits in 2012. The first period was mostly an orientation visit, intended to get a feel of the region, which I knew only from my earlier trip in 2006. Most of the ethnographic material was collected at two field sites: an urban, tsunami-affected neighborhood in Banda Aceh and a rural village in Aceh Besar, referred to in this book respectively (and pseudonymically) as Blang Daruet and Jurong. Interviews and conversations took place in Indonesian. The Acehnese, like most other people in Indonesia, do not generally consider this to be their first language; however, most people speak it, and virtually everyone understands. Although I was able to learn some Acehnese, I never succeeded in speaking it fluently. I did obtain a good level of passive understanding, which made it possible to follow conversations that were not explicitly directed at me. Archival data collected in the Netherlands and Indonesia complete the material presented in this study.

In 2008, I lived on the university campus in Darussalam, Banda Aceh, which hosts the Syiah Kuala University (Unsyiah) and the State Islamic Studies Institute (Institut Agama Islam Negeri, IAIN; presently Universitas Islam Negeri, UIN) Ar-Raniry. During this period, I stayed in the house of Professor Darwis Soelaiman, a retired professor of educational sciences, and his wife Mariani. One of my objectives was to familiarize myself with the Acehnese network of religious schools (*dayah*). Although I do not focus in this book specifically on the *dayah* setting, it is important to emphasize that these institutions function as an important frame of reference for Acehnese religious life more generally. Differences in the education system, for instance, reflect the basic doctrinal and sociological differences between the two largest Islamic organizations in Indonesia, Nahdlatul Ulama (NU) and Muhammadiyah.[8] Assisted by Muhajir al-Fairusy, then an undergraduate student at the IAIN, I visited some twenty *dayah* in Banda Aceh and Aceh Besar. We would usually arrive at these places unannounced, by motorcycle, trying to meet leaders, teachers, students, and villagers. We did not conduct extensive interviews. Although we asked about scholarly networks, curricula, and institutional histories, my primary intention was to observe some of the everyday routines and practices at the *dayah*. Many young men and women in Aceh, particularly in rural areas, live in a *dayah* for at least a few years, and religious teachers and students are frequently invited by villagers to perform or assist in basic religious rituals. I therefore look back on these visits as highly formative for my research, even if this is not clearly evident from the ethnographic descriptions presented in this book.

Muhajir's willingness to be my guide was significant for several reasons. Although a university student, he was highly interested in the *dayah* curriculum. Once or twice a week he attended lessons at Dayah Darul Ulum, in the village of Ateuk Long Ie (about ten minutes from the university campus), a school founded in 1962 by the venerated ulama Teungku Usman al-Fauzy (d. 1992). He was thus familiar with different forms of religious instruction. Even within Aceh, the world of the *dayah* is known as insular. As a foreigner and a non-Muslim, it was important to be accompanied on these first, unannounced visits by someone who spoke Acehnese and who was familiar with unwritten rules and codes. Muhajir took great care in explaining to me the importance of introductory rituals, appropriate gifts (such as sugar, or coffee for the students), and, above all, patience. There was also another reason why I was lucky to have him at my side at this early stage of my research. Muhajir is a grandson of Teungku Dahlan al-Fairusy (d. 2007), the former leader of Dayah Tanoh Abee, a well-known and prestigious religious school located in the subdistrict of Seulimeum, Aceh Besar. During our visits to the *dayah*, Muhajir usually mentioned this pedigree, which is not at all strange or obtrusive in the Acehnese context, where kin and place of descent are the most common ways of introduction. I am sure that this made some of our visits easier, or at least more informal.

One day in November 2008, Muhajir and I visited a school that I refer to in this book as Dayah Darul Hidayah. My first impression of it was colored by amazement. The school, which accommodated hundreds of students, seemed very well taken care of. The largest buildings were multistoried and built of concrete. Most student dwellings were simple, built of brick or wood with thatched roofs, but still better kept than the ones we had seen in other places. Students walked around industriously with brooms and rakes, buckets full of stones and gravel taken from the riverbed, and large bundles of palm leaf. The *dayah* leaders were absent, so a caretaker told us about the history of the school, the status of its grounds, and the origins of its students. A week later we returned to meet Abuya, the head of the *dayah*, who received us in a large, beautifully decorated *balai* (shelter or place for religious instruction) in front of his house. Afterward, we strolled to the adjacent village to pay a courtesy visit to the *geuchik*, Ilyas. When he heard about my research, we were invited to join the weekly religious lesson (*pengajian*), which would take place that same night in the village communal hall (*meunasah*). We ended up staying overnight, sleeping in the *meunasah*. A week later I visited again, this time alone. A young man I call Agus invited me to stay at his house. This village was Jurong, and in 2009–2010, Agus's family, which included his father, Hasyim, and his mother, Adhinda, would become my host family.[9]

Jurong was part of a cluster of eight villages surrounding a market town just off the main road to Medan. With 115 households and little over 500 inhabitants, it was a community of intermediate size (figure 2). The village itself did not have a mosque. There was one at the market and one at the *dayah*, both of which were used by villagers for Friday prayers. Jurong was located between the road and the banks of the Aceh River (Krueng Aceh). Most commercial activities took place at the market and on the side of the road. The only businesses in the village itself were a few tiny roadside shops and a coffee shop (*kedai*). The village was separated from the road by a small rice field (*sawah*). Another, much larger *sawah* was located at a twenty minutes' walk, on the other side of the river, accessible via a pedestrian bridge. Besides the river and the *sawah*, the community bordered on the walled *dayah* compound and a complex of gardens (mostly coconut, vegetables, pepper, and banana).

Inhabitants of Jurong generally described their village as poor, explaining that most of them were farmers and that few actually owned the land on which they worked. Only ten households owned *sawah* land, Agus's family being one of them. Although 80 percent of the population were officially registered as farmers (*petani*), few people lived exclusively off the land. Most were also active in construction, transport, petty trade, odd labor, or, in the case of women, home industries. Seven people were officially registered as traders. Twelve households lived on civil servant salaries. A list of "poor people" (*fakir-miskin*), drafted by the village administration a few years earlier by order of the subdistrict (*kecamatan*), counted fifty-nine families. Overall, the people of Jurong were not very highly educated. Most of them had only finished primary school or junior high school. Of the adolescents and young adults, the percentage attending senior high school or vocational training was higher. In 2009, six people studied at an institution of higher education.

When I came to Aceh in October 2009 for a full year of fieldwork, my plan was to stay for a few days with my friend Nurdin, look for a place to live in a Banda Aceh neighborhood, and start my research there. I would then

FIGURE 2. "Jurong," Aceh Besar (August 2010). Photo by the author.

go back to Jurong and decide whether it was possible to conduct research in both places. Eventually I decided to stay in Nurdin's *kampung*, Blang Daruet. I rented a house in the compound of an elderly couple. Yusuf was originally from Daruet. He had worked most of his life in the cement factory in Lhok-nga, located near Banda Aceh on the West Coast. After his retirement he had started a business of his own in the transport sector. His wife, Mila, was a nurse in Banda Aceh's main hospital. Yusuf and Mila belonged to one of the few wealthy families in Daruet. They had a good name. Yusuf made a point of hiring people from the neighborhood and invested considerable sums of money in communal facilities, such as the Daruet mosque. My house was separated from their own (much larger) residence. While Yusuf and Mila took very good care of me, our relationship was that of tenant and landlord and thus different from the more personal relationship I had with my host family in Jurong. I did, however, develop close relationships with some other families in the neighborhood, who were mixed in terms of their economic situation. Besides being my most regular interlocutors in Blang Daruet, they would ask me to join them on family visits and trips to local fairs, festivals, or the beach.

Desa Blang Daruet is relatively close to the sea and stood no chance when the tsunami smashed into the city on December 26, 2004. The neighborhood was completely destroyed. Apart from a few larger buildings, everything

FIGURE 3. "Blang Daruet," Banda Aceh (November 2009). Photo by the author.

(mainly houses and shops, but also warehouses) was razed to the ground. In the mayhem, a staggering total of 75 percent of about 3,000 inhabitants died. In the following years, Blang Daruet was physically reconstructed with the help of two international NGOs. When I first arrived, almost all survivors had been given a house to live in. Yusuf and Mila were among the very few who were able to reconstruct their house. The large majority of villagers lived in so-called *rumah tsunami*, concrete houses comprising three rooms (a sitting room and two bedrooms), a miniature bathroom, and a kitchenette (most "tsunami houses" in Banda Aceh look roughly like this) (figure 3). My own house was also a tsunami house. It had been granted to Yusuf and Mila before they rebuilt their own house. In 2009, the neighborhood consisted of 1,325 inhabitants, including many newcomers.

Once, Blang Daruet belonged to a cluster of villages situated between Banda Aceh and the coast. In 2009, it was an integrated part of the urban conglomeration. Like Jurong, it was not a wealthy community. According to the *kampung* secretary's calculations, it had a poverty rate of around 50 percent. By far the largest part of the working population was registered as skilled or unskilled laborers (*buruh*), artisans/craftsmen (*tukang*), and traders (*pedagang*). About a hundred people worked in the private sector (*swasta*), and thirty-three people were registered as civil servants (Pegawai Negeri Sipil, PNS). The bulk of economic activity took place on a reconstructed main road that cut across the neighborhood. On one side there was the neighborhood mosque, which was also the geographic center of the original settlement. Before the tsunami this area had been very populous. In 2009, it was still more densely built than the area on the other side of the road, which, not so long ago, was mostly *sawah* land. My house was located in this "new" part of the neighborhood.

Overall, my decision to conduct research in Jurong and Blang Daruet worked out well. I enjoyed the close relationship with my host family in Jurong, but it was also pleasant to return regularly to my more independent life in Banda Aceh. My official residence was Daruet, where I registered as a inhabitant. As a result, I was always a visitor in Jurong, regardless of the length of my stay. After a while, I established a rhythm in traveling back and forth. Usually I spent between ten days and two weeks in Jurong. The periods in Banda Aceh were somewhat longer, usually between two and three weeks, not because I needed more time for my research in Daruet, but because other activities—interviews, university meetings, formalities—kept me in the city longer. In contrast to Jurong, Daruet had its own office for village administration and its own mosque, both of which were good places to meet people and talk about current issues. On the other hand, Jurong was smaller and more separated from neighboring communities because of the physical boundaries formed by rice fields, gardens, the *dayah*, and the river. Thus it was generally easier to find out what was "going on" in Jurong than in Daruet, certainly in the beginning. One of the major disadvantages of the choice to divide my time was the fact that I sometimes missed important events or developments, simply because I was not there. In such cases, I tried to find out as much as possible afterward from the people who were directly involved. Of course, the information I gathered in this way could never match direct observation.

A brief closing remark about my position as a non-Muslim and a Dutch national is in place. Like other personal traits, such as my age, gender, and education, these identities influenced my daily interactions. People often told me, especially at first meetings, about the inherent beauty of Islam. This was prompted, at least in part, by a perceived need to counter mistaken "Western" images of Islam as an intolerant or even violent religion. As we came to know each other better, my interlocutors expressed their hope that, at some point in the future, I would decide to become a Muslim. I never experienced brash attempts at conversion. In rare instances, my identity as a non-Muslim became a source of tension. For example, a man I had not met before once told me that, as a non-Muslim, I should leave the Daruet mosque during Friday prayers. I explained that the leadership of the mosque had granted me permission to attend and listen to the sermon. In fact, I was more than happy to leave in order to prevent a conflict, but before I could make this clear, some of my local acquaintances interfered and told the man—who neither came from nor lived

in Blang Daruet—that my presence was none of his business. The discussion
became rather heated but was also quickly solved when I said that I would
sit at the back, near the exit. My identity as a Dutch researcher was a topic of
occasional questions and conversations about the colonial past, as well as jokes
that I had come to try and "colonize Aceh again" (which made me feel awk-
ward, but not attacked). As Anton Stolwijk (2016) has shown, memories of the
war against the Dutch are still very much present in contemporary Acehnese
society, often in surprising ways. My research did not focus on the remnants
of the war, however, and people rarely brought it up. As my relationship with
my interlocutors deepened, both my Dutch nationality and my identity as a
non-Muslim became less and less prominent as a topic of discussion.

Organization of the Book

The first two chapters of this book focus on the impact of Islamic reformism
on Acehnese society, from the late colonial period until the early 1970s. They
are based on different types of sources. Chapter 1 is based entirely on library
sources and materials collected in the colonial archives in Leiden, The Hague,
and Jakarta. Chapter 2 is based partly on archival sources (including documents from the provincial archive in Banda Aceh) and partly on the field notes
of Chandra Jayawardena (d. 1981), an anthropologist who conducted extensive
fieldwork in the subdistrict of Indrapuri, Aceh Besar, in the mid-1960s and
early 1970s. Chapters 3, 4, and 5 each show a different but crucial aspect of
the constitution of religious agency in contemporary Aceh: respectively, the
transformation of traditional religious authority, flexible engagements with
normative Islam, and self-perceived moral failure as a part of individual projects of ethical improvement. These three chapters are based almost entirely on
my own ethnographic fieldwork. Before I proceed, let me briefly outline the
individual chapters and their contribution to the argument.

Chapter 1 discusses the main political, economic, and religious forces that
have shaped Acehnese history. It describes the heyday of the Acehnese sultanate around the turn of the seventeenth century, the subsequent decline of
royal power, and the emergence in rural areas of religious experts (the ulama)
as a new and influential social group. The chapter then investigates the role
of colonialism in the imagining of Aceh as a particularly "pious" place. In the
twentieth century, agents of the colonial state and Islamic leaders converged
in their tendency to frame religious identity and pious expressions in scripturalist (rather than, for example, pluralist or syncretistic) terms. The resulting discourse of Acehnese exceptionalism was reproduced and reconfigured
in the period of Indonesian independence, influencing in complex ways the
interactions between state and religious authorities on the one hand, and the
majority of lay Muslims on the other.

Chapter 2 focuses on Aceh Besar, more specifically the subdistrict of Indrapuri, which is known historically as a hotbed of reformist and militant Islam. On the basis of an analysis of archival sources and the field notes of the late Chandra Jayawardena, I show that although Islamic scripturalism was attractive as a political currency in the mid-twentieth century, its impact on Acehnese religious life was actually limited. Under the influence of the state asserting itself more strongly at the village level, religious and political authority became increasingly intertwined. Ordinary villagers complicated this process by appropriating the expressions of formalized religious authority to address their own religious and nonreligious concerns.

Chapter 3 elaborates on the theme of state assertion by analyzing a conflict between ordinary villagers and the leaders of Dayah Darul Hidayah. Rooted in a deeply seated contestation about power and resources, it reveals a fundamental, for a large part generational, difference in ideas about moral leadership. The chapter shows that young adults are prepared, much more than their elders, to view traditional institutions such as the village and Islamic boarding schools as part of the state. This difference connects to an important historical shift, as young people have become increasingly pragmatic consumers of religious authority without abandoning or deeming irrelevant traditional institutions.

Chapter 4 returns to the question of Acehnese exceptionalism. Shifting the view to Blang Daruet, it places the study of Aceh squarely in debates about the global Islamic resurgence. The chapter describes how a young man, feeling attracted to the forces of global Islamism, adopted a strongly "outward" pious lifestyle. In the wake of the destruction caused by the 2004 tsunami, his behavior was accommodated, rather than categorically resisted or rejected, by his family. Drawing on the concept of moral ambivalence, and focusing in particular on the stances, practices, and narratives of his parents, I demonstrate how, within a single family and in the context of a neighborhood being reinvented after the disaster, religious practices and experiences were connected in different ways to contested concepts of kinship, community, money, social security, and class.

Chapter 5 further develops the concept of religious agency. It explores the ways in which ordinary Acehnese Muslims deal, in thought and action, with the problem of sinning. While sinfulness seems to be primarily a matter of discipline, this chapter shows that even the basic concern of dealing with bad behavior is marked by considerable measures of flexibility and creativity. This is important, because it influences the ways in which ordinary people approach and respond to the legalistic moral frameworks formulated by the state, most notably through the recent implementation of shari'a law. This chapter elaborates in particular on experiences associated with specific life stages, and the question of how these experiences enable ordinary Acehnese Muslims to build on self-perceived moral failure—sinning, in this case—as they work, assertively

FIGURE 4. View of Banda Aceh, as seen from Kapal Apung (January 2010). Photo by Eliza Jacobi.

and creatively, on their ethical selves. It demonstrates how, rather than simply rejecting or adopting state and public discourses, ordinary Acehnese actively select and appropriate officialized discourses of ethical improvement when they make moral decisions, approach dilemmas, and justify behavior, acts that are part and parcel of the process of becoming better Muslims.

1

History and the Imagining of Pious Aceh

> Here, everything speaks of struggle, resistance, hatred.
> Everything, except for the people.
> —DR. J. TIJSSEN (1933)

This chapter discusses the history of Aceh until the end of the Dutch presence in 1942, with a special focus on the late colonial period. I concentrate on the question of how Aceh came to be imagined, in the course of this history, as a particularly "pious" place. To a large extent, this is a question of authority: What groups, institutions, and individuals were able, in consecutive periods of time, to lay claim to the "correct" interpretation of Islam, and how was this connected to the construction of Aceh as a meaningful social, cultural, and political space? Although Islam was a constitutive force in the political and ideological foundations of the sultanate state, I argue in this chapter that ultimately the image of pious Aceh was a product of the colonial encounter, understood here as a shared cultural project, in which, despite the unequal relationship of power, both colonizers and colonized had stakes (see Comaroff and Comaroff 1988; Cooper and Stoler 1997).

The chapter starts by placing Aceh in its broader historical context of maritime Southeast Asia and competing imperial powers. In the sixteenth century, the Sultanate of Aceh—strategically located at the entrance of the Strait of Malacca—developed into one of the most powerful kingdoms of the eastern Muslim world. Political and religious authority were closely intertwined and concentrated at the royal court. The sultan (or sultana) acted both as a symbol of moral virtue and as a patron of religious scholars. The latter often hailed from abroad. They were cosmopolitan figures, who engaged in religious and doctrinal debates that transcended oceans and world regions. Important changes took place, however, in the eighteenth century. In the wake of the increasing maritime dominance of European powers and the gradual integration of the Acehnese interior in the globalizing economy, new and competing sources of political and religious authority emerged in coastal towns and rural areas. A new class of locally based religious teachers appeared, with moral and intellectual horizons that diverged considerably from those of the scholarly elite who resided at the court. As a result of this shift, local communities became increasingly prominent as sites of religious debate and contestation.

In the nineteenth century, the sultanate benefited from a resurgent trade with British Malaya. As a result, it was able to regain some of its prestige. The trading routes around northern Sumatra became the subject of fierce rivalries and complex diplomatic relations among the Acehnese, the British, and the other major power in the region, the Dutch. This lasted until 1873, when the Dutch colonial government in Batavia, after signing a treaty with the British, acted on its imperialist ambitions and decided to incorporate Aceh—the last indigenous kingdom in the western archipelago—into the Netherlands Indies. When the sultan refused to respond to an ultimatum, a military expedition invaded the shores near Banda Aceh, marking the beginning of a long and brutal war of conquest.

The Dutch-Acehnese war initially drove state and religious authorities further apart. As local chiefs were co-opted and absorbed into the colonial order as symbolic "heads" or indirect rulers, the colonial army was forced to direct itself against a radical faction of ulama, who perceived the struggle as a "holy war" and had taken over the leadership of Acehnese resistance. However, as large-scale violence subsided in the early twentieth century, both the Dutch stance toward Islam and Acehnese Muslims' stances toward the colonial project became more ambiguous. On the one hand, the Dutch government saw Aceh's religious leaders as their fiercest adversaries. On the other hand, the fact that the Acehnese resistance had come to be cast in Islamic terms forced the government to think in terms of managing religious sensibilities. As Harry Benda (1958) and Michael Laffan (2011) have argued, contrary to the common image of Dutch colonialism as being rather neutral toward religion, agents of the colonial state were deeply implicated in the making and legitimization of Islamic discourse and, ultimately, in the definition of Islamic orthodoxy.

The final decades of Dutch colonial rule were a period of rapid social change. In 1918, a civil governor was installed at the head of what had become Aceh "province." As the violence decreased, and the colonial government worked to integrate the region into the administrative and economic structures of the Netherlands Indies, ordinary Acehnese acted on emerging opportunities. The number of Acehnese children going to colonial and indigenous schools rose.

New technologies were embraced, and affluent youngsters in urban centers adopted new, "modern" lifestyles. A range of both political and nonpolitical associations emerged, which expressed an abundance of ideological affiliations and ideas about the future, thus transforming and reinvigorating the public sphere.

This pluriformity of society has been driven from memory, however, by the activities of one group. Founded in 1939 by reformist ulama from Aceh Besar and the North Coast, PUSA (Persatuan Ulama-Ulama Seluruh Aceh, All Aceh Association of Ulama) advocated a revitalized and purified interpretation of Islam, freed from corruptions and deviations. This interpretation, put forth by the so-called young generation (*kaum muda*), prescribed modern education, brotherhood, and individual moral development through pious practice rather than the hierarchical models of religious knowledge and authority associated with the old generation (*kaum tua*). What distinguished PUSA from other, kindred organizations (such as Muhammadiyah) was its regionalist focus, its role in the expulsion of the Dutch in the early 1940s, and its ultimate transformation, during the Japanese occupation and the subsequent Revolution, into a factor of political and military significance.

The PUSA model of Islamic scripturalism combined with an Acehnese ethnic self-awareness is often presented as the main (or even single) indigenous expression of modernity in Aceh (see, e.g., Aspinall 2009; Morris 1983; Piekaar 1949; Reid 1979; Siegel 1969; Sulaiman 1985). This chapter takes issue with this tendency to reduce the colonial experience to a continuous, uninterrupted history of Islamic activism and resistance. For many Acehnese, the recovery from the war was charged with the promises of change and progress, including (but not limited to) ideas about religious revitalization. However, as I argue toward the end of the chapter, a combination of factors, including the memory of the war, protracted colonial and anticolonial violence, and the deeply repressive nature of the late colonial state, also limited the space for debate and alternative images, thus reproducing and strengthening the imagining of pious Aceh.

Reconfigurations of Authority

Between the tenth and the thirteenth century CE, rising demands on both ends of the Indian Ocean and the decline of land-based trading routes following the collapse of the Pax Mongolica caused a sharp increase in Asian maritime trade (Chaudhuri 1990). In the wake of this trading boom, the rulers of several coastal polities (*negeri*) lining the Strait of Malacca adopted Islam as the religion of state. The oldest archaeological and textual evidence of such a conversion stems from thirteenth-century Pasai, a kingdom located near present-day Lhokseumawe (Guillot and Kalus 2008). This trend continued eastward. From Sumatra, along the North Coast of Java, and all the way to the southern Philippines, indigenous rulers converted to Islam, both because of the economic advantages it offered them in a trading system dominated by Muslims and because of the legitimacy that Islamic legal traditions were able to bestow on them and on their courts (Reid 1993, 140–73).

Not much is known about the early history of Aceh. Legend has it that "Aceh" was the name of a Hindu princess who got lost and was eventually found in Sumatra by her brother, upon which she became queen of that land (G. P. Tolson, cited in Djajadiningrat 1911, 145–46). The Acehnese language suggests Chamic influences, locating the origins of the Acehnese-speaking people in southern Vietnam (Sidwell 2005). The first evidence of Islamic influences is found in the form of several twelfth-century tombstones discovered in Lamreh (near present-day Banda Aceh) (Montana 1997). A richer picture emerges with the appearance of court chronicles—the fifteenth-century *Hikayat Raja-Raja Pasai* (Story of the kings of Pasai), and the seventeenth-century *Hikayat Aceh* (Story of Aceh) and *Bustan al-Salatin* (The garden of kings) (Djajadiningrat 1911; Iskandar 2011)—and the reports of European traders. According to the *Bustan al-Salatin*, Nur al-Din al-Raniri's history of the Acehnese sultanate, the first ruler of Aceh to convert to Islam was Ali Mughayat Syah (r. 1515–30) (Nuru'd-din ar-Raniri 1966, 31), who was known in Portuguese sources as Raja Ibrahim (Djajadiningrat 1911, 144–53).

After the conquest of Malacca by the Portuguese in 1511, Indian and Chinese Muslim merchants redirected their routes to other ports in and around the Strait. Reinvigorating places such as Johor, Patani, Banten, Brunei, and a string of ports on the North Coast of Sumatra, these contacts strengthened local rulers' attachment to Islam (Laffan 2011, 10; Prakash 1998, 34; Reid 2006b, 106). It was in this context that the Portuguese apothecary and diplomat Tomé Pires (1967 [1515]) wrote about the rise of the "kingdom of Achin." He also wrote that Pidie and Pasai, located to the east of Aceh, were more powerful, populous, and prosperous. Their main source of wealth was the pepper trade. However, in the 1520s these ports were conquered and absorbed—one by one—by Aceh under Ali Mughayat Syah. The incorporation of Pasai in 1524 was particularly significant. This kingdom had converted to Islam and integrated Islamic elements into its administrative system centuries before Aceh. By appropriating the fame of Pasai, the rulers of Aceh were able to legitimize their position more forcefully than before on the basis of an Islamic understanding of kingship, fashioned in turn after the great Islamic empires to the west (the Mughals, the Savafids, and the Ottomans) (Andaya 2008, 114).

In the sixteenth century, Aceh developed into a wealthy and powerful kingdom. Illustrative of its military strength, Malacca was besieged in 1568, and several naval battles were fought against the Portuguese, Aceh's main rival in the Indian Ocean trade (Subrahmanyam 2012, 133–37; 2009; cf. Borschberg 2010).

In the 1560s, Sultan Alauddin Riayat Syah al-Kahar (r. 1537–68) established diplomatic relations with the Ottoman Empire. Presenting himself as a vassal of the caliph, he was able to obtain a modest amount of military assistance (Reid 2006b, 56–57). While this increased the authority of Aceh as an Islamic kingdom (Peacock and Teh Gallop 2015, 2), other transoceanic connections were forged by itinerant scholars, traders, and pilgrims. The Acehnese court actively attracted ulama from the Middle East and South Asia to teach and study subjects such as Islamic law, jurisprudence, and mysticism. Sufi orders or "brotherhoods" (*tariqa*) facilitated the dissemination of religious knowledge across the Indian Ocean (Azra 2004; Ho 2006; Kraus 2010, 203; Laffan 2011). As a consequence, Aceh became a center of scholarly inquiry and, at times, fierce debates about Islamic doctrines.[1] Under the rule of the legendary sultan Iskandar Muda (r. 1607–36), Aceh became the political and cultural leader of the Malay world, both superior in terms of military might and authoritative in terms of scholarly production. State revenues were used to build and maintain an increasingly splendid court (Hadi 2004; Ito 1984; Reid 2005).

The sultan of Aceh was a principal among equals, who emanated from a class of rich traders known as *orangkaya* (lit. "rich men"). The *orangkaya* maintained the relationship between the center and the interior. They operated from Banda Aceh and other, smaller ports. Some of them held military titles, such as *uleebalang* or *panglima*, a practice modeled on examples in the Muslim world, notably the Ottoman Empire and the Mughal dynasty in South Asia (Andaya 2008, 132). From the seventeenth century onward, the *orangkaya* were integrated into the administrative structure of the state through a royal seal, the *sarakata*, that legitimized their privileged position, but also tied them to the sultan as vassals, obliging them to pay revenues in times of peace; to provide military service in times of war; and, increasingly, to serve as officers of the state (Snouck Hurgronje 1893–94, 1:91–93). The relationship between the sultan and the *orangkaya* was ambiguous, however. Although the sultan depended on the nobility, he also competed with them over commercial interests. This was not a fair competition, for the sultan could use his military power to create monopolies (see, e.g., Kathirithamby-Wells 1986). This situation caused perpetual friction and alternating periods of political stability and unrest.

It is sometimes claimed that the sultanate state enforced on its subjects a strict Islamic normative code. Evidence to support this is scarce. Certainly, there is much to suggest that, at times, Islamic norms were taken very seriously by the court. For example, Sultan Alauddin Riayat Syah Sayyid al-Mukammil (r. 1588–1604) is described in the *Bustan al-Salatin* as a just and God-fearing king, who received many ulama, told his subjects to keep to God's law, and commanded the nobles at his court to dress in Arabic-style clothes. Iskandar Muda was reported to enforce particular religious prescriptions, such as the daily prayers, as well as Islamic interdictions, such as those against gambling and consumption of alcohol, and to have "executed at least two drunken Acehnese by 'pouring molten lead down their throats'" (Reid 1988, 143). In Banda Aceh, a criminal court administered justice on the basis of a combination of Islamic and *adat* law. Cases were brought before the court by inhabitants of the city and by "guards" (*panghulu kawal*) who patrolled the various quarters (Beaulieu 1705, 743–44). Yet the available evidence suggests that, in many cases, *adat* took the upper hand (Peletz 2002, 27–29). At the same time, very little is known about the administration of other ports, let alone the interior. The French commander Beaulieu (1705, 744), author of the most detailed description of Banda Aceh during the rule of Iskandar Muda, mentioned a "watch of two hundred horse that patrols every night in the country and along the shore." He also wrote that the *orangkaya* presided personally over their province or country-district, "where [they] give orders, and [administer] justice to the inhabitants," but provided no further details. Although a relatively complex judicial system thus served to maintain order in a bustling and increasingly heterogeneous confluence of people and commodities—explaining, perhaps, the "severe, draconian and sensationalistic punishments" (Peletz 2002, 29) reported in the early seventeenth century—there is neither evidence to support that this system reached far beyond the confines of the city, nor reason to imagine a uniform, or evenly spread, enforcement of Islamic norms and regulations.

This discussion raises important questions about conversion and the formation of Muslim subjectivities beyond the confines of the court. Like other *negeri*, Aceh did not exert strong territorial claims. Its power was based on maritime trade, and its priority was to control the sea rather than the land. The religious scholars who visited Aceh engaged with the court and the transoceanic networks of which they were part rather than with the interior (Laffan 2011, 18–24). Islam did penetrate territories and social spaces beyond the court, but this was not a top-down process. As the port cities in the Indian Ocean region became "saturated with overriding Islamic values," questions of purpose or direction seem to be of limited relevance. Religious change was driven by multidirectional processes of internal networking, rather than by acts of proselytization (Hall 2001, 225–26).

After the rule of Iskandar Muda, the power of the sultanate started to crumble. His daughter, Sultana Safiyyat al-Din Syah (r. 1641–75), who became queen after the death of her husband, Iskandar Thani, inherited a troubled realm. Her father's futile military excursions to Malacca and tight domestic control over agriculture and trade had exhausted the interior (Reid 2006b, 60). In contrast, Aceh's old rival Johor experienced a revival as a result of the Dutch conquest of Malacca in 1641.[2] In 1699, Aceh's fourth queen in succession, Sultana Kamalat Zainat al-Din Syah, was forced to abdicate.[3] By then, the Acehnese sphere of influence had shrunk to the northern tip of Sumatra (Lieberman 2009, 862–63). A long and unstable period of foreign rule followed, in which sultans succeeded each other rapidly. In 1726, Sultan Jemal al-Alam Badr al-Munir, the last of a brief dynasty of Arab sultan-*sayids*, was overthrown by (the ethnic Bugis) Sultan Alauddin Ahmad Syah, who is regarded as the progenitor of all subsequent Acehnese sultans until the institution was abolished by the Dutch in 1903 (Snouck Hurgronje 1893–94, 1:92–95).

Although Banda Aceh remained an important port, the presence of European traders diminished local opportunities for long-distance trade. To secure their wealth, the sultan and the *orangkaya* were forced to turn to the interior, where they levied, in the words of the English traveler Thomas Forrest (1792, 39), the "land and industry of [its] inhabitants." Rural production was revived, and pioneering chiefs opened up large swaths of land for the cultivation of cash crops, notably pepper. As a result, large Acehnese-speaking migrant communities appeared on both coasts (Dobbin 1983, 87–108; Lee Kam Hing 1995; Reid 2005, 108–109; 2006b). The effect of these shifts was a gradual but significant restructuring of the Acehnese polity. The power of the sultan vis-à-vis the *orangkaya* was reduced (see, e.g., Forrest 1792; W. Marsden 1811 [1783]). The entrance into the archipelago of English and American traders ignited a new pepper boom. By the early 1820s, Aceh was responsible for more than half of the world's production (Lieberman 2009, 858). An increasing number of ships traded directly at the ports of the West Coast, thus evading the sultan's toll (see, e.g., Gould 1956). Taking control of local production, the *orangkaya* positioned themselves increasingly as local autocrats. Although they remained formally tied to the sultan by the *sarakata*, their political authority was based on their wealth and on kinship, which bound them to the clan-like communities that inhabited their territories.

In this context of social and political change, a new class of local religious teachers emerged in rural areas.[4] Unfortunately, we know little about these figures and their institutions. In West Sumatra, the increasing prominence of religious teachers was closely connected to the transformation of local communities by the booming trade in cash crops. Rapid social and economic change gave rise to moral anxiety and increasingly heated doctrinal contestations, religious activism, and even violent conflict (Dobbin 1983, 118–41). In the coastal traverse between West Sumatra and Aceh, religious teachers affiliated with the "globally salient" Naqsyabandiyah Sufi order objected to the allegedly syncretist practices associated with the Shattariyah order (Laffan 2011, 41–44; Kraus 2010, 213–14). The call for purification—as well as the resistance against it—became a central religious trope in this area (see, e.g., Suryadi 2001). It is difficult to overemphasize the significance of these transformations. Although religious treatises written in the sixteenth and seventeenth centuries were sometimes meant as personal guides for moral development—Abdurrauf al-Singkili's commentary on the Qur'an is an important example (Johns 1998)—these were always intended for a scholarly elite. From the eighteenth century onward, religious instruction, debate, and doctrinal contestation became increasingly a concern of local teachers and ordinary villagers.

Social and religious reconfigurations were not limited to coastal areas. The turn toward the interior also brought significant changes to the fertile Aceh River valley known as Aceh Besar (Greater Aceh). In the nineteenth century, this became the domain of the "three Sagis" (lit. "corners"), confederations of smaller territorial units known as *mukim* (a collection of villages centering on the presence of a mosque). In the mid-nineteenth century, a three-way divide of power emerged among the court, the sagis, and the farther flung territories controlled by local rulers. The result was a profoundly decentralized social and political order (van Langen 1988). At the same time, religious institutions became an intrinsic part of local administrative structures: "In every neighborhood there is a place of worship, binasah [*meunasah*] or mandarsah [*madrasah*], where meetings are held and religious training is provided" (van Langen 1988, 19). This situation was reinforced by a set of royal decrees, which made the dissemination of religious commands a responsibility of local chiefs and judges.[5] It is in this context of fragmented authority that the Dutch invaded Aceh in 1873.

Islam and the Imperial War

The official reason for the Dutch assault on Aceh was the sultanate's alleged support of piracy and contraband. Today, the war is generally interpreted in the context of imperial conquest (Tarling 2001, 135–44). In terms of agricultural production, prominence in regional trade, and diplomatic relations with other regional powers, Aceh in the mid-nineteenth century was going through a revival. The rise of nearby Penang, as an entrepôt, a center for regional business, and a principal dock for pilgrims making their way to the holy land, contributed strongly to this development (Gedacht 2013, 201–205). The opening of the Suez Canal in 1869 further increased the importance of the Strait as a gateway between Europe and Asia. Two years later, a treaty with the British "allocated" the whole of Sumatra to the Dutch sphere of influence. It was consequently decided to integrate one of the last remaining independent kingdoms into the Dutch colonial empire (see Reid 1969). Sultan Mahmud Syah (who was not consulted for the treaty) sought allies in Turkey, France, and America, but to no avail. While the first campaign was beaten off, a second invasion in 1874 forced the sultan to move his court to the village of Keumala, Pidie. He died, in the same year, of cholera. Under the leadership of the guardians of his under-age son, Keumala in subsequent decades grew into "a considerable center of agriculture and trade" (Reid 1969, 205) and the heart of anticolonial resistance.

The Dutch believed that the subjugation of Aceh would be a short and straightforward campaign. Instead, it turned into a grinding and extremely bloody affair, which, as the Dutch journalist Paul van 't Veer (1969) argued, never really came to an end. Until the 1890s, the Dutch controlled only a small territory, comprising a number of defensive works connected by a tramline. The momentum changed, however, with the arrival in 1891 of the scholar-cum-adviser Christiaan Snouck Hurgronje, who was commissioned by the government to write a secret report about interelite relationships and popular sentiments. He discovered that, behind the "line of concentration," a bitter conflict over arms, resources, and authority had broken out between the traditional nobility (the *uleebalang*) and a number of ulama, who saw the struggle as a "holy war" (*jihad*). A genre of epic poetry known as the *Hikayat Perang Sabil* (The story of the Holy War) or *Hikayat Perang Kompeuni* (The story of the war against the Dutch) circulated widely and, according to the Dutch, persuaded ordinary villagers to join the struggle by praising the martyrs who had died in battle against the "infidels" (Ac. *kaphe*). According to Snouck Hurgronje, the ulama became the de facto leaders of the resistance, first, because their religious "fanaticism" inspired the (inherently ill-disposed) Acehnese to take up arms, and, second, because their network of relatively secluded rural institutions enabled them to set up an organization that was difficult to upset. As a result, he wrote, these ulama had acquired unprecedented authority among the population.

In his "Aceh report" (*Atjeh-verslag*), Snouck Hurgronje advised the colonial government to actively support the *uleebalang* and, at the same time, ruthlessly persecute the ulama and anyone who might associate with them (Gobée and Adriaanse 1957–65, 1:47–125). This strategy eventually shifted the balance to the advantage of the Dutch. In 1903, after the capture of his family, Sultan Muhammad Daud Syah (the son of Sultan Mahmud Syah, who was only a child when the war began), capitulated. He was brought back to Banda Aceh and eventually, after being accused of masterminding the ongoing resistance, exiled to Java.

If the war turned out to be a grave problem for the Dutch, for the Acehnese it was simply devastating. The assault was total. The invading army attacked the port city, the palace of the Sultan, coastal fortifications, and other strategic places, but also, from the outset, the villages of the interior. The population was decimated. Thousands fled to the Malay peninsula. Thousands more became internal refugees. Complete villages, rice fields, and irrigation channels were destroyed, and the pepper production collapsed.[6] Acehnese leaders were co-opted or killed, and the areas that were brought under Dutch control were fundamentally reshaped. This was a period "in which one out of eight Atjehnese was killed or displaced and in which the economic base of Atjehnese society was drastically altered" (Siegel 1979, 229).

Part of the Dutch strategy to subdue (or, to cite a contemporary term, "pacify") Aceh was to cut the region off from the political, economic, and religious networks that formed the basis of its dynamism and strength. As Joshua Gedacht (2013, 213) has shown, this was done half-heartedly. The military blockade of Acehnese ports was at odds both with British interests and with the idea that "cosmopolitan" Acehnese traders and chiefs might be convinced "to join, or at least passively tolerate, the invasion rather than aggressively seeking to thwart it." An alternative policy of shipping regulations, introduced in the 1890s, could not prevent Aceh from being sent on a "slow drift of isolation" (Gedacht 2013, 199). Economic policy was beneficial to foreign rather than local entrepreneurs. A "dual economy" (Ismail 1996) emerged, split between a local peasant economy and a world of European capital based on Javanese migrant rather than indigenous labor. As the pepper trade declined, Acehnese men in particular became marginalized and impoverished (Siegel 1969, 90–97).

In the twentieth century, the "Aceh report" was turned, gradually, into a political doctrine. The so-called Aceh policy (D. *Atjeh-politiek*) consisted of three elements. First, it stipulated that the "*adat* chiefs" (*adathoofden*) were recognized as natural rulers in their respective realms. In return for their loyalty, which was officialized through the signing of a contract (the *Korte Verklaring*, "Short Statement"), they were allowed to govern as *zelfbestuurders* (self-rulers) under the authority of the colonial government. The *zelfbestuurders* were responsible for matters of law and order, resolving conflicts between "natives"—as long as these did not concern matters of state security—before indigenous courts (*musapat*). Second, the Aceh policy implied a gradual abolition of military rule. Civil institutions were established to regulate and stimulate the economy, improve communication and infrastructure, and advance a system of Dutch-style education. Third, the policy ensured a continuous military crackdown on every form of organized resistance, as well as all groups or individuals who were suspected of disseminating the "seeds" of *kafir*-hatred or anti-Dutch sentiment among the population. According to A. G. H. van Sluys, who was appointed in 1918 as the first nonmilitary governor in three decades, what was needed above all was "peace, and again, peace." Aceh, he believed, was ready to be "normalized."[7]

Despite the efforts of van Sluys and his successors, violent resistance continued, especially on the West Coast. Particularly frightening for the Dutch were the assaults known throughout the archipelago as the "Aceh-murders" (D. *Atjeh-moorden*). This was a term used by the Dutch for the persistent suicide attacks directed at the lives of European residents (mostly Dutch), committed by individual Acehnese hoping to become *syahid* (martyrs to the Islamic faith). As I have discussed in more detail elsewhere (Kloos 2014a), administrators commissioned scientific investigations (including psychiatric reports about the Acehnese "mind") to find an explanation—and a solution—for the problem. Such initiatives were based on older ideas, including those advanced by Snouck Hurgronje, about the long-term decline of Aceh and the associated "degeneration" of the Acehnese race.[8] Smoldering anger and discontent, resulting from the experience of the war and the inequalities and forms of marginalization typical of Dutch-style colonialism, were met with wariness about the so-called false doctrines (D. *valsche leer*) and "fanaticism" (D. *geestdrijverij*) that were prevalent among the inherently "suggestible" Acehnese. Military leaders and civil administrators conceived of the Acehnese "kafir-hatred" as a repressed, generally unarticulated but widespread pathological condition. Religiously motivated violence might break out at any time and any place, but especially in those "isolated" regions—Central Aceh and the South and West Coasts in particular—where colonial modernity had not been able to reach sufficiently deep to change the Acehnese mind for the better.

Colonial ethnography and the dichotomies it produced played an important role in the development of these ideas. The earliest ethnographic description of an Acehnese community known to me deals with the town of Idi, on the North Coast, and is found in a memoir published in 1877 by the naval officer J. A. Kruyt (1877).[9] The people of Idi, it reports, were diligent in prayer and the fast, and, encouraged by a growing number of "priests" (i.e., hajis), kept strictly to Qur'anic prescriptions such as the rejection of pork (Kruyt 1877, 67). At the same time, they believed firmly in "miraculous events"; "visions and dreams"; the apparition of "ghosts," "spirits," and "monsters"; the possibility of obtaining supernatural powers such as invulnerability (*kabal*); and talismans (*jimat*), as well as other magical objects and forms of divine protection. The town itself was thought to be founded at the instigation of a dangerous supernatural being, called "Ma-Edi," who had "only one breast protruding in the form of a cinnamon bread or mortar-shell, and fiery eyes the size of coconuts" (Kruyt 1877, 67–68). Twenty years later, Julius Jacobs (1894, 1:393) wrote in similar style about the mixing of "general Muhammadan considerations" and "original demonism" by villagers in Aceh Besar.

Snouck Hurgronje's *De Atjèhers* (1893–94)—a scholarly elaboration of the first (ethnographic) part of the original Aceh report—also described a fusing of Islamic teachings and pre-Islamic or "animist" beliefs. What makes this text fundamentally different from earlier ethnographic accounts, however, aside from being generally more extensive, systematic, and innovative, is its focus on a politically useful dichotomy between an acceptable, rational, and "true" understanding of Islamic law and its potentially dangerous aberrations. "Proper" Islamic scholarship, according to Snouck Hurgronje, was based on the three pillars of doctrine (*tauhid*), law (*fiqh*), and mysticism (*tasawuf*). Mystical traditions, in turn, covered a continuum between "orthodox" doctrines (including the teachings of the Naqsyabandiyah) and beliefs and practices that should be placed wholly outside the Islamic tradition "proper." The latter included the pursuit of a state of "unity" with God (Ac. *eleumee sale*), as well as a range of other knowledges ("ilmoe's"), including spells and formulas (*rajah*); special prayers (*doa*); magical objects; amulets (*jimat*); and the interpretation of signs, omens (*alamat*), and dreams.[10] Viewed from an Islamic legal perspective, Snouck Hurgronje argued, the Acehnese were followers of the "orthodox" Shafi'i school. Their everyday practices, however, revealed a "direct continuation of Hamzah [al-Fansuri]'s heresy" (Snouck Hurgronje 1893–94, 2:1–20, 33–49).

De Atjèhers is more comprehensive and nuanced than the original Aceh report. Its political impact was indirect. While Snouck Hurgronje considered some expressions of mysticism, such as *rateb* (a practice of chanting religious formulas) or *seudati* (a kind of dancing and chanting contest performed by young boys dressed as girls) to be harmless, the opposite was argued with regard to the practices linked to invulnerability (Ac. *eleumee keubaj*), invisibility, martial arts, the control over weapons and ammunition, and the practice of bringing warriors into a state of religious ecstasy. Snouck Hurgronje's writings on these matters were useful for the colonial government. They distinguished between "good" and "bad" Islamic practices and, as such, offered an intellectual instrument for the creation of a state-sanctioned discourse on Islamic orthodoxy. This discourse was reproduced and elaborated by administrators who sought to take preemptive action against the possible flaring up of the "holy war," often in collaboration with religious scholars intent on denouncing such mystical expressions as heretical or disruptive.

While debates about "correct" and "incorrect" religious practices took place on a regular basis before the indigenous courts (*musapat*), the distinction between "good" and "bad" Islam was particularly salient where it concerned matters of order and security. By the late 1910s, resistance in the densely populated areas of Aceh Besar and the North Coast had been effectively suppressed, which meant that the Dutch could concentrate on the "pacification" of other areas. In the mountainous and thickly forested areas of Central and West Aceh, roaming bands of "rebels" (as they were now called) continued to challenge colonial authority and attack military posts. According to the Dutch, there was a direct relation among remoteness, mystical practices, susceptibility to ideas about the "holy war," and the outbreak of violence. At the same time, and rather paradoxically, administrators and military leaders were concerned about the porous borders with North Sumatra and Tapanuli. Dutch intelligence reports from the 1920s and 1930s are rife with references to "unreliable" or "unpredictable" elements present among the continuous stream of workers, traders, students, political activists, *tarekat* leaders, religious teachers, proselytizers, and adventurers making their way along the coastal trail. "Here nor in West Sumatra," wrote Governor Hens in 1923, "would it be possible to regulate individuals travelling back and forth, especially when it concerns ordinary kampong [village] folk."[11] Still, considerable effort was invested in the attempt to lift these areas from their so-called isolation, connecting them—through the building of new roads, improved communication, and administrative integration—to the parts of Aceh (Banda Aceh and the North and East Coasts) that were considered to be more developed, both economically and intellectually.

Official investigations of local outbreaks of violence typically revealed a range, and sometimes a combination, of Islamic, millenarian, and communist influences. These complexities faded, however, as knowledge about particular events and circumstances made its way "up" from local accounts to the reports about the Acehnese "situation" more generally (cf. Stoler 2009). In such instances, racial explanations, including the emphasis on the "typical" Acehnese hatred toward unbelievers, took over. Thus, in the early 1930s, Governor O. M. Goedhart (1925–30) lamented the "neglect" of the West Coast, where the people were "too isolated" and where the "old mentality" (D. *oude geest*) of the Acehnese persisted. His words were echoed by Governor A. Ph. van Aken (1932–36), who spoke of the need to open up these areas for the "enlightening" effects of Western-style education and modernization.[12] These views reflected both the paternalistic and conservative nature of the late colonial state (Bloembergen and Raben 2009) and the established discourses of disconnection and racial degeneration in Aceh. According to Snouck Hurgronje, who was quoted time and time again in the reports and letters of colonial administrators, Aceh (as a whole) had come to relish a state of self-isolation.[13] This view was reproduced by other influential scholars, such as R. A. Kern, who stated in 1920 that "influences from outside, except for those coming from the center of Islam" were "largely lost" on the Acehnese. Such views would persist until the end of Dutch rule, despite the general atmosphere of change that pervaded Aceh—much as in the rest of Indonesia—during the late colonial period.

Belief and Practice in a Society in Flux

According to Dutch observers, people in Aceh took their faith seriously, in the sense that they prayed regularly, observed the yearly fast, and paid religious tithes, while showing an aversion to impurities (such as pork or objects touched by dogs) (figure 5). Snouck Hurgronje found that diligence in religious observance varied from village to village, depending on the encouragement of village leaders or the awe (or lack thereof) excited by religious authorities (Snouck Hurgronje 1893–94, 1:65). Almost thirty years later, an itinerant eye doctor and philanthropist, J. Tijssen, observed that young men traveling along the West Coast "would spread out [their] headscarf on the road to perform their prayers, regardless their exact location, whenever the time for prayer was drawing near" (Graadt van Roggen 1934, 12). During Ramadan, he added, ordinary life came to such a standstill that it was impossible for him to carry out his work. Collecting taxes in Aceh Besar in the early 1930s, civil servant J. J. van der Velde became used to the sight of male villagers congregating in the *meunasah* to conduct the evening prayer (van de Velde 1982, 53).

In the early 1930s, political reports spoke of a "revival" (D. *opleving*) of public religiosity in Pidie, expressed by an increasing attendance of congregational

FIGURE 5. Friday sermon in a *meunasah* (communal hall) in Calang, West Aceh (May 1922). Photo by Friedrich W. Stammeshaus. Courtesy of John Klein Nagelvoort. Reproduced with permission.

prayer. This was thought to be a direct result of the rapid expansion in the same period of religious schools, meetings, and public sermons (*tabligh umum*).[14] Education had always been part of the pacification strategy of the Dutch, yet decades of warfare had made people wary of indoctrination by "kafir schools" (*sekolah kafir*). In response, the government told the *zelfbestuurders* to "convince" their subjects to send their children to Dutch-style primary schools (D. *volksscholen*, lit. "people's schools"). This was unsuccessful at first, but by the mid-1930s, 328 such schools had enrolled more than 36,000 students (Jongejans 1939, 254). Initially, teachers came from outside the province (most of them having a Minangkabau, Batak, or Mandailing background), but gradually more Acehnese teachers were trained. Two hundred and one schools already taught in Acehnese, besides the common Malay medium. In the same period, mixed religious/secular schools established by reform-minded ulama began to provide a serious alternative. In the 1920s, these schools popped up "like mushrooms from the ground," especially in Aceh Besar and along the North Coast.[15] Like the Dutch schools, these reformist *madrasah* taught girls as well as boys.

Another conspicuous change was found in the attitude toward Western medicine. In 1933, van de Velde reported:

> In the past [Acehnese villagers] were afraid of injections. An old man told me, with a big smile on his face, that for a long time after the war, the Aceh-nese were so mistrustful, that they called the injections "ie kaphé," water of the unbelievers, the aim of which was to bring the Acehnese from their true faith, Islam. (van de Velde 1982, 53–54)

Ordinary villagers regularly asked van de Velde for quinine against malaria and injections against framboesia (a skin disease). Similar experiences were related by Tijssen, who performed operations throughout Aceh, often successfully. Reflecting on a 1932 trip to Bakongan, a region on the West Coast notorious for an outburst of anti-Dutch violence in 1925–26, he recalled:

> Everything speaks of struggle, resistance, hatred. Everything—except for the people. In this region, no [military] officer will ever enter the kampong [village] without a soldier with a loaded carbine in his trail. And yet—while I lived among these people, unarmed, for weeks in a row, no one touched a hair on my head, and when you ask me why here, exactly here, the situation was always so turbulent, I have to answer: I don't know, and I have never understood. (Graadt van Roggen 1934, 11)

Tijssen worked, alone or in the company of a Javanese assistant, in areas where the state failed to provide care. The government, as part of its modernization policy, set up medical posts in many small and medium-sized towns, but as Tijssen told a journalist, whom he met by chance aboard a ship on its way to the Netherlands, Acehnese villagers would never come to these hospitals

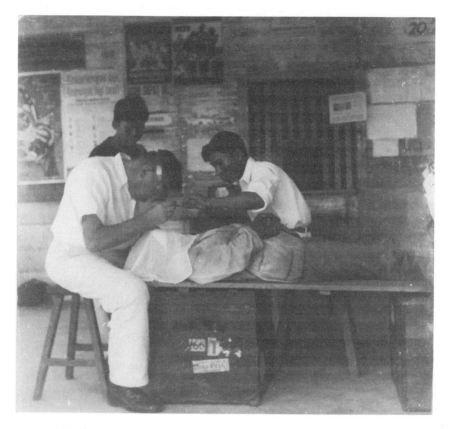

FIGURE 6. Eye doctor J. Tijssen carries out an operation in the post office of Bakongan, South Aceh (February 1939). Photographer unknown. Source: Leiden University Library, KITLV 18675. Reproduced with permission.

spontaneously (Graadt van Roggen 1934). Yet, as Jean Taylor (2011, 231) notes, photographs of Tijssen performing his surgeries show that "the Acehnese were willing to undergo a risky and scary operation—one that was a product of Western medical practice; [and that] they were not refusers or rejecters of modern medical achievements" (figure 6).

A particularly rich description of the changes taking place in Acehnese society comes from the hand of the conservative writer and journalist Henri Zentgraaff, an acute observer who was well equipped to note down the developments that were lost on the eyes and pens of many of his contemporaries.[16] According to Zentgraaff, Aceh in the 1920s was catching up with modernity, and it was doing so quickly:

Not so long ago, everywhere you would see the larger part of the population in typical Acehnese clothes, the men with headscarf or the familiar uleebalang-topi [*uleebalang* hat], the women in trousers and bad-joe [blouse].

Well, on the East Coast these have become exceptions. In short, it is astonishing how significant the change is; almost everywhere I see people wearing that meaningless and insipid garb, which appears to have become the one and only common ideal of the "Indonesians," with the familiar dark little cap. Women appear almost everywhere in sarong [cover] and badjoe. As for the younger men, they seem to obtain their clothing . . . from the "horror-chamber of Western dress," as they go around in jackets with Schiller-collars, sometimes with startling, thick knitted caps, that well-known breeding place of bugs. (Zentgraaff 1928, 221–22)

European dress was not new in Aceh. Several decades earlier, Kruyt (1877, 21–22) had described Acehnese nobles in Idi wearing a combination of European-style garments and "local" clothing. However, in the 1920s a growing number of people seemed to be discarding "traditional" dress altogether. A typical example was the attempt by a local administrator in Lam Meulo (Pidie) to have thirty *uleebalang* appear in "typical" *adat* clothing for a visit of the governor general. It turned out to be impossible. Zentgraaff reported: "[The controleur] had to settle for a different kind of headwear; [for] the [traditional scarf] had become a curiosity" (Zentgraaff 1928, 222). Personally, Zentgraaff was ambivalent about these changes. On the one hand, he lamented the loss of "local identity." On the other hand, he saw the development as a sign that the Acehnese were turning their backs on the resistance. Instead, what he observed was a new—and rather content—group of young people, who "go to the cinema . . . bring comfort in their lives and feel that they can no longer do without some degree of leisure and enjoyments." This, Zentgraaff pondered, was essentially a good thing: "When I see those lanky youngsters, wearing a modern flannel costume with a collar at one of those small stations of the Atjeh-tram, I am certain that these are not the men for long stays in the jungle, for months-long wanderings in the 'mud,' or fanatical klewang-attacks" (Zentgraaff 1928, 215).

Dutch administrators, according to Zentgraaff, failed to see these changes. Scathing was his critique, therefore, of the obsessive attempts to track down and destroy remaining copies of the *Hikayat Perang Sabil*. Citing a conversation with Panglima Polem, a former resistance leader and one of the most prominent *zelfbestuurders* in Aceh (see chapter 2), he noted perceptively that, in terms of mobilizing power, the Malay-language press had taken over from vernacular expressions many years ago, at least in Banda Aceh and on the North and East Coasts (Zentgraaff 1928, 281–82).

Language, indeed, was central to the atmosphere of change. Literacy was a feature of the growing middle class, or what John Bowen (1991, 95–96), writing about Takengon in the Gayo highlands, referred to as a new "cultural elite," defined by its engagement with a range of "new cultural forms—literary, political, religious, musical, athletic—[that] had in common a supra local and contemporary perspective on society." A rapidly expanding body of popular literature in Malay—the lingua franca—allowed Aceh (and other regions) to form new relationships with the Netherlands Indies and, through translation, with the world at large (Siegel 1997). This included popular works written in vernacular Malay, and, from the late 1910s onward, the use of a "proper," standardized, and edifying Malay by institutions such as the state-owned publishing house Balai Pustaka. According to Siegel (1997, 134), a central theme in the novels of Balai Pustaka was the clash between the "culture of the regions" (typically denoted as *adat*) and "a certain 'modernity' that reflected Dutch influence but was at the same time often thought of as 'nationalist.' " Balai Pustaka publications presented "a nationalism that was not at odds with colonial authority." As a paradigmatic example of the Balai Pustaka novel, Siegel discusses *Djeumpa Atjeh* (Flower of Aceh), a novel by the Acehnese author Zainoe'ddin, which narrates a tragic love story of two Dutch-educated Acehnese youth and their struggle against the conservative and restrictive custom of arranged marriages (Siegel 1997, 134–60).[17]

Ideas about modernity and the emergence of an educated middle class in colonial Indonesia are often analyzed in support of the macro-narrative of the Indonesian nation. In reality, however, expressions of progress and modernity did not necessarily (or, indeed, very usually) result in political action. As Henk Schulte Nordholt (2011b) argues, the totalizing narrative of Indonesian nationalism is problematic because it privileges the views and concerns of the politically engaged. Using alternative sources, such as advertisements and school posters, he suggests that "the majority of the indigenous native middle classes were not primarily interested in joining the nationalist movement." They aspired, rather, to a particular lifestyle, which "could be obtained by joining the framework of the colonial system" (Schulte Nordholt 2011b, 437–38). His argument resonates with that of Jean Taylor, who scrutinized colonial era photographs from Aceh for "clues for writing social histories to complement the political histories that already exist" (J. Taylor 2011, 234). Some of these photos reflect the "emergence of an Acehnese urban class that was being integrated into the colony, at a time when the colony was moving towards becoming Indonesia" (J. Taylor 2011, 233). Like elsewhere in the colony, in Aceh race and ethnicity "trumped" class in official colonial discourse, while "class was self-evident, but implicitly regarded as operating within separate communal arenas" (Sutherland 2011, 823). For some segments of the middle class, these communal arenas were tied to the Netherlands Indies and to global intellectual and cultural networks rather than to the region (Mrázek 2002;

Siegel 1997). It is important to keep this in mind as I move, in the next section, to the dynamics of religious activism, proselytization, and the emergence of an Acehnese regionalist discourse.

Islamic Activism

Associational life in early twentieth-century Aceh was extremely diverse. Organizations listed in a 1920 inventory range from branches of major political movements—such as Sarekat Islam and Boedi Oetomo—to specific interest groups such as the Association of Railway and Tram Personnel, local charity initiatives, and reading clubs. Officially, the government stance toward indigenous associational life was neutral. This was expressed, for example, in its refusal to intervene in worker strikes, which happened quite often.[18] The same was not true for religious organizations, however, despite the official mantra that religion and *adat* should be considered, above all, "indigenous" affairs.

The first significant Islamic organization active in Aceh was Sarekat Islam (SI, originally Sarekat Dagang Islam, "Association of Islamic Traders"), which was also the first Indonesian mass movement to claim a social basis in Islam. It was particularly popular among educated youth and the middle class. In Aceh, these were found mostly among the *uleebalang*. An Acehnese branch was founded in Tapaktuan (South Aceh) in 1916. Although Dutch officials predicted that the movement would not flourish in "conservative" Aceh, it grew quickly in membership. In 1920, Governor van Sluys thought that SI might well become the preeminent popular movement in Aceh, and its activities came to be closely watched.[19] In 1921, three SI "propagandists" and two *zelfbestuurders* were exiled for creating an "anti-Dutch atmosphere."[20] What worried the government the most was the organization's secretive character. Suspicion was raised by the alleged practice of taking a holy oath, which included a promise of loyalty to the leadership of the organization. In 1922, the governor general in Batavia warned the chairman of the People's Council (D. Volksraad) that this oath might be perceived as "stronger" than the loyalty sworn by the *uleebalang* to the government.[21] At the same time, the practice reminded the Dutch of the oaths sworn by fighters in the holy war. The success of SI did not persist, both because of the persecution of SI leaders and because of the increasing polarization between *kaum muda* and *kaum tua*. Particularly fierce within the multiethnic populations of large and middle-sized towns, these religious contestations undermined the class-based and business-oriented networks that facilitated the spread of SI.

Other Islamic associations were asserting themselves. The originally West Sumatran organization Sumatra Thawalib established its first Acehnese branch in Tapaktuan in 1919. In 1930, it changed its name to Persatoean Moeslimin Indonesia (PMI). Another reformist organization, Muhammadiyah, established its first Acehnese branch in Banda Aceh in 1927. Political reports consistently stated that Sumatra Thawalib and Muhammadiyah were attractive primarily to ethnic outsiders (particularly Javanese, Minangkabau, and Malays). It seems, however, that Acehnese membership was structurally understated by the Dutch. Muhammadiyah was active mostly in urban settings, and in the late colonial period these were indeed markedly multiethnic. However, when the first Muhammadiyah school opened in Banda Aceh, twenty-seven of the ninety-nine students were ethnically Acehnese.[22] This was a minority, but not an insignificant one. Several *uleebalang* (and "other important Acehnese people"), including the leader of the Acehnese branch, Teuku Moehammad Hasan of Glumpang Payong, were present at the opening.

Sumatra Thawalib and Muhammadiyah were in the first place educational movements. As such, they raised less suspicion than Sarekat Islam. Like in West Sumatra, however, Sumatra Thawalib members were occasionally suspected of having communist sympathies.[23] This was certainly not the case with Muhammadiyah. Dutch officials were quite sympathetic to Muhammadiyah, which they regarded as doctrinally moderate, politically quiescent, and a modernizing influence because of its focus on education and development.[24] Still, even Muhammadiyah was seen, ultimately, as a mixed blessing. The Acehnese, it was thought, were so self-conscious about their religion, so inherently conservative, and so easily brought off balance, that any Islamic movement from the "outside" might cause a disturbance. Again, geographical framing played a role. In Banda Aceh, Sigli, and Lhokseumawe, Muhammadiyah branches were regarded as a positive influence, because they might have the ability to absorb *kaum muda* factions and keep them from radicalizing. In West and South Aceh, however, the population was considered to be too "orthodox" to accommodate reformist influences peacefully. In these areas, the presence of these movements was a priori considered undesirable.[25] In Tapaktuan, Muhammadiyah propaganda was first discouraged and later (in 1936) forbidden.[26]

In the 1920s, a number of reform-minded, locally based Arab and Acehnese (*dayah*-educated) ulama began to establish new schools and organizations throughout Aceh, often under the patronage of sympathetic *zelfbestuurders*.[27] Active reformers, they did not limit themselves to teaching but traveled around to spread their ideas in public meetings (*tabligh*). Although they included the leaders who would be involved, later, in the establishment of PUSA, it is important to emphasize that, at this point in history, there was no "Aceh-wide" association of ulama. Instead, a wide range of initiatives, shifting alliances, and collaborations emerged, which were all, one way or another, associated with the *kaum muda* current. The reformist movement was neither homogeneous nor progressively moving toward a clearly defined goal. Many initiatives were place specific, responding to local (village- or neighborhood-level) concerns. A 1933 article in the Acehnese newspaper *Muslimin* stated: "In Moentasik, there is Djadamnja; in Blang Pase there is Djami'atoek Diniahnja; in Mt. Ol. Doea there is Al Moeslimnja.... [T]here is the establishment of schools standing by themselves. They do not have a bond with each other, whether in the affairs of organization or in the affairs of teaching and training. This is who we are!" (cited in Gedacht 2013, 252).

A small booklet summarizing the content of a gathering in Banda Aceh and a "Great Tabligh" in a village in Aceh Besar in 1936 nonetheless speaks of a shared reformist agenda.[28] According to the program, representatives of ninety-two organizations and schools attended the meeting. Of these, forty were located in Banda Aceh and Aceh Besar, twenty-six on the North and East Coasts (including Pidie), twenty-four on the West and South Coasts, and two in Takengon. Before discussing both events, the booklet praises the "renaissance" of Muslim consciousness, emphasizing the importance of bringing "clarity" into the "true goal and meaning of the religion of Islam," and of countering the false teachings, "propaganda," and attacks of Yusuf Nabahani (a Sufi and poet from Palestine, who campaigned against reformist thinkers such as Muhammad Abduh and Jamal al-Din al-Afghani). The meeting brought together a select group of ulama, sympathetic chiefs, and other dignitaries at the house of Teuku Njak Arif.[29] After everyone had been given the opportunity to speak, the assembly decided that neither Islam nor shari'a prohibited the study of "worldly sciences," that the study of these subjects should be considered obligatory (*wajib*), that including these was "indeed the intention" of those schools, and that there was no objection to women teaching men.[30]

The subsequent *tabligh* featured a number of reform-minded ulama and reportedly attracted an audience of "more than 10,000 Muslims and Muslimahs." Also present were Teuku Moehammad Hasan, the *zelfbestuurder* of Glumpang Payong (and former leader of Muhammadiyah in Aceh), as well as other *zelfbestuurders* from Pidie and Aceh Besar. After a short opening address, a speech was given by Teuku Njak Arif, who warned the audience that "Islam does not permit fragmentation and division." Different ulama subsequently discussed issues such as the history of Islam, from the Prophet Muhammad to the "services to the *umma*" offered by Shaykh Muhamad Abduh, the "obligation of men to teach women," the crucial importance for the *umma* of modern education (including sciences such as geography and books with pictures), and the discrepancy between Islam and the Malay and Acehnese practice of holding ritual feasts (*kenduri*) for the deceased.[31]

Three years later, in May 1939, a conference was held in the village of Matang Glumpang Dua (Bireuen, on the North Coast), which featured many of the same speakers. This meeting, a joint initiative of Teungku Abdul Rahman, head of the Al-Islam school movement in Peusangan, and Teuku Mohamad Djohan Alamsjah, the influential *uleebalang* of that district, resulted in the establishment of the All Aceh Association of Ulama (Persatuan

Ulama-Ulama Seluruh Aceh, PUSA). Unfortunately, we have little information about the content of the conference. According to a Dutch observer, the intention of the organization was "to join together all those involved in Muhammadan education, to raise the level of [Islamic education] . . . to standardize it more or less, and to adapt it to the demands of modern times."[32] The participants agreed, moreover, that modern Islamic education in Aceh depended too much on Muhammadiyah. The network of religious schools and teacher training colleges should be adapted not only to "modern times," but also to "the specific qualities of the land and its people."[33] Daud Beureueh, an ulama from Mutiara (Pidie), was elected as chairman, probably because of his talent as an orator and youthful charisma.[34] Despite its name, PUSA was open to both lay Muslims and religious teachers. Its headquarters were in Sigli. Daud Beureueh's first initiative was to go on a promotional tour to the West Coast, together with Ismail Yakub, a teacher and writer who claimed—decades later—to have been one of the driving forces behind the establishment of the organization.[35]

In April 1940, PUSA held its second conference in Sigli. Apart from attracting thousands of people, this meeting was significant for a number of reasons. First, the idea of an Acehnese "reawakening" had become very prominent, both in speeches and in the pamphlets distributed.[36] Second, PUSA-affiliated ulama presented themselves as leaders of a mass-based popular movement, founding chapters such as the PUSA Youth (Pemuda PUSA), led by Teungku Amir Husin al-Mujahid, and a women's section, Muslimat PUSA, led by Nyak Asma (Daud Beureueh's wife). Existing organizations, such as the Islamic scouting movement (Kashfatul Islam, based in Bireuen), affiliated themselves formally with PUSA. Third, PUSA began to advocate its reformist ideology more widely. A special council—the Majlis Tanfidziyah Shariyah, under the chairmanship of Teungku Hasballah Indrapuri—was established to issue fatwas on legal issues, and a periodical, *Penjoeloeh*, was established as a platform for reformist views on different matters ranging from correct Islamic practices to international politics. Finally, PUSA was affiliated with the Indonesia-wide network of Islamic associations called Majlis Islam Ala Indonesia (MIAI).[37]

Although PUSA presented itself as a regionalist alternative to Muhammadiyah, a gradual process of radicalization caused both organizations to draw closer together rather than move apart.[38] Instead of emphasizing mutual differences, they sharpened their profile by rallying against shared enemies. The Dutch would come to occupy this place, eventually, but before that happened, a target was sought in the "deviant" Ahmadiyah sect, a messianic movement founded five decades earlier in Qadian, India. In terms of membership, Ahmadiyah in Aceh was negligible. Yet in the view of Islamic scripturalist reformers it posed a serious threat to the integrity of the Muslim community. Anti-Ahmadiyah rhetoric was an effective means of drawing crowds. In these campaigns, reformists found an ally, rather than an opponent, in the colonial government. For the Dutch, who worried about the potentially destabilizing influence of "foreign propagandists" (D. *vreemde propagandisten*), the outbreak of anti-Ahmadiyah propaganda was a sign of the "conservative" and "orthodox" nature of the Acehnese.[39] Thus, when an Ahmadiyah follower was advised by a meeting of prominent ulama to leave Aceh to avoid a beating, he was told by Governor van Aken that, "however tolerant and beautiful" his teachings may be, it would be wise not to choose Aceh as a ground for propaganda, for he would harvest only hatred and conflict.[40] In a report, van Aken wrote that the Acehnese aversion to Ahmadiyah was so great that the police "had to protect its propagandists." In practice, this protection meant persuading these people to "leave Aceh alone."[41]

Violence and the Transformation of the Public Sphere

In histories of Aceh, changes during the late colonial period are often placed in the service of explaining the Indonesian Revolution and subsequent events. The problem with this framework is that it presents PUSA as the first and foremost—or only—"natural" agent of vernacular modernity, the logical or even inevitable reaction to colonialism.[42] However, for most people in Aceh, including many of those involved in the blossoming of associational life, it was probably not very clear what the future would, or should, bring. I reject the common tendency to look at Acehnese history solely or primarily from the perspective of the next war coming (cf. Blom 2008, 4). Rather than viewing the colonial encounter from the perspective of the events that followed it, I suggest treating it as an open-ended process, a sense of "premonition" (Mrázek 2002, xv), perhaps, but not a predetermined route toward an inevitable future.

This section offers two final reflections on the colonial period. The first bears on the misleading use of the concept of "Islamic modernism." The second is a comparative note about the impact of the war and the nature of the public sphere. Both reflections are intended to add nuance to a historiography that, in my view, has been overly concerned with the idea of "total transformation." Contemporary calls for the remaking of society merit a longue durée and comparative perspective that brings into focus both the continuities at work and the reasons why the calls for radical change did not meet the resistance that might be expected from a complex and plural society.

Recovering from a decades-long war, Aceh in the late colonial period was permeated with the promise of progress. This involved new lifestyles, a thirst—near-unquenchable in the 1930s—for schooling, and a variety of attempts to reconcile long-standing religious traditions, changing religious ideas, and secular knowledge. As James Siegel (1997) has argued for the Netherlands Indies more generally, for the emerging middle class, modernity meant nothing less than the creation of a new kind of person. PUSA stood at the forefront of this development. Its view of society implicated a "movement from one state to the next: from darkness to light, from disorder to unity, from backwardness to modernity, from sleep to awareness" (Siegel 1969, 130–31). Such a total transformation was to be achieved through strengthening, by way of education, worship, and individual religious development, the bonds between Muslims. Modern society, in the ideology of PUSA, was a "manifestation of ibadah [worship]" (Siegel 1969, 116). However, as I have argued in more detail elsewhere, expressions of Muslim selfhood and individual moral responsibility were by no means tied to a twentieth-century, or "colonial era," modernity. The tradition of Acehnese epic poetry suggests that an individualized religious ethics, as expressed in abstract concepts of harmony, loyalty, chastity, patience, sacrifice, and piety, had already emerged in the eighteenth and nineteenth centuries, thereby replacing previous, more ritualized and hierarchical conceptions of religious personhood (Kloos 2015a).

My critique of modernity as a framework for understanding religious change should not be confused with the more general critique of the concept of modernity as a "model held up before colonized people" (Cooper 2005, 115–16). Modernity, as Cooper notes, "has been a claim-making concept" for colonizers and colonized alike. At the same time, it is "only one of the terms in which claims can be made." To present the emergence of an Acehnese version of "modernist" Islam as the primary indigenous expression of social and religious change negates alternative, established, and above all less "political" expressions of change and moral consciousness. In particular, it fixes notions about the transformation of the self to the colonial project, thereby reifying a very particular ideological framework—PUSA's call for a "total transformation" based on an activist, scripturalist, and regionalist version of Islam—that was developed in and against its fold.

This brings me to my second reflection, namely the space for contesting normative Islam more generally. In many respects—such as the professionalization of religious authority, the growing influence of transnational religious movements, and the impact of the printing press—the situation in Aceh was quite similar to that in other regions in the archipelago. One of the main differences was that, in Aceh, these changes took place to an important extent outside a colonial context, and that, once colonial forces did enter the scene, it was with such intensity and violence that the space for contestation and ambivalent political and religious commitments was relatively limited. Let me elaborate on this point—and its implications—by drawing a brief comparison with two other Indonesian regions with a history of Islamic reformism and colonial violence: Java and West Sumatra.

In Java, rulers such as Sultan Agung (r. 1613–46), Pakubuwana II (r. 1726–29), and Dipanegara (1785–1855) reconciled Islamic and "Javanese" religious identity to produce what Merle Ricklefs has called a "mystic synthesis"

(Ricklefs 2006). Fusing a commitment to Islamic norms and local spiritual forces, this became the dominant religious form in Java, embraced by elites and commoners alike. The mystic synthesis was not just a matter of religious practice. It was also a major source of resistance against colonialism, which, from the eighteenth century onward, was increasingly led by religious leaders and presented (much like in Aceh) as a "holy war."[43] In the second half of the nineteenth century, an increasingly strong and pervasive colonial state and a large number of pilgrims returning from the Hejaz together put an end to the mystic synthesis as the major strand of Javanese religion (Ricklefs 2007). Javanese society became polarized between pious Muslims on the one hand and nominal Muslims and Christians on the other, while the mystic synthesis survived as a marginal stream. By the early twentieth century, Javanese religious life had become characterized by an ongoing negotiation between old and new forms of piety, and between quiescent local elites and shari'a-minded reformers who were essentially, but not usually very openly, dismissive of non-Muslim rule (Ricklefs 2007; cf. Blackburn 2008, 85–90; Federspiel 2001; Nakamura 2012, 18–118; Shiraishi 1990).

A comparable process took place, though under very different circumstances, in West Sumatra. In the early decades of the nineteenth century, a disruptive conflict broke out between Islamic reformers-cum-moralizers known as the "Padris" and an alliance between the Minangkabau royal family and Dutch forces. As Jeffrey Hadler (2008) has shown, after the defeat of the Padris in 1833, Minangkabau Muslims were confronted for a long time with a variety of religious and ideological currents. These contestations, a dynamic contest between the ideological principles of the traditional Minangkabau matriarchate, reformist Islam, and the colonial state, became part and parcel of the West Sumatran public sphere. Reaching a climax in the 1920s, this contest focused to an important extent on the private domain of the house and the family.[44] The "continual, everyday interrogation of essential cultural definitions," starting with the Padri War and persevering throughout the colonial period, thus became a source of great energy within Minangkabau society (Hadler 2008, 154–55).

Aceh, too, was a site of contestations between the representatives of *adat*, religion, and the state. But the timing, scale, and intensity of the colonial intrusion were very different. When, in the late nineteenth century, the Dutch annexed the area associated with the sovereignty of the Acehnese sultan, it was with such brutal violence that the space for negotiation and the formation of flexible and adjustable relationships was smaller than in other parts of the archipelago. When the debate about the Minangkabau family reached its apex, people in Aceh had barely begun to recover from the disaster that had struck their society. As Joshua Gedacht has shown, Dutch military leaders were less "pragmatic" than elsewhere. In West Sumatra, workable relations were negotiated, eventually, with religious leaders. At the same time, Dutch strategies in Aceh chased away moderate actors, including the traders and "savvy cosmopolitan operators striving to reach some sort of resolution" (Gedacht 2013, 113–15, 230). Most importantly, perhaps, the nature of the war in Aceh prevented a "vibrant urban sector" from materializing, as in Java and West Sumatra, in the first decades of the twentieth century (Gedacht 2013, 242–43).

When a dynamic public sphere did emerge, eventually, in the 1930s and early 1940s, it was in the context of a deeply militarized society and under the purview of an increasingly conservative and paranoid colonial administration (see Kloos 2014). It also had very little time to mature. This analysis differs from the more positive picture of the public sphere drawn by other scholars of the region. Michael Feener, for instance, emphasized the "high profile debates" between Islamic modernists and traditionalists as they appeared in newspapers, pamphlets, sermons, public meetings, study sessions, and so forth. Although I do not deny the significance of these debates, certainly not from a religious (doctrinal) perspective, it is important to emphasize that these debates did not take shape until the mid-1930s. A similar qualification may be added to John Bowen's (1993, 27) contention that "confrontations and debates [between modernists and traditionalists] were the hallmarks of the years 1928–1942, the formative period for developing a scripture-based conception of religion in the Gayo highlands." Setting aside the argument advanced earlier in this chapter (and based partly on the work of Bowen himself) that public debates in this period were not just about religion, this thirteen-year period may have been crucial but also—compared to the more drawn-out histories of religious and ideological contestation in Java and West Sumatra—very short. Religious debates, writes Bowen (1993, 28), were dominated by modernists, because they were the ones who "called for open debates on religious matters." To this I add that there was neither time nor a very conducive atmosphere for their critics to formulate a strong response. Both in Aceh and in the Gayo highlands, the public sphere developed late and in a tense political context. The outbreak of the Pacific War in 1941 released the Acehnese and the Gayo from the shackles of Dutch colonial rule, while setting the stage, at the same time, for a new round of political violence and social upheaval.

Conclusion

Only two decades separated the installment of a civil administration and the end of colonial rule. In the intervening period, Aceh was a social, cultural, and political pressure cooker. While the war continued, on a lesser scale, until the late 1930s, the promise of peace and progress came with a range of new aspirations and possibilities, new and more complex relations between the Acehnese and the colonial state, and new religious ideas. In the meantime, and driven by their determination to crush the remaining Acehnese resistance, Dutch administrators and military leaders created a sharp distinction between a traditional Aceh that was wild, mystical, and belligerent and a (future) modern Aceh that was rational, civilized, and transformed by a mundane strand of Islamic reform.

This dichotomy was not solely of Dutch making. In this chapter, I have analyzed in some detail the social and organizational dynamics that preceded the establishment, in 1939, of the Acehnese reformist organization PUSA (All Aceh Association of Ulama). While PUSA is commonly regarded as an "anticolonial" phenomenon, owing to its role in the expulsion of the Dutch, the Japanese occupation, and the Indonesian Revolution, conspicuous analogies existed between the views of Islamic reformers and colonial administrators. These included a strong propensity to declare expressions of Islamic mysticism as deviant, backward, and antithetical to the expression of a true, orthodox, and forward-looking interpretation of Islam. Both groups had very different ideas about the place of Islam in the public sphere and the way in which Acehnese society should be organized. Yet out of the dialectic a new, shared narrative emerged, which tied particular ideas about the history of Aceh—as a place turned in on itself—to a particular vision of the future. Despite the very different terminologies in which this future was cast—one secular, one religious—this was a narrative with a specific direction, pointing toward the total transformation of Aceh on the basis of a paradigm of progress, modernity, and moral restoration.

If the image of pious Aceh was politically potent, it was also contingent and exclusivist, a construction based on the social concerns and political interests of specific groups and people. Although there is no question that Acehnese society in the late colonial period was experiencing significant change, both the language of pacification and the call for a new and transformed religious "consciousness" conceal continuities, slower processes of adaptation and adjustment, and persistent ambivalences about the role of political and religious authorities (cf. Kloos 2015a). The often-used concept of Islamic modernism negates alternative vernacular expressions of religious emancipation. At the same time, the colonial war continued to cast its long shadow. The main reason why the imagining of pious Aceh made such a strong and lasting impression is that the scale of the violence and the intensity of the campaign to "normalize" and "modernize" Acehnese society left very little room for reflection and debate about competing religious dispositions and practices. The next chapter analyzes the impact of the Islamic reformist movement in the mid-twentieth century. It does so by elaborating further on the relationship between state and religious authority, and the space available for both individual and collective action.

2

The Limits of Normative Islam

There are too many factions in this village.

—TEUNGKU JAHJA (INDRAPURI, 2008)

This chapter investigates the impact of state and reformist Islam on the religious lives of ordinary Acehnese in the early decades of Indonesian independence. Ever since the state was brought "back into" the study of politics and society (Evans, Rueschemeyer, and Skocpol 1985), works on Aceh have tended to focus on the forces that mobilized the Acehnese either in support of, or against, the central state (see, e.g., Aspinall 2009; Kell 1995; Morris 1983; Reid 1979; Sjamsuddin 1985; van Dijk 1981). While these studies have increased our understanding of local politics, the frequent use of Aceh as a case study for examining rebellion, separatism, or center-periphery relations also contributes to an essentialist understanding of Acehnese identity. Instead of viewing the Acehnese as pitted against the national, secular state, this chapter asks how the state was embedded in Acehnese society (cf. Aretxaga 2003; Barker and van Klinken 2009; Gupta 1995) and how this process influenced local contestations about religious practice and authority (cf. Beatty 2009; Bowen 2003; Feener, Kloos, and Samuels 2015; Guinness 2009; Hadler 2008; Hefner and Horvatich 1997; Peletz 2002; Siapno 2002).

The dominant narrative of the Indonesian nation has long been a secular one. In recent years, however, historians have drawn attention to the religious foundations of the Indonesian nation and the accommodative stances toward normative Islam on the part of the secular state (see, e.g., Fogg 2012; Formichi 2014; Laffan 2003; Ricklefs 2012). In Aceh, a pro-Republican government emerged from the violence of the Revolution (1945–46). Led by PUSA (Persatuan Ulama-Ulama Seluruh Aceh, All Aceh Association of Ulama) chairman

Daud Beureueh, it catered simultaneously to regionalist, nationalist, and Islamist sentiments. Once in power, PUSA leaders employed the state to redefine, disseminate, and impose Islamic norms on society. Tensions soon arose, however, and in 1953 a radical faction, led by Daud Beureueh, decided to revolt against the central government under the banner of Darul Islam (Abode of Islam). At the same time, a more moderate segment of Aceh's political and religious leadership entered the service of the state. The rebellion ended in 1962. Suharto's military "New Order" regime, established in 1965, subsequently switched to a more blunt strategy of co-optation, placing the interpretation and dissemination of Islamic norms in the service of state power and the need to uphold social and political "order" (see Feener 2013).

My perspective on these changes and events is informed by an important essay by Joshua Barker and Gerry van Klinken (2009), who, following Philip Abrams (1988), suggested that we regard the Indonesian state simultaneously as a "system" and as an "idea." To study the state as a system involves "disaggregating the state, lowering the level of analysis below the national, studying interactions anthropologically, and looking for social forces rather than static structures." Studying the state as an idea requires from researchers "an exercise in unmasking an ideology" (Barker and van Klinken 2009, 40). This approach is useful because it offers conceptual backing for understanding the state as a means or an arena for contestation, as well as an actor.[1] How were Islamic norms produced, reproduced, strengthened, changed, or discarded as reformist ulama and political leaders worked to make Aceh into a more "properly" Islamic society? How should we assess the role of the state? And how should we understand the negotiations among state agents, religious experts, and ordinary Muslims as they sought to protect or expand their religious agency?

A brief comparative note helps to sharpen my approach. As Michael Meeker (2002) demonstrated, in provincial Turkey the creation of a secular polity facilitated, rather than obstructed, the dissemination of normative Islam. For many centuries, local, place-specific beliefs and practices existed side by side with the more standardized, shariʻa-minded system of practice and authority that facilitated commercial contacts across geographic and ethnic boundaries. However, during the course of the twentieth century a developing national culture, in combination with a more egalitarian state system associated with secular modernity, contributed to the formation and increased prominence of a normative model of Sunni orthodoxy. Likewise, in Malaysia, a strong connection has been observed between the advances of normative Islam and the attempts by the secular state to increase its control over those segments of society, such as the Islamic judiciary, that used to be largely autonomous from it. "The largest threats to civil society," writes Michael Peletz (2002, 289), "lie not with one or another facet of Islamic jurisprudence . . . or with some other aspect of Islam, but with the thoroughly secular state." As I will show, these observations resonate strongly with my view on twentieth-century Aceh. At the same time, it is important to emphasize, as both these scholars do, that Islamic norms were never simply imposed on society by the state or by other powerful actors. Rather, they were the result of social and political interactions, taking place to an important extent at a local level.

This chapter concentrates on the subdistrict of Indrapuri. This was the base, from the 1930s until the mid-1950s, of PUSA ideologue Teungku Hasballah Indrapuri, and the place where Daud Beureueh declared his allegiance to the Darul Islam revolt in 1953. My analysis is based partly on archival materials and partly on the work of the late Chandra Jayawardena, a Sri Lankan–born, British-trained anthropologist, who carried out fieldwork in British Guyana, Fiji, Burma, and Indonesia, and who lived in Indrapuri in 1964, 1971, 1972–73, and 1981. Jayawardena published three articles about Aceh: one on kinship (1977b), one on marriage customs (1977a), and one on village politics (posthumously; 1987). He intended to publish a monograph, provisionally entitled *Land, Labour and Society in Acheh Besar*, but in 1981 he passed away, suddenly and untimely, before completing the manuscript. His notes about Aceh were donated by his wife, Yvonne Jayawardena, to Macquarie University, Sydney, where he had been a founding professor of anthropology in 1969. On the initiative of Kathryn Robinson, they were digitized and made available for students as an online resource.[2] The notes cover a wide range of phenomena, from agricultural cycles and religious rituals to the details of Acehnese history, politics, and conflict. Viewed as a whole, Jayawardena's work provides an unparalleled insight into Acehnese rural society during the early years of the New Order.

According to Robinson (2006, 242), Jayawardena's work "illustrates, even prefigures, the path taken by anthropology in moving beyond a preoccupation with the boundedness of the social worlds we study, the isomorphism of people, place, social structure and culture, to an appreciation of the complex manner in which local communities engage with the social dynamics of a wider world." The relationship between inequality, social conflict and the "tensions between ideologies in embedded forms of sociality" had his particular interest. Although Jayawardena studied anthropology in the Malinowskian tradition of structural-functionalism, by the end of his life he had come to consider Max Gluckman as "one of his greatest intellectual influences" (Kapferer 1987, 17–18). It is not surprising, then, that the observations and analyses in which he connected major ideological tensions (centralist versus regionalist, Islamist versus secularist) to the microdynamics of social life turn out to be particularly rich.

This chapter discusses the Indonesian Revolution in Aceh, the rocky path of the region's incorporation into the nation-state, and the establishment—at the local (district and village) level—of the New Order. I will argue that the impact of reformist Islam, championed by PUSA and Darul Islam, was more limited than commonly assumed, and that the attempt by the government to adapt and incorporate reformist Islamic norms and interpretations created opportunities as much as constraints. The New Order was based to a significant extent on coercion. At the same time, ordinary villagers were part of the state in various ways. As I will show, partly on the basis of the work of Jayawardena, people in Aceh were able to contest the state and to advance their own particular religious and nonreligious interests and concerns as they solicited and utilized state resources and institutions. To substantiate this argument, I single out two themes, namely the reformist objection to "un-Islamic" practices and village conflict. Let me begin, however, by providing more context, extending the narrative from the end of the colonial period to the early years of the Suharto regime.

Occupation, Revolution, Rebellion

In February 1942, anti-Dutch violence broke out in Aceh Besar and the areas around Sigli (Pidie) and Calang (West Aceh). Although different "malcontent elements" (Piekaar 1949, 77–78) were thought to be responsible for the revolt, it soon became clear that PUSA played a central role. Reformist ulama had joined a fifth column (known as Fujiwara Kikan or "Komite F"), which prepared the ground for the imminent Japanese invasion (cf. Reid 1979, 85–90). One month later, Aceh was occupied by Japanese forces and purged of the Dutch (Piekaar 1949). The system of government was initially left intact. The *uleebalang* were even strengthened as they were granted the offices of former Dutch officials. PUSA and the PUSA Youth, despite their support for the new power holders, were told "not to interfere in government matters."[3] However, in subsequent years they were increasingly involved in the bureaucracy and government propaganda, and ultimately the Japanese went much further than the Dutch in their creation of a separate Islamic officialdom. This included a religious advisory council (the Madjelis agama Islam oentoek bantoean kemakmoeran Asia Timoer Raja di Atjeh, or Maibkatra) and a system of religious courts (Mahkamah Agama), in which the chairmanship of the *uleebalang* was replaced by an Islamic judge (*kadi*), who operated directly under the authority of the Japanese.

Realizing that the war might be lost, the Japanese initiated a process that was expected to lead, eventually, to Indonesian independence. In September 1944, PUSA leader Daud Beureueh spoke of "two celebrations," namely Hari Raya Idulfitri (the celebration of the end of Ramadan) and Hari Raya Kemerdekaan (the celebration of independence), declaring that it was "impossible to say which one was the greatest of the two."[4] The Japanese surrendered to Allied forces in August 1945. The Dutch, caught up in revolutionary violence in Java and North Sumatra, never returned to mainland Aceh.[5] Hoping to fill the vacuum, paramilitary groups affiliated with PUSA and individual *uleebal-ang* became locked in a bloody struggle for power that has come to be known, rather euphemistically, as a "social revolution." Eventually, it was PUSA that emerged as the strongest of the warring parties. In a brief but furious contest, the traditional Acehnese nobility was eliminated from the political stage (see Reid 1979). Several *uleebalang* families escaped to Medan or Jakarta. Others were incarcerated in internment camps as "enemies of the Republic." Many were killed or executed as traitors to the Acehnese people. In July 1947, the Republican government in Yogyakarta appointed Daud Beureueh as the military governor of Aceh, Langkat, and Karo (Morris 1983, 151).

PUSA leaders framed the Revolution as a continuation of the "holy war" against the Dutch.[6] Daud Beureueh continued to give speeches across Aceh, admonishing his audience to abolish "un-Islamic" practices and rituals. Under his rule, the Islamic courts were strengthened and reformist schools were made part of a government-funded system of Islamic education (Morris 1983, 164–65). PUSA's power was contested by different groups, however. *Uleebalang* in Medan and Jakarta used the press to accuse the new government of abuse of power, self-enrichment, corruption, violence, and murder.[7] Langsa, East Aceh, developed into a center of communist activities.[8] In rural areas, especially in West and South Aceh, conservative ulama challenged the government's puritanical message. At the same time, lay officials and bureaucrats showed less and less affinity with PUSA's religious ideals. Having affiliated with the organization primarily to pursue the goals of the Revolution, they were much less prepared to confront the central government on the grounds of Islamic reform. As a result, the government's attempt to restructure Acehnese society on the basis of Islam was stalled. Rather than making compromises, Daud Beureueh stepped up his attempt, announcing that people engaged in sinful practices (such as gambling and adultery) would soon be "interned in the interests of 'public security'" and that intercession rituals and the veneration of saints would be banned (Morris 1983, 160–62).

In the early 1950s, Indonesia was "still in search of a centre." Although Sukarno "came home" to Jakarta in December 1949, "the Outer Islands took a different trajectory" (Schulte Nordholt 2011a, 387–400). The relationship between Aceh and Jakarta turned sour. In a move designed to curb the power of PUSA, military units loyal to the organization were transferred and replaced by non-Acehnese, leading to tensions on the ground, as well as violent confrontations between the Indonesian army and local communities.[9] Meanwhile, Jakarta forced the provincial government to return possessions of non-Acehnese that had been confiscated during the Revolution.[10] The situation escalated after 1951, when the central government decided to incorporate Aceh into a newly formed province of North Sumatra, thus severely curtailing Aceh's regional autonomy. The lucrative barter trade with Penang and Singapore, which had flourished since the surrender of the Japanese, was restricted in Aceh to better favor Medan, the capital of the new province (Sjamsuddin 1985, 71–75).

The attempt to create an Islamic polity was further thwarted when funding for religious education was cut and shari'a courts were degraded. In March 1953, President Sukarno publicly repeated his rejection of an Islamic state during a visit to Aceh.[11] Less than half a year later, Daud Beureueh withdrew his support for the Republican government. According to the PUSA leader, Sukarno had promised him, in a personal conversation in 1947, that Aceh would be allowed to implement shari'a law. When the province of Aceh was abolished and its new Islamic regulations nullified, this was regarded as betrayal. In September 1953, and followed by the more radical segment of PUSA, he pledged loyalty to the "Islamic state of Indonesia" (Negara Islam Indonesia, NII), also known as the Darul Islam (Abode of Islam) rebellion, which had been declared more than ten years earlier by Kartosoewirjo in West Java (see Formichi 2014; van Dijk 1981).

After a failed attack on Banda Aceh, the rebels gathered at the base of the ulama and PUSA leader Teungku Hasballah in Indrapuri. There, Daud Beureueh proclaimed the NII in Aceh "in a big ceremony" (Sjamsuddin 1985, 96–97, 179) and in front of a "huge crowd . . . which then proceeded to uproot the railway and march on Seulimeum."[12] In subsequent years, the rebels succeeded in taking control over large parts of the countryside, particularly in the Aceh Besar and Pidie districts, where they established an alternative government of sorts, including a "parliament" (Majelis Syura) and an "executive council" (Dewan Syura). Their main sources of income were smuggling and taxes, including "war fees" (*infaq*) that were imposed on local populations (Sjamsuddin 1985, 209–12). Justice was administered at ad hoc courts.[13] In areas where the Darul Islam was strong, close relationships were forged with local administrators, thus blurring the distinction between the rebellion and the government.

It is difficult to assess the level of popular support for the revolt. Morris (1983, 204–205) wrote that "for the most part Darul Islam rebels had no difficulty obtaining support from villagers," and that "in the early stages of the rebellion no distinction could be made between the populace and the rebels as tens of thousands of villagers had participated in the first wave of mass attacks on the towns." This support was based to an important extent on the idea— cultivated during the Revolution—that a "ritualized egalitarian community of believers" could be achieved only through struggle (Morris 1983, 205–209). However, support declined rapidly after 1954, when the rebellion was realigned on the basis of a military structure and placed under the supreme command of Daud Beureueh. No attempts were made to appoint local level "officials." Instead, government functionaries and community leaders were forced to cooperate (Sjamsuddin 1985, 197–212). Violence, or the threat of violence, against local populations became a central element in the rebels' strategy.[14] In the meantime, negotiations between the government and a more pragmatic segment of PUSA mitigated Acehnese grievances. In 1956, Aceh's provincial status was restored. In 1959, provincial autonomy was reestablished in the fields of religion, education, and *adat*. Aceh was now officially recognized as a "special region" (*daerah istimewa*), on a par with the cities of Jakarta and Yogyakarta (van Dijk 1981, 335). For the majority of Acehnese, few reasons remained to follow the leaders of the Darul Islam into a violent and uncertain future. In 1962, Daud Beureueh gave up his struggle on the condition of amnesty for the remaining combatants.

Other significant developments were taking place. In the mid-1950s, the government started to fill the places left empty by local administrators who had joined the rebellion. Potentially loyal groups included the (descendants of) *uleebalang* and conservative ulama.[15] The first head of the newly autonomous province, however, came from the PUSA camp. Ali Hasjmy, an ulama, youth leader, republican, and career administrator from Montasik (Aceh Besar), had been incarcerated for a few weeks in 1953 because of his alleged involvement in the preparation of the Darul Islam rebellion. He then continued to play a mediating role in the conflict and, while residing in Jakarta, was "groomed to serve as the new governor of Aceh" (Feener 2013, 38). At the same time, religious differences crystallized in the political party system. Conservative ulama mobilized in the Acehnese branch of the (originally West Sumatran) Perti (Persatuan Tarbijah Islamijah; Islamic Educational Association). Sympathizers of the Darul Islam gathered in Masyumi (Partai Majelis Syuro Muslimin Indonesia; Consultative Council of Indonesian Muslims, formed during the Japanese period), while the majority of PUSA's lay members joined Partai Sarekat Islam Indonesia (PSII), the successor of Sarekat Islam that had split from Masyumi in 1947 (Sjamsuddin 1985, 6–7, 263–64). Masyumi was banned in 1960 during Sukarno's "Guided Democracy," leading its members in Aceh either to become active for religious associations, such as Muhammadiyah, or to join PSII (Soeyatno 1977, 72).

The autonomy formula did not last long. In 1965, General Suharto seized power. The first year of his "New Order" regime was marked by the systematic destruction of the Communist Party and its (alleged) sympathizers. In Aceh, thousands were killed by Islamic youth groups in collaboration with the military.[16] The first fatwa of the newly formed provincial Ulama Council (Majelis Ulama)—the predecessor of the national Majelis Ulama Indonesia (MUI) founded in 1975—outlawed communism, branding it as "atheist, anti-God and anti-Religion" and conflating it with neo-colonial ideology.[17] Military officers were appointed as district heads (*bupati*). In the following decades, New Order policies (and abuses) would contribute to the development of a distinct style of Acehnese nationalism, ultimately embodied by Gerakan Aceh Merdeka (GAM). It is important to emphasize, however, that during the 1960s and much of the 1970s there was no GAM, and that the Acehnese case was an example of "Indonesianization" rather than the "rediscovery of regional identity" (Aspinall 2009, 35). For many Acehnese, Indonesia was changing from an "abstract ideal" into an "increasingly intrusive presence in people's daily lives," with state institutions and instruments tuned "ever more purposefully" to the objective of nation building. In contrast to earlier periods, the reform-minded elite in the 1950s and 1960s "consisted of various social classes, [including] ulama, schoolteachers, youth [groups] and students, and village intellectuals carrying the status of civil servant" (Soeyatno 1977, 67). During the early New Order period, these groups were woven, much more forcefully than before, into the fabric of the state, from the provincial government all the way down to the village. In the next section, I discuss more specifically the social and political history of Aceh Besar by focusing on two important exemplars of reform: Panglima Polem and PUSA ideologue Teungku Hasballah Indrapuri.

Exemplars of Reform

One of the wealthiest and most influential "autonomous rulers" (*zelfbestuurders*) in colonial Aceh was the former resistance leader and head of the "Sagi of the twenty-two Mukims," Panglima Polem Sri Muda Perkasa Muhamad Daud. His base was the village of Lam Sih, in the heart of Seulimeum. Like elsewhere in Indonesia, indigenous chiefs in Aceh vied for influence by combining business endeavors with an attempt to strengthen their position in the colonial bureaucracy and indigenous institutions (cf. Sutherland 1979). Although physically their territories were (relatively) fixed, the boundaries between their spheres of authority were fluid and continuously renegotiated. Religious affairs were an important dimension of this struggle. Panglima Polem sought to increase his control over religious sites (such as mosques or sacred graves), rituals (such as the Friday prayers), and the administration of religious tithes. He collected *zakat*, in the form of *padi* (unhusked rice), throughout the sagi.[18] According to Jayawardena's older interlocutors, the proceeds were used to pay the allowances of religious judges and teachers and to establish new schools and mosques.[19] Among lower ranked *uleebalang*, this was a source of great irritation.[20] In the eyes of Dutch administrators, however, he was a "true" Acehnese, culturally conservative and with great knowledge of *adat* and Islamic law.

In the mid-1920s, Panglima Polem campaigned against a new kind of dance, called the *seulaweuet* (salutations) and performed exclusively by women, which had become very popular among the younger generation. Like other *uleebalang*, he regarded this trend as a threat to public morality.[21] Thus, when a band of dancers from Padang Tiji once arrived in Seulimeum to give a performance, he summoned the leader, bought off the arrangement, and ordered him to "withdraw with his dancing girls" (Zentgraaff 1928, 223–24). His stance toward the *kaum muda* was generally supportive. The reformist Perguruan Islam school in Seulimeum enjoyed his protection, and he even founded his own reformist school, the Madrasah Islamijah Menengah, in Lam Paku. He agreed, moreover, with the idea of enriching the curriculum of Dutch schools with religious lessons (Piekaar 1949, 61; Zentgraaff 1928, 298). There is no indication, however, that he entertained a particularly scripturalist attitude toward indigenous law. The *musapat* in Seulimeum, for which he was responsible, privileged *adat* over Islamic law in marriage and divorce cases. One of the reasons for this was that shari'a was thought to give women "few rights" (van de Velde 1982, 48–52). His reformist agenda, I suspect, reflected a struggle for authority and social control rather than a clearly articulated ideological program.

The same cannot be said, however, about the religious scholars who enjoyed his patronage. When Panglima Polem returned to Seulimeum in 1903, after his surrender to the Dutch, one of his priorities was to restore the local religious infrastructure, which had suffered badly from the war. Jayawardena was told that, in the late 1910s, Panglima Polem asked Teungku Eumpetrieng, a well-known ulama from Sibreh, to restore the site of the Indrapuri mosque, the oldest surviving mosque in Aceh.[22] This scholar, possibly in a joint petition with other ulama from Aceh Besar (Hasbi Amiruddin 2003–2004, 1:38), responded by persuading Teungku Ahmad Hasballah, an ulama from Montasik who had migrated to Malaya during the war, to return to Indrapuri and take up the task of reestablishing the *dayah* there. Hasballah had received extensive religious training in Aceh, Malaya, and Mecca. After returning to Aceh, he established a school in Lheuch, a village close to the market of Indrapuri. The school was called Madrasah Hasbiyah and included a special section for girls, called Al-Madrasah lil Ummahat (Hasbi Amiruddin 2003–2004, 1:37–39). Although we have few details, it seems that his relationship with Panglima Polem was rather close. According to Jayawardena, it was said that Hasballah was the only imam in the *sagi* who "dealt directly" with the Panglima, instead of with his religious advisor, the *kadi* in Lam Sih. It was also said that he received a monthly salary and that he was supported by the Panglima in his opposition to non-Islamic beliefs and practices.[23]

According to Jayawardena's older interlocutors, Hasballah had married a woman from Lheueh, and, for a certain period, lived there. His activities caused a split in the community. Frictions emerged as Hasballah and his supporters attacked "beliefs in the intermediaries between an individual and God, and the belief in supernatural beings other than God," as well as "a whole series of folk practices such as sacrificial feasts (*kenduri*), the worship of 'sacred' graves (*keramat*), several funeral practices such as the *talkin*, the *rateb*, several harvest rites, and so on" (Jayawardena 1987, 36). Things "came to a head" when "bands of youth under Hasballah's influence" started to destroy old graves. Conservative ulama, in turn, considered his school heretical because it taught the same subjects as Dutch schools, put boys and girls in the same classroom, and used textbooks with pictures.[24] An important source of protest was the village of Tanoh Abee (which is considered one of the oldest centers of Islamic learning in Aceh Besar). Some of his fiercest adversaries were related, by blood or by marriage, to the family of Teungku Tanoh Abee.[25] Jayawardena was also told, contrary to James Siegel's (1969) thesis about the gendered nature of Islamic modernism in Aceh, that women in Lheueh were generally more sympathetic to the school than men, and that it was built, eventually, with their support.[26]

Teungku Hasballah was politically active from the moment of his return to Aceh. Initially, he joined Sarekat Islam. When this association was banned, he established a local reformist organization, called Jamiah al-Ataqiyah al-Ukhrawiyah (Hasbi Amiruddin 2003–2004, 1:39). In 1939, he was one of the founding members of PUSA. Together with other ulama from Aceh Besar, as well as the son of Panglima Polem, Teuku Muhammad Ali, he played a leading role in the 1942 revolt. Muhammad Ali, who was known as "almost explicitly anti-Dutch" and to have mingled with "extreme nationalist circles" in Java, had been appointed "out of convention" after the death of his father in 1940. His cooperation with PUSA was based on the organization's "anti-Dutch evolution" rather than its religious program (Piekaar 1949, 57–81). Unlike Teuku Muhammad Ali and the Pemuda PUSA, who represented the "progressive and militant" part of the Acehnese youth, Hasballah was able to mobilize an older, more conservative segment of the rural population. As such, he contributed significantly to the making of a popular movement, in which "the PUSA-youth and the elderly gampongman" struggled "side by side."

Compared to Pidie and other parts of the North Coast, Aceh Besar was relatively quiet during the Revolution. The old nobility was politically marginalized but allowed to keep much of their land. After the outbreak of the Darul Islam, and in the context of a sudden but brief revival of the *uleebalang* class, Muhammed Ali was appointed, to his own surprise, as the Bupati of Pidie, to be "honorably dismissed" again in 1955. He moved to Jakarta, where, in December 1958, he was arrested and incarcerated "at the request of the authorities in Aceh." In 1959, he was set free, and shortly thereafter appointed as a representative for Aceh at the newly established "temporary parliament" (Madjelis Permusjawaratan Rakjat Sementara). In 1968, he finally returned to Aceh and tried to regain his possessions (Ali Panglima Polem 1972, 47–51). He died in 1974. When Jayawardena came to Aceh Besar in the mid-1960s, there were no more descendants of Panglima Polem living in Lam Sih. They had sold their land, piece by piece, and lived "scattered in Banda Aceh and elsewhere." In the words of the villagers, they had "blended" into society (*sudah masuk masyarakat*) and become "ordinary people" (*orang biasa*).[27]

While Teuku Muhammad Ali withered, the status of Teungku Hasballah steadily increased. During the Japanese occupation he became one of the

leading members of the Maibkatra and the head of the Islamic court in Indrapuri. Whereas Daud Beureueh was groomed into the charismatic face of
Japanese propaganda, Hasballah came to be seen as his intellectual counterpart
(Piekaar 1949, 224, 268). After the Revolution, he became a leader of the Acehnese branch of Masyumi (Sjamsuddin 1985, 7). By now, he was a figure to be
reckoned with.[28] After the outbreak of the Darul Islam, he disappeared into
the mountains. His band consisted partly of religious students and partly of
PUSA supporters who were fearful of being rounded up by the army. During
the early years of the rebellion, Teungku Hasballah acted as the head of the
Darul Islam "judiciary." He did not witness the resolution of the conflict, however. He died in 1956 of natural causes.

The Limits of Normative Islam

People in Indrapuri supported the Darul Islam in different ways. In the village in which Jayawardena lived, "most of the residents . . . had joined the
rebellion."[29] Some acted as "rebels" during the night and as ordinary citizens
during the day. Others disappeared for long periods in the mountains and returned to the village during harvest time, where they were sheltered from the
authorities by fellow villagers. Yet others assisted by stocking mountain camps
with food and basic necessities. In their hiding places, Jayawardena was told,
the combatants formed a "society of their own." Their activities included the
preparation for armed confrontation but also communal prayer and religious
discussion. Life was "pure" (suci), they said.[30]

There was also aversion to the rebellion. Jayawardena heard that arbitrary
killing took place on both sides and that people who disagreed with the revolt
were forced to take refuge in Banda Aceh. One person said that he refused to
support the rebellion because "the first duty of an individual is to the state"
and because "religion is a personal business."[31] Many rebels gave up their struggle after the negotiation of a ceasefire in 1957. One of Jayawardena's regular
interlocutors, a former Tentara Islam Indonesia (TII) captain, recalled that
they camped on the coast or on the roadside, "uniforms and all." Personally,
he continued the struggle because he "agreed with Daud Beureueh that the
Sjariat Islam must be enforced throughout Atjeh."[32] By the late 1950s, however,
the situation in Aceh Besar became untenable. Too few of them were left and
popular support had crumbled. Many rebels were persuaded to surrender on
the condition of amnesty. Jayawardena's informant returned to his former job
as a TNI officer, although he was no longer required to report for duty. By the
early 1970s, he was spending most of his time in the village.

Although it is important to consider the violence, the impact of the Darul
Islam should not be reduced to an analysis of armed conflict and its justifica-
tions alone. Teungku Hasballah and Daud Beureueh were charismatic leaders

who inspired people, acquired followers, and succeeded in making the rebellion hold sway, at least for some years, over a large part of the Acehnese countryside. How should we assess the impact of their call to "purify" society, and their attempt to bring Acehnese society into accordance with the laws of God?

One of PUSA's main objectives was to stop the practice of *ziarah*, the visiting of sacred graves, and the ritual of *kenduri kematian*, the communal meals during which the deaths of loved ones as well as important spiritual leaders and saints were commemorated. Such practices, reformists argued, falsely suggested the possibility of intercession by the deceased between God and human beings.[33] A formal ban by the (PUSA-led) government had denied access, temporarily, to the tomb of Syiah Kuala (Morris 1983, 161–62). This was close to Banda Aceh. In rural areas, the prohibition was difficult, if not impossible, to enforce. In the mid-1960s, Jayawardena noted, several graves in the Indrapuri area were considered *keramat* (holy sites). The most important of these were the graves of Teungku Chik di Tiro (one of the leaders in the Aceh War), Teungku Chik Eumpetrieng (the ulama who facilitated the arrival of Teungku Hasballah), and Teungku Lam Djamee. These places were frequently visited, both by locals and by people from further away, and they were popular sites for holding *kenduri*.

The practice of *berziarah* served different goals. Securing one's livelihood was one of them:

> When cattle and buffalo are sick the animals are brought thither. *Doa* [supplicatory prayers] are offered at the grave; and a bit of earth, mixed in water, is daubed over the head and face of the animal. Or recently born calves are brought there. Some come there after the harvest with the animals who had worked the season. Especially brought there are young buffaloes who, in their calf-hood, shed their fur once or twice. The animals suffer greatly from the heat during this time, and more often than at other times, die. The *teungku meunasah* [of] Lheueh, whose *sawah* are near the tomb say that people still come. . . . Hasby, [a] tailor from Meusale says that people come often.[34]

In fact, the practice was not limited to rural areas. Jayawardena did not mention the grave of Syiah Kuala, but he did observe another famous site in Tanjong, just outside the city. The grave of Nek Rabi belonged to a woman who, according to local traditions, had been killed for committing adultery (*zina*). Such ghosts or spirits of women who had led an "adulterous life" were known as *burong*, a creature similar to the Sundanese *kunti* or *kuntianak* or the Javanese *sundel bolong* (Snouck Hurgronje 1893–94, 1:417). Nek Rabi was ascribed the power to "close the womb" of pregnant women, making the delivery of children difficult and dangerous.[35] At her grave, blessings were "transferred" to the visitor's body by washing the face, using water mixed with soil from the grave, preferably taken from its "centre," "the location of the navel of the corpse," or by "rub[bing] the headstone with one's hands and then . . . rub[bing] one's face."[36]

Pregnant women regularly visited the tomb to make offerings. It was not even necessary to visit the grave in person:

> In some parts, old women (perhaps men too) announce that they have been appointed "duta" [emissary] for that area by Nek Rabi—so that people could intercede with Nek Rabi through them, without going all the way to the tomb.[37]

The grave was guarded by local descendants. Alms were collected by a *teungku* some kilometers away, who shared them with local residents.

The reformist movement did influence *ziarah* practices, but this was contingent on time and circumstances. Consider, for example, Jayawardena's notes about *djirat adjar*, the "tomb of the hermit," located close to the village of Lheueh. For as long as people remembered, this place was *keramat*, a favorite location for *kenduri blang* (communal meals related to the harvest) and rituals performed in the wake of disaster (such as the outbreak of disease). By the 1970s, most people had stopped visiting this grave. According to the *geuchik* of Lheueh, this was a direct result of Panglima Polem's and Teungku Hasballah's admonitions. Visitors were mostly descendants of the people buried in the compound (the newest grave was six months old). This was an exceptional case. With the reformist influence "greatly lightened" by the 1970s, there were signs of a "resurgence" of *ziarah* practices.[38] During a visit to the grave of Nek Rabi, Jayawardena was told that, two days earlier, a party of thirty people had come all the way from Sigli (Pidie). At the grave of Teungku Chik Eumpetrieng, the buried ulama's son confiscated offerings and forbade people to come to the grave and engage in practices such as taking earth, burning lamps, and hanging flags. "People were annoyed," Jayawardena wrote, "but most dissuaded. However, a few continue to worship it."[39]

More sensitive than the practice of *ziarah* was the work of healer-diviners and their dealings with supernatural beings. The people of Indrapuri were mindful of a wide variety of supernatural phenomena, including *jinn* (spirits) and *hantu* (ghosts). These beings inhabited trees or other objects and occasionally revealed themselves in front of human beings in the form of an "incandescent glow." They were generally thought malevolent, able and willing to attack careless people at night. Jayawardena was told that, up until the 1950s, it was quite common for villagers to make offerings to *hantu*. Spirits possessing a human being would cause the latter to "become stiff" or "get the shakes." They would demand "specific kinds of food and drink" and depart when their wish was fulfilled. In stark contrast to the practice of *ziarah*, the custom of making offerings to *hantu* was "dying out fast." If it happened at all, it happened secretly. The reason was, at least partly, the campaign against heretical practices. Allusions to such activities were enough to cause anger or embarrassment.[40]

Of course, the reformist challenge was not the only factor that explained these changes. The concept of *hantu* was intimately connected to ideas about health and disease, and improvements in healthcare and technological change came with a certain measure of disenchantment. "It is . . . said that the [Japanese] caused a change because they hacked down trees which were invisible, built roads and trenches over graves etcetera, and people saw that no harm came to these people."[41] This change seems to have been of a more lasting nature. Although people in Aceh today take into account the presence of a wide variety of spirit forms, according to my own experience it would be very unusual for people to openly engage in, or even speak about, the practice of making offerings to *hantu*.

Healer-diviners are designated in Jayawardena's notes with the (Malay) term *pawang*.[42] He provides some fascinating descriptions of their work. Take, for example, the following passage:

> The illnesses [caused by *hantu*] are cured by the *"pawang"* whose usual method of treatment is blowing on water. The *pawang* is a "white" magician while there are sorcerers too . . . who practice *"ilmu."* They obtain this power after many ordeals, and are said to possess special qualities—such as being invulnerable—and to be under special taboos—water may not touch their bodies. They also may not read the Qur'an—in contrast to the *pawang* who are said to be in accord with the Qur'an, and who may also—probably—invoke it in their practices.[43]

Healing practices were targeted by reformers because they were thought to be based on non-Islamic beliefs. "Teungku Hasballah used to dramatically hack at tabooed and sacred trees to prove that it can do no harm and [that] the belief [is] superstition."[44] Ordinary villagers, in defense of their community's religious integrity, said that there were more *pawang* in "remote" districts, such as West and Central Aceh, than in Aceh Besar.

Still, even the practice of offering to spirits was not fully eradicated at the time of Jayawardena's stay, as we learn from a meeting between him and Suleiman, a *pawang* from South Aceh, who had come to Indrapuri many years earlier. Suleiman had learned his skills from different teachers in Bakongan (south of Tapaktuan). Diseases, he explained, may have a natural cause, requiring medicines (*obat*) based on "herbs, leaves, ground wood, the skins of tigers, monkeys etcetera," but they might also be caused by less tangible agents, such as *burong, jinn, hantu*, or ancestral or personal "wickedness." A *pawang* was able to learn the cause of the disease by looking at the behavior of the patient, or by speaking to the *burong* or *jinn* by which he or she had come to be possessed.

> When an individual is affected by a *burong*, the general cure is to ask the *burong* what it wants. The *burong* replies—meat, or fish or whatever. This is offered, and then the *burong* is exhorted to leave the patient. Each *pawang*

also seeks to obtain the services of a *burong*. He does this by lying naked on the grave of a man who died by homicide or a woman in childbirth. He does this for seven nights, repeating *doa*. On the seventh, out of the navel of the corpse comes a *burong*, which he traps. The *burong* is a small being, about the size of the tip of one's finger, and it shines like a light. It is trapped in a bottle which is kept at home. It can be sent on errands to inflict people, and then it comes back.[45]

Jayawardena was acquainted with an older couple who were treated regularly by Suleiman. The woman's illness had been diagnosed by doctors in Medan as a form of cancer against which "no amount of Western medicine helps." Her husband was blind and wished to regain his eyesight. They had a couple of daughters, who, according to Jayawardena, did not seem to object to Suleiman's procedures, even though their "orthodox" husbands clearly did. "The interesting thing is that the Muslim husbands [*sic*] have not [forbidden] the services of the *pawang*. They, as it were, turn away with a condescending tolerance and make it clear that it is a woman's matter they have nothing to do with."

Jayawardena's observations show that, even in times and places in which a militant, puritanical movement holds sway, established religious practices condemned as heretical do not necessarily, or all of a sudden, disappear. A comparison might be drawn here between Indrapuri in the mid-twentieth century and the Minangkabau villages controlled by the Padris one and a half centuries earlier. Far from an assault on local customs and practices, the Padris established their authority within particular villages by respecting, to a large extent, the practices and forms of authority central to everyday village life (Dobbin 1983, 128–41). The representatives of the Darul Islam could not afford to alienate local populations, nor did they have the power to fully impose their religious views. As the purist pressures surged and waned, however, a deeper, more sustained change occurred in the capacity of local communities to accommodate and appropriate the forces of normative Islam. The next two sections shift the focus from contestations about doctrinal issues to the gradual intrusion, during the early New Order period, of the state.

Villages in the New Order

The early New Order years—the period of Jayawardena's travels to Aceh—have been characterized as an intermediate phase between Sukarno's Guided Democracy and the extreme centralization of the 1980s. It would be a mistake, however, to underestimate the administrative reforms of this period, which included Law No. 5 (1974) on the structure of the government and the Village Law of 1979. It is clear, nonetheless, that the New Order was "far from being a strong government," and still needed to "establish control and to impose [its] authority . . . on the whole country" (MacAndrews 1986, 11). In rural areas particularly, the government's modernization policies regularly led to "critical contest and dispute between peasant and administrator" (Hansen 1971, 63). This section deals with four different effects of the changing relationship between state and Islam, respectively bearing on the propagation of religious norms, the collection of religious tithes, the position of the village head, and the 1971 general elections.

The "Province of the Special Region of Aceh" (Propinsi Daerah Istimewa Atjeh) was headed by a governor and divided into seven districts (*kebupaten*) and two municipalities (*kotamadya*).[46] These were in turn subdivided into subdistricts (*kecamatan*). The lowest administrative unit was the village (I. *desa*; Ac. *gampong*). The supra-village unit of the *mukim* was recognized as an *adat* institution but not formally included in the government structure. Indrapuri, one of the twelve subdistricts in Aceh Besar, counted seventy villages. The large majority of its inhabitants lived off agriculture or small trade. The administrative center, with the *bupati*'s office, the *camat*'s office, the police station, a military compound, and the local branch of the Office of Religious Affairs (Kantor Urusan Agama, KUA), was the market town of Indrapuri.[47]

In 1967, the *bupati* of Aceh Besar issued an "appeal" (*seruan*), in which he called on "all Muslims" in his district to "enliven (*meramaikan*) the mosques, *meunasah* and *musholla* by engaging in communal prayer every time, [or] at the very least at the *magrib, isya* and *subuh* prayer-times." The document was drawn up in accordance with the provisions of the Republic of Indonesia regarding "religion, education, and culture"; the proclamation (*pernyataan*) of the provincial parliament regarding the "effectuation of shari'a regulations"; the 1965 instruction of the *bupati* about the "obligation to follow religious study for all inhabitants of the Aceh Besar district"; the 1967 decision of the district parliament about "mental development"; the notion of religion as "an essential ingredient of nation and character building"; and the notion of communal prayer creating a "sense of Islamic brotherhood" and a "solid and lasting unity." The document concluded by declaring that community leaders (*Kepala Mukim—Imam Mesdjid—Ketjhik dan tengku Menasa*) were "responsible for the implementation of this appeal."[48] I linger on these admonitions—and their formulaic aspect—with a reason. Regulations of this kind reflected the emergence during the early New Order of a state-driven discourse that emphasized the grounding of Acehnese society in Islam. To translate this discourse into practice, the provincial and district governments handed down instructions about religious "rules" and "duties" to the local KUA, which were expected to "socialize" these norms among community leaders.

The report of a meeting held in the *mukim* Gle Jeueng, in April 1966, gives a good impression of this process.[49] Led by the *camat* of Indrapuri, participants discussed regulations under the headings of "village discipline," "agriculture and cattle breeding," "marriage," "education and worship," and "health." These domains officialized and adapted social norms by putting them into an idiom of public order and state security. "Village discipline" implied that "the village head has the right to know about guests staying overnight in a village, [so] the person receiving the guest is obliged to report [this] to him." Also, "there should be no people roaming the village after ten at night." Villagers were told to conform to prosaic communal responsibilities, such as keeping their houses clean, contributing to communal labor (*gotong royong*), and ensuring that free-ranging cattle would not endanger people or houses. More generally, community leaders were expected to disseminate the message of mutual respect and prevent "envy" (*hasud*) and "slander" (*fitnah*). "Education and worship" stood for "communal prayer in every *meunasah*" and religious study for adults and children. Village leaders were obliged to gather in the mosque every Friday for religious study.

A contentious aspect of this developing body of local Islamic regulations was the management of religious tithes (*zakat* and *fitrah*). In November 1962, Governor Ali Hasjmy established a provincial Islamic Treasury (Badan Harta Agama Islam Daerah Istimewah Atjeh), an agency designed to advise the government and to register, order, collect, distribute, and altogether take care of "all forms of Islamic wealth and property."[50] In 1964, a district-level branch was established by the *bupati* of Aceh Besar, who appointed himself as chairman, the senior public prosecutor (Djaksa Madya) and the head of the KUA as his deputies, and a mix of officials and ulama as other members.[51] The office distributed forms, on which village leaders could fill in amounts of *zakat* given and the names of givers, and assisted in its distribution. This officialization of *zakat* collection became a source of conflict. The Indrapuri files contain several references to local disputes, focusing on the place where *zakat* was supposed to be delivered, and accusations of fraud.[52] This problem was also noted by Jayawardena, who wrote that village heads in particular were charged with misconduct or corruption. In a village called Lam Bentong, accusations of the *geuchik* "fiddling" with *zakat*, "selling the paddy when prices were high and replacing it when the prices were low," led to a crisis. In the village of Manggra a very similar problem emerged.[53] These cases reflect the emergence of a new type of intravillage conflict rather than a general dissatisfaction with the government. New institutions such as the Islamic Treasury constituted a direct and unprecedented interference in the religious lives of ordinary Muslims. At the same time, both villagers and village leaders made use of the government infrastructure to complain and point out local abuses.

A central aspect of these frictions was the changing position of the village head (*geuchik*). In Aceh, this institution is traditionally vested with considerable authority, perhaps more than in other parts of Indonesia. However, the intruding state caused a significant increase in terms of responsibilities, expectations, and discontent, both on the side of the state itself and on the side of ordinary villagers.[54] Both factors, those of traditional authority and lurking disappointment, were recognized and put to use at a very early stage by the government. For example, in response to the "psychological pressure experienced by the village heads," in 1965 the *camat* of Indrapuri suggested that a new regulation was needed to accelerate the procedure of replacing village heads, to raise their salaries, and to elevate their status, for example, by providing them with "a new official uniform (*pakaian dinas*) once every year."[55] Jayawardena observed how the position of the *geuchik* was being transformed through the process of "Golkarisation."[56] In the run-up to the 1971 elections, all government officials, including the *geuchik*, were forced to choose between joining Golkar—the regime's new tool for managing bureaucratic and political careers—or being dismissed. The *geuchik* were given an annual fund of 45,000 rupiah (and a bicycle) for "village development," and "advised" to use a part of this money for the election campaign. These strategies did not make the *geuchik*'s office much easier. Some of Jayawardena's informants suspected a strategy to "militarize" the village. Others said that the concentration of power in the hands of the *geuchik* would lead to "intolerable oppression" because it struck at the root of traditional village organization, defined as a "balance of powers which resolves itself through *musjawarah* (consultation)."[57]

The elections of 1971 were the first of the New Order. They were intended primarily to provide Golkar with popular legitimacy. In Aceh Besar, Golkar won the largest share of votes, beating Parmusi (Partai Muslimin Indonesia; the successor of Masyumi, established in 1970) by a slight margin, but trailing far behind the "Islamic" vote as a whole.[58] According to Jayawardena, this result— and the strategies used by Golkar—caused "much bitterness" in the Indrapuri area.[59] The fact that Aceh was one of the few provinces in which Golkar failed to win a majority in the face of the "Islamic bloc" (with the reform-minded PSII and Parmusi on one side and the conservative NU [Nahdlatul Ulama] and Perti on the other) has been regarded as a sign of Acehnese "piety" (see, e.g., Brown 2003, 105; Morris 1983, 291). It would be wrong, however, to frame this event exclusively, or even primarily, as a struggle between "Islam" and the secular state. Such a view obscures the differences that existed within the ranks of political Islam as well as the agencies of those groups and individuals who were increasingly, but never entirely, tied down by Suharto's political machinery.

A dynamic that tends to be overlooked, first, is the revival in the 1960s and 1970s of Perti. In his analysis of local politics in Sibreh, one of Indrapuri's bordering subdistricts, Soeyatno (1977) shows how this traditionalist Islamic party used the elections to raise its profile and strengthen its social base.[60] This was part of a prolonged strategy on the part of conservative religious leaders to present the party as a dynamic, activist, and locally grounded alternative to the Darul Islam. Second, and somewhat paradoxically, the very fact that local officials were forced to join Golkar—while probably, in many cases, their sympathies lay elsewhere—mitigated the constraints placed on other parties and created space for negotiation and cooperation. According to Jayawardena, this especially benefited the supporters of PSII.[61] Let me now turn, in the final section of this chapter, to a village conflict—described in detail by Jayawardena—that reveals some of the implications of these shifts, and the changing relationship between state and society in the mid-twentieth century.

The Lheueh Dispute

On November 22, 1972, Jayawardena noted that "there is an area called [Darang] which is regarded sometimes as belonging to [Lheueh]; but is also sometimes referred to separately as [Darang] because it has its own *masjid* [mosque]."[62] In the following months, contestations about the status of Lheueh and Darang, and the relationship between both places, boiled over. Jayawardena wrote about this conflict in an essay that was completed just before his death and published posthumously as part of a memorial volume devoted to the work of Max Gluckman. The case deserves discussion here, because it speaks directly to the relationship between religious agency and the state. I start by summarizing Jayawardena's analysis. I conclude with a reference to his original field notes, illuminating some observations—bearing on local contestations about religious authority and the state—that are less salient in his article yet strongly relevant for the argument of this book.

Formally, Lheueh was one village. However, as Jayawardena was told by his older interlocutors, there used to be three villages, called Lheueh Jeumpa, Meunasah Baro, and Meunasah Darang. During the war against the Dutch, the region of Indrapuri became so underpopulated that some villages were forced to join together to keep functioning as communities. The village of Lheueh was the result of such a merger. The *geuchik* was Budiman, a former schoolteacher from a neighboring district, who had been appointed in the run-up to the 1971 elections after his predecessor, Ibrahim, had refused to join Golkar. Budiman's home base was the newly built mosque of Lheueh, which he saw as "the centre of his operations and wished to make the focal point of the village" (Jayawardena 1987, 37). He had been accused of selling *wakaf* land in order to finish the building, however, and as a result the mosque was avoided by most villagers (who kept going to the old mosque of Indrapuri instead). This was not Budiman's only problem. A former PSII member turned Golkar, he had difficulty establishing his authority among both "modernists" and "traditionalists." His style caused irritation. To strengthen his position, he divided the village bureaucratically into three "sectors," a measure that conflicted starkly with the organic way in which the original core communities had coagulated in previous decades.

In the course of 1972, a series of *rateb* (devotional chanting) sessions were held in the *meunasah* of Darang.[63] Jayawardena was intrigued, because he had been under the impression that such practices had disappeared under the influence of the reformist movement and the Darul Islam. In subsequent months, he gradually discovered that the staging of the *rateb* was part of a broader conflict that was quickly growing in intensity. When the Darang group was told by Budiman that they were not allowed to continue, and that in any case they should have asked him for his permission, they "petitioned the government for their separation under their own *keuchik*" (Jayawardena 1987, 37). Budiman subsequently told the villagers of Darang to pay their yearly religious tithes (*fitrah*) to the mosque instead of to their own *meunasah*. This was perceived in Darang as a badly concealed attempt to strengthen his own institutional basis and, at the same time, "denigrate" the status of the Darang community. They refused to comply with what they saw as a rancorous act as well as a flagrant "departure from custom" (Jayawardena 1987, 37).

According to Jayawardena, the staging of the *rateb*, a practice that was clearly audible throughout the village and affronted the village's leading "modernists," was a persistent strategy to undermine Budiman's authority. It put him in an impossible position. One night, a few weeks after the clash over the collection of the *fitrah*, a *rateb* session held in the presence of Jayawardena as well as several people from a neighboring subdistrict (again without formal permission) was disturbed, brusquely, by the *geuchik* and his assistants. Budiman was told off and forced to retreat. Two days later, the leader of the group, Daud, was arrested on the order of the *camat* and brought to the police headquarters in Seulimeum. The police chief, who thought it was a "local matter concerning art and culture and should be settled locally," was reluctant to pursue the matter (Jayawardena 1987, 35). Daud was briefly questioned and released. However, later that same night he was arrested again, together with two others, and locked up in the *camat*'s office. This aroused a crowd of villagers to gather in front of the office. Their presence was sufficiently intimidating for Daud to be released again, under the condition of signing a letter, "in which he agreed to cooperate with the government, not to oppose its policies and not create popular disturbance" (and which he probably could not read because he was illiterate) (Jayawardena 1987, 35). The people of Darang, meanwhile, celebrated the whole episode as a victory.

Jayawardena analyzed the staging of the *rateb* and the arrest of Daud as a "social situation," evoking Max Gluckman's (1971 [1940]) use of the concept in his famous essay on the opening of a bridge in northern Zululand. The concept is useful, he argued, because it helps to "reveal the patterns of conflict and cooperation that regulate the interactions of the participants [of the event]" while at the same time enabling the sociologist or the anthropologist to "relate his observations to the flow of time, to the stream of history." Three different "sets of events" had led to this particular social situation, namely the "schism" between modernists and traditionalists in the early twentieth century, the Darul Islam rebellion, and the subsequent "encroaching direct control of the Achehnese by the central government" (Jayawardena 1987, 36). The pretext was formed by the 1971 elections. It had been the job of the *camat* and the *geuchik* to "rustle up support for Golkar and the government." In practice, their actions had raised opposition by violating long-standing village traditions. "The quarrel with the administration took the ostensible form of a dispute about a *kolot* ["traditionalist"] ritual though basically it was one about village autonomy."

Jayawardena's essay advances an important argument about the capacity to resist the state in the early New Order period. The tension between Darang and Budiman inspired local youth to provoke the authorities. At night, they swung their machetes openly in the vicinity of the *geuchik*'s house, instead of wearing them inconspicuously as usual. In the weeks after Daud's arrest, people were less reluctant to criticize the government. Their behavior, Jayawardena argued, showed the possibility of future action. "The truculence of the Achehnese, part regionalist, part Muslim, was evident in their persistence in holding the *rateb*. . . . The Achehnese of [Darang] accepted government repression of the *rateb* (up to a point) but in the event also revealed the sources on which they could draw for further rebellion against the government" (Jayawardena 1987, 43). This focus on resistance and rebellion distracts, to some extent, from the fascinating insights that Jayawardena's research gives into the changing relationship between villagers and the state, and the significance in this process of the struggle for religious authority. Let me elaborate on this by looking more closely into his notes and by discussing two additional observations.

The first observation concerns the "status" of Darang and its inhabitants' appeal to the "traditional" right to elect their own *geuchik*. Budiman's predecessor, Ibrahim, had been very popular, especially in Darang. He had been elected (in contrast to Budiman, who was appointed) but only, as we learn from Jayawardena's field notes, after *his* predecessor, Arab, had been accused of abusing his office and "persuaded" by the *camat* to resign.[64] Shortly after becoming *geuchik*, Ibrahim was himself accused of irregularities by Budiman. He was protected by the *camat*, and Budiman had been forced to leave the village for a few years. The significance of these observations lies in the fact that, when the villagers of Darang petitioned the government—first the *camat*, then the *bupati*—for their separation from Lheueh, this was based on earlier interventions by state actors as much as village "tradition."[65] Equally significant, in this regard, is the atmosphere in which Daud's arrest took place. When the police chief released him, Jayawardena wrote, he did this angrily, exclaiming that the whole matter had "nothing whatever to do with regulations."[66] Clearly, the state in Lheueh had multiple faces, and these were not all necessarily unsympathetic to the interests of the villagers in Darang.

The second observation concerns the apparent revival of traditionalist (*kolot*) practices and sites. Although the village of Lheueh consisted of three core communities, by the time of Jayawardena's stay a fourth "basis" or "locus" of power had emerged. This was "Tgk Yussuf's *balai* [place of religious instruction] . . . which he was seeking to be recognised as a [*meunasah*]" (Jayawardena 1987, 37). The field notes contain more information about this intriguing development. Teungku Yussuf (a pseudonym for Teungku Jahja) was the *kepala mukim*. He was also one of Budiman's most important allies in the conflict over Darang. The *balai* he was building had a strongly traditionalist constituency (Teungku Jahja's father-in-law used to be one of Teungku Hasballah's strongest opponents).[67] The *balai* was built on the site of the former *dayah* of Teungku Tjhi di Lheueh, an ancestor of both his wife and the imam of Lheueh Djeumpa, who was a prominent Perti supporter. Gravitating to the *balai* was "the rump of Perti followers in Lheueh," who were led by the *imam meunasah* of Djeumpa.[68] Kicking up some dust, the *kepala mukim* and the *imam* once brought down "two motors [trucks?] full of Perti ulama's and followers from Lam Baroh" to make the funeral of his mother-in-law a "full Perti display, with *tahlil* and *dhikr* by the graveside." Reform-minded villagers objected to this practice. However, there was little they could do except for advancing the formalistic argument that the *imam* of the mosque—rather than the *imam meunasah* of Lheueh Jeumpa—should be seen as responsible for funeral rites in the village. Religious authorities from "outside," they said, should not officiate at a burial.[69]

Jayawardena convincingly argues that the tensions in Lheueh were "not entirely doctrinal." At the same time, it is clear that the struggle for religious agency played a central role in the conflict. His observations reveal that, in the decades that separated the eruption in Darang and the arrival at the beginning of the century of Teungku Hasballah Indrapuri, the state had become an increasingly important site for contestations about religious practice and authority, not just at the provincial level but at the village level as well. In the early 1970s, community leaders such as Ibrahim and Budiman became agents of the state. Yet they also remained villagers, who sympathized or strategically allied themselves with different—sometimes opposing—groups or "factions" of villagers who shared particular ideas or interests. As the case of Lheueh shows, this could lead to festering conflicts. In a rather ironic turn of events, Teungku Jahja (the *kepala mukim*, who was responsible for the "fourth locus of power" in Lheueh) responded to the dispute by calling a meeting, in which he warned the villagers that there were "too many factions" (*kompani*) in the community and that these internal conflicts were affecting village "principles."

Conversely, groups like the Darang youth recognized in the intruding state an important resource, a collection of means and instruments that could be employed to advance their own concerns and interests. Jayawardena shows, in meticulous detail, that this was not merely a struggle for power. Religious authority, and the control over particular places, institutions, and rituals, comprised a moral resource with the capacity to strengthen or mitigate the role of the state in social interactions. Despite the persistent, and at times very successful, universalizing message of Islamic reform, local networks and appeals to "tradition" remained essential repertoires of action. This was a matter of appropriating rather than undermining a state that was perceived as enabling and constraining at the same time.

Conclusion

This chapter has looked at religious practices and expressions of religious authority, in relation to the changing nature of the state, in rural Aceh Besar from the final decades of the colonial period until the early New Order. I have argued that to assess the impact of the reformist movement on the lives of Acehnese villagers, it is necessary to take into account both the changing position of the ulama and the ways in which normative Islam was embedded, negotiated, and adapted at the local level.

The project of remaking Acehnese society on the basis of Islamic (scriptural) norms was initiated by PUSA and subsequently driven by a wide range of state- and non–state-affiliated groups and individuals. This process was ambiguous and uneven as much as it was forceful. I have made extensive use of the work of Chandra Jayawardena, who lived in the Indrapuri area in the mid-1960s and early 1970s. A mixed picture emerges from his work. Owing partly to the imposing presence of Teungku Hasballah Indrapuri and the earlier activities of his patron Panglima Polem, PUSA was strong in the area. Some practices that used to be widespread, such as the offerings made to spirit-forms, stopped or disappeared from sight. However, in the early 1970s conservative Islamic organizations and once undisputed dispositions and practices, including the practice of *ziarah* and the intercession rituals commonly categorized as *kenduri kematian*, became the subject of a conspicuous revival. Jayawardena's notes, combined with archival materials from the same period and place, describe a set of complex interrelationships between this development, the intrusion of the state, and the bureaucratization of religious authority. They reveal a dynamic interaction between a gradually maturing state religious ideology, a reformist thrust to "standardize" religious forms and institutions, and a number of resilient and unpredictable, hyperlocal factors of kinship, property structures, collective interests and individual temperaments, and "traditional" Islamic practices that turned out to have a stronger hold on certain segments of Acehnese society than they seemed to have had in previous decades.

In the early 1970s, contestations about religious norms were part of the fabric of social life in rural Indrapuri. The state was ascribed a dual role in this process. On the one hand, state agents and institutions acted as mediators between individual villagers and the representatives of organized religion. This was the secular state in Indrapuri. On the other hand, the state functioned as a normative force in itself, which could be shaped and adapted to serve particular interests, including those religious ideas that were subject to doctrinal dispute. State practice continually disrupted and complicated the religious and ideological dividing lines that seemed, at first sight, cut and dried. The state reinforced normative pressures and provided space for alternative—individual or collective—action at the same time. The fact that villagers interacted with, and were personally involved in, the development of state institutions bespeaks of considerable agency on their part in the negotiation of religious norms. The forces of state and religious authority, as powerful yet flexible domains of moral practice and disposition, simultaneously allowed for and obstructed the adjustment and adaptation of normative Islam.

As the state imposed itself on, and was actively drawn into, local communities, people discovered a vast range of new instruments suitable for advancing personal interests and protecting or increasing their religious agency. The next chapter further elaborates on this argument by investigating the relationship between the villagers of Jurong and a group of influential religious leaders in the early twenty-first century.

3

Village Society and the Problem of Moral Authority

We don't listen to Abuya, we listen to the *kitab*.
—PUTRA (JURONG, 2009)

In November 2008, Muhajir and I visited Teungku Faisal Ali, the founder of Dayah Ulum al-Aziziyah in Sukamakmur, Aceh Besar. Teungku Faisal was the chairman of the Aceh branch of Nahdlatul Ulama (NU) and the leader of HUDA (Himpunan Ulama Dayah Aceh, Association of Acehnese Ulama). This organization was founded under tense circumstances in 1999, when the conflict between the military and Gerakan Aceh Merdeka (GAM) had reached boiling point. In Banda Aceh, large demonstrations were held to demand a referendum about independence (see Aspinall 2009, 129–34). HUDA joined the referendum movement, which was spearheaded by the Aceh People's Congress (Kongres Rakyat Aceh, KRA). It was forced to keep a low profile, however, after both the government and GAM expressed their suspicion of traditionalist ulama reasserting themselves in local politics (McGibbon 2006, 334–36).

One of the topics we discussed with Teungku Faisal was the changing position of the ulama in Acehnese society. Reflecting on the distinction between different currents in Islam (*aliran*), Teungku Faisal stated that "80 percent" of the *ulama dayah* in Aceh, including himself and most members of HUDA, were intellectual descendants of Syaikh Muda Waly al-Khalidy (1917–61), the charismatic Perti leader and founder of the prestigious Dayah Darussalam in Labuhan Haji, South Aceh (see Feener 2013, 30–31). In response to this ostentatious affirmation of Islamic traditionalism, I wondered—provocatively perhaps—whether HUDA might be regarded as the first attempt by Acehnese ulama to "unite" (*bersatu*) since the founding of PUSA in 1939. Apparently, this was not a very appropriate remark. While the conversation had seemed spontaneous up until this point, Teungku Faisal suddenly looked cautious. He curtly responded to my suggestion by stating that the founder of PUSA, Daud Beureueh, was a "soldier, not an ulama." Not much later, the conversation was over, and Muhajir and I were on our way again.

The ulama in Aceh are in somewhat dire straits. They continue to offer important religious services to local communities, especially in rural areas, from religious education and counseling to guidance in life cycle rituals. They also remain a standard symbolic element of local political culture.[1] At the same time, their political position is marked by ambivalence. People are often suspicious, if not outright disenchanted, about the way in which many ulama have aligned themselves with the central state, especially during the conflict. The result, some observers believe, is that the ulama can no longer claim the popular authority they once had. What seems clear is that, although the recent implementation of shari'a law has created possibilities for a renewed political role, the provincial government has not been very keen on granting formal power to the ulama (Nur Ichwan 2011). Although the latter have a formal role in the state-funded Ulama Council (Majelis Permusyawaratan Ulama, MPU), the question of who holds "legitimate authority in the determination and defense of Islamic orthodoxy in contemporary Aceh" has been a subject of contestation between the ulama and the provincial government (Feener 2013, 126). Finally, their influence has been compromised by pervasive social, theological, and political differences within their own ranks.

This chapter deals with the relationship between the people of Jurong and the leaders of Dayah Darul Hidayah, located adjacent to their village. This was a tense relationship, described by villagers and religious leaders alike as a "crisis of solidarity" (*masalah kekompakan*).[2] The leaders of the *dayah* had become influential figures in recent decades, both in their district and beyond. Many villagers saw this as a sign that the ulama no longer cared for ordinary people. Others, however, argued that they cared too much, as they interfered on a daily basis with "village affairs" (*urusan kampung*) and actively blurred the boundary between village and *dayah*. In my analysis of the changing relationship among state, ulama, and villagers, I will focus in particular on generational differences. As I have argued in the introduction, age and life phase constitute a major, but also underestimated, aspect of the approach of ordinary Acehnese to state and religious authority.

Beyond the Politics of Violence and Grief

Several scholars have written about the "crisis of authority" in contemporary Islam (see, e.g., Bulliet 2002; Eickelman and Piscatori 1996; Mandaville 2007;

F. Robinson 2009; Roy 2004). The general argument is that the advent of modernity has undermined traditional Islamic leadership, modes of religious knowledge production, and hierarchies of authority. In recent years, the threat of jihadism and the perceived reluctance of Muslims to dissociate themselves from it has added to the perception that it is unclear, today, who "speaks" for Islam (Bulliet 2002, 34).

According to Francis Robinson, the crisis of authority has been long in the making, developing first between 1800 and 1920 as a consequence of the conquest of the Muslim world by non-Muslim forces. The crisis intensified in the second half of the twentieth century, during "the next great movement of globalization" (F. Robinson 2009, 339). Although Robinson discusses different factors, his focus is on the ulama. Over the course of two centuries, he writes, the age-old tradition of person-to-person transmission of religious knowledge has broken down:

> Lay folk have come forward to challenge the authority of the *'ulama* as interpreters, indeed, increasingly each individual Muslim has come to arrogate to his or herself the responsibility for interpretation. Lay folk and some *'ulama* have come to challenge the authority of past Islamic scholarship. Scholarly authority has become fragmented; old hierarchies have been flattened; the old interpretative disciplines have been sidelined. All kinds of new interpreters of the faith have come forward; all kinds of new interpretations have been promulgated. . . . [N]o one now knows who speaks for Islam with authority. (F. Robinson 2009, 345)

By clearing the space for interpreters coming from outside traditional educational institutions, Robinson argues, the ulama effectively struck at the roots of their own authority.[3]

At the same time, the sources and expressions of Islamic authority have been placed increasingly under the surveillance of the state. Throughout the Muslim world, governments have taken control of key domains of authority, such as mosques, courts, schools, endowments, and other institutions central to the production of Islamic knowledge. This process has changed the position of the ulama. In classical Weberian terms, if the ulama used to be exemplars of "traditional" or "charismatic" authority (and often a combination of the two), modern state practice has led to a gradual replacement of these sources of authority with a form of legitimacy that is impersonal and bureaucratic in nature (see, e.g., Starret 1998).

In nineteenth century Aceh, a clear distinction was made between the people addressed as *teungku*, a common title used for "all those [with] a religious function, or who distinguished themselves from the mass of the population through higher knowledge or a more faithful practicing of the religion," and the people known as ulama, the experts in religious law and doctrine, who taught independently in their *dayah* and were venerated for their specialized knowledge and, in some cases, for their supernatural powers and personal charisma (Snouck Hurgronje 1893–94, 1:68, 74). In the course of the twentieth century, the *dayah* and the village remained, to an extent at least, separate realities, characterized by different norms, rules, and aspirations (Siegel 1969). At the same time, however, state, village, and *dayah* became increasingly intermeshed. Reformist ulama gave up their institutional independence in the 1950s, as they allowed their schools to become part of the state education system. In subsequent decades, former PUSA supporters were transformed from a loose collection of activists into an "upper class" of conservative state agents. In the 1970s and 1980s, this group, which included many descendants of reformist ulama, became known as the "technocrats."[4] Although the *ulama dayah* remained, in contrast, a distinct social group, they also followed in the footsteps of their reformist counterparts as they were co-opted, bought, or intimidated into political quiescence by the New Order.[5] By the turn of the twenty-first century, it has been argued, the ulama had become estranged from the general population.[6] A particularly stinging critique, voiced inside and outside Aceh, was that the ulama had failed to respond to, or were actually complicit in, the grief inflicted on the Acehnese people during the conflict.

Recent studies have both elaborated and complicated this debate. According to Edward Aspinall (2009, 207), the separatist conflict contributed to a gradual convergence of religious authority and the state, resulting in a "precipitous decline of the independent political role of the *ulama*." This process, it may be added, continued after the signing of the 2005 peace treaty (Nur Ichwan 2011). A somewhat different perspective has been offered by Michael Feener (2013) in his work on the implementation of shari'a law. The ulama, he argues, have been involved in the cultivation of a state-centered, shari'a-minded ethics since the 1960s. The "shari'a project" was instrumental in the process of aligning religious leaders with the ideological principles of the New Order regime, as it molded Islamic norms and practices (and their scriptural justification) in the straightjacket of security and economic growth.[7] Rather than the process of co-optation, then, Feener emphasizes the active role played by the ulama in the officialization of ("traditional") religious authority.

To assess how the nature and the roles of religious authorities have changed, these state-centered accounts must be complemented with an ethnographic perspective. In particular, it is necessary to take into account the perceptions, practices, and strategies of those people who are not regarded—and who do not regard themselves—as religious experts. Authority exists by grace of an interest in obedience. Organized religion, or the "professional organization for the cure of the soul," owes its existence to a "need of salvation" (Weber 1946, 272–73). This means that even if it is agreed upon, at the very least, that the ulama have increasingly identified with the state, their choices and positions should not be detached from the agencies of ordinary Muslims, who often have stakes in this process of religious officialization themselves. In particular, I think it is important that the analysis of religious authority in Aceh does not become overly dominated by the separatist conflict. As I have explained in the introduction, this book makes a case—however difficult this may seem in the context of real suffering—for looking beyond violence and grief as a central organizing principle for studying Acehnese lives.

In 1977, after the establishment of GAM but well before the escalation of the conflict, the Acehnese sociologist Alfian stated that, for the ulama, the main challenge was not their formal role in state structures (as was the case during the Darul Islam revolt), but rather the increasing authority of a class of "new intellectuals" (*cendekiawan baru*) that had been groomed by the educational institutions of the secular state. The new intellectuals came from different social strata and included the children of ulama, *uleebalang*, civil servants, farmers, traders, and soldiers. Because of their strategic positions in the government and the bureaucracy and their capacity to influence public discourse—their success, in other words, in exerting real power—they were essentially rivals of the ulama (Alfian 1977, 215–16). One of the ways in which the ulama responded to this was by diversifying their own role in society through entering new domains of social and intellectual activity, including state institutions. This process continued in the early twenty-first century, despite the dominant language of separatism and counterinsurgency, which pitted the idea of local, "authentic," and perseverant religious institutions against its corruptions by the central state.

As a result of this process, formerly meaningful distinctions have faded. "Traditional" institutions have become more "professional," and "modern" institutions have sought to reinvent traditional styles of learning. While this is just one aspect of the state becoming more embedded in society, the position of the ulama is particularly important (and complex) in the sense that, by guarding the distinctions between formal and informal, public and private, local and national (and transnational), and, of course, "right" and "wrong," they must be regarded as central agents with respect to the ways in which these boundaries have shifted.

While writing this chapter, I was struck by the similarities between my own observations in Aceh and Andrew Walker's (2012) analysis of village society and political power in northern Thailand. In recent decades, peasant life in Thailand has become economically diversified, less dependent on agricultural income and tied in multiple ways to the state. As a consequence, the Thai peasantry can be regarded, simultaneously, as a class dominated by political elites and as a significant political force itself (expressed, for example, in the so-called red shirt movement). Today, the Thai state supports the peasantry through subsidies instead of extracting surpluses. Walker refers to this new configuration as a "rural constitution," stating that "it is not just formal written constitutions that regulate and channel the power of the state in Thailand," but also the "extensive network of relationships that makes up political society" (a term adopted from Partha Chatterjee). The rural constitution "is premised on the view that the state can enhance local power by providing new modes of authority, additional resources, and innovative forms of symbolic capital that can all be selectively drawn on to pursue security, status, and livelihood enhancement" (Walker 2012, 29).

Aceh is characterized by similar links between rural society and the state. Like several other provinces of Indonesia, Aceh lacks industrial complexes or commercial hubs the size of those in Jakarta or Medan. The provincial capital, Banda Aceh, fits the category that Gerry van Klinken calls "Middle Indonesia," a particular sociopolitical domain comprising Indonesia's hundreds of middle-size provincial administrative centers, which are home to "surprisingly assertive (lower) middle classes" (van Klinken 2014, 7) and generally characterized by economies that are "pre-industrial, dominated by the state and by trade" (van Klinken 2009, 880). It is ironic, then, that even in the context of the separatist conflict, one of the most important resources for social mobility in Aceh has, in fact, been the state. "Traditional" leadership plays an important role in the contestations over state resources, which are often played out at a local level. This chapter investigates some of these struggles as I observed them in the village of Jurong in the early twenty-first century.

A Crisis of Solidarity

There are three access roads to Jurong. One unpaved road leads from the main thoroughfare, through vegetable and coconut gardens, to the *meunasah*. The second is a small foot path, which leads from a suspension bridge over the river, connecting rice fields and other villages, also to the *meunasah*. The third is a paved road that leads from the market, along Dayah Darul Hidayah, to the other side of the village. The *dayah* borders directly onto the village and is separated from it by walls. When I lived in Jurong, I observed that the students of the *dayah* had little direct contact with the villagers. They could access the main road and the market without crossing the *kampung*. They passed through only when they were looking for construction materials (such as gravel from the river or palm leaves). Female students were also rarely seen in the village. This used to be different, however. In the past, before a separate, walled section was built especially for them, the *santriwati* were taught right in the middle of the village, where they lived in simple bamboo huts. Women told me that they used to do the laundry in the river, side by side with the *santriwati*, who were friendly, but also shy to engage with them.

This scarcity of direct contact between villagers and religious students should not, in itself, be seen as remarkable. James Siegel (1969, 56) noted that, traditionally, the *pesantren* functioned as a retreat from the "world of the village." The reluctance of the *santriwati* to talk to the villagers, even though they were close neighbors, may be the result of them being actively discouraged to do so. That said, I was also told by several villagers that, over the years, students of the *dayah* had been less and less prepared to engage directly with the villagers. They thought that this was due, at least partly, to the size and prestige of the *dayah*. Some of them called the students arrogant (*sombong*), and stated that, on returning to their own villages, there would be little to distinguish them from other people. Opinions varied, however. Other villagers claimed that the relationship with their "friends from the *dayah*," some of whom had lived in Jurong for many years, had remained unchanged.

Dayah Darul Hidayah was founded in 1946 by Abu Nazir, a Perti member who had studied in Dayah Mudi Mesra in Samalanga, North Aceh. The school was not originally located in Jurong. In the mid-1970s, Abu Nazir decided that the original location—some kilometers away in the same subdistrict—was no longer suitable. The people of Jurong, his wife's place of birth, granted permission to move the *dayah* to their village. On the banks of the river there was still space. In the late 1980s, the leadership of the *dayah* was transferred to his son, referred to in this chapter as Abuya ("father"), who studied in Samalanga as well. Abu Nazir passed away in 1997. When I lived in Jurong, the *dayah* compound consisted of two separate sections for male and female students and six large residences. One of these was occupied by Abu Nazir's widow (and former leader of the women's section), Umi ("mother"). The remaining five houses were inhabited by Abu Nazir and Umi's children and their families, including (besides Abuya) Abi, Bang Ali, and Anwar. Abi (also "father") was appointed as the leader of the women's section when his mother became too old to teach. Bang Ali, the oldest of the children, taught several weekly religious lessons (*pengajian*) in Jurong and surrounding villages. He was also the *imam meunasah* of Jurong. Teungku Anwar was also a religious teacher but he did not focus on the *dayah*. Instead, he specialized in audiences of adult women, providing regular lessons in his own house and several *meunasah* in the surrounding area.

Before I elaborate on the relationship between the village and the *dayah*, let me briefly illustrate how the *dayah* leaders, Abuya and Abi, perceived their own position in the region. Like Teungku Faisal Ali, Abuya cultivated his traditionalist credentials. He emphasized his father's membership in Perti and the "destructive" role of reformist ulama who, in the early decades of Indonesian independence, had tried to bring Aceh in line with the ideas of PUSA (*memPUSAkan Aceh*). He mocked their intellectual capacity, which in his view contrasted sharply with that of "charismatic" (*karismatik*) ulama like his father (and himself). PUSA, he explained, rejected age-old scholarship. What they were good at was "making bombs."

Abuya carried on his father's role as a district leader of Perti, which today is no longer a political party but a network of ulama engaged in advancing religious education and proselytization (*dakwah*). He saw himself as a religious leader who served, in the first place, a specific locality. At the same time, he believed that the role of the ulama was per definition translocal. If something important happened in Banda Aceh or West Aceh, a "political matter" deserving his attention, he might decide to talk "straight to the governor." Although the ulama should not aspire to become a part of the government, he regarded it his duty to judge the government on its religious merits. For Abuya, there was no need to stay far from politics. Quite the contrary. "It is our task to engage the government, to work together with government officials (*umara*)." Rather than aspiring to executive offices, the ulama may choose to take a seat in parliament or become a member of advisory bodies, such as the Ulama Council (MPU). In fact, Abuya and his brother Abi had been involved in the establishment of a new political party led by *ulama dayah*, called the Aceh Sovereignty Party (Partai Daulat Aceh, PDA).[8] This, Abuya said, was to push the government to develop the system of religious education and thus advance the moral condition of the *umma*. He rejected the idea that traditional *dayah* should refuse state support.

Abi, the leader of the women's section, agreed that the ulama and the government should not be "separated." His arguments were more formalistic, however. "In Aceh, we have two types of education, a formal type [i.e., state education] and a non-formal type [the *pesantren*]. It would be unfair if the government supported only one type." I asked him whether he was not afraid that the *pesantren* would become too dependent on the government. He answered: "No, not if we request support that is unbinding, that does not direct us." When I wondered how this could be guaranteed, he mentioned institutions such as the Badan Dayah (a relatively new body responsible for the development of religious boarding schools) and associations such as HUDA (of which Abi was a branch leader). According to Abi, these organizations functioned as intermediaries, pointing to the gradual professionalization of the *dayah* system. When I asked for a concrete example of this process, he suggested that, in the future, *dayah* leaders might be able to pay their teachers a salary, making their schools less dependent on alms (*sedekah*). Since *sedekah* was typically regarded, in Jurong and elsewhere, as the "purest" form of support given to traditional *dayah*, I considered this a remarkable statement.

Besides being a *dayah* leader, Abi was also the head of the Jurong village council (*teuha peut*). In this position he engaged, much more frequently than Abuya, with the everyday affairs of the village. Abi explained his role by referring to the Indonesian political system. The ulama, he declared, were obliged to "help the village." He had joined the *teuha peut* because this institution was like the "legislative" power (*legislatif*) assessing the *kampung* "government" (*pemerintah desa*). Help from the *dayah* was important, he argued, because the people of Jurong, including the village head (*geuchik*), were generally poorly educated. For him, this justified the stance of the *teuha peut*, which was more proactive than its counterparts in many other villages. Village affairs were not yet well administered and "clearly written rules" were still lacking. When I asked him for an example, he mentioned the distribution of Raskin (*beras orang miskin*, government aid for poor people in the form of uncooked rice). In principle, Abi explained, there were clear rules, and a number of villagers had even received formal training. Still, conflicts occurred quite regularly, and it was his role to intervene. It was only natural, he concluded, that good local administration should develop slowly. He pointed to the experience of the conflict. People in Aceh were still "scared and traumatized" and often did not understand or want to accept government rules and regulations.

Abuya was widely regarded, within and beyond the district, as an influential ulama. His most important public forum was a weekly religious lesson on Friday night. This *pengajian* was attended by hundreds of people, many of whom visited each week from Banda Aceh, and some even from as far as Sigli. Another sign of Abuya's stature was the fact that the *bupati* paid frequent visits to the *dayah*. Among the villagers of Jurong, Abuya was regarded as the highest local authority on Islamic law. Take, for example, a conversation I had with Adhinda, my host mother, which was prompted by a recent conflict over the settlement of an inheritance:

> DAVID: What do people do when there is an argument (*ribut*) about inheritance?
>
> ADHINDA: We ask the *imam* [i.e., Bang Ali, Abuya's older brother] for a judgment.
>
> D.: And what if one of the parties does not accept Bang Ali's decision?
>
> A.: Then we go to Abuya.
>
> D.: And how about the religious court (*pengadilan agama*)?
>
> A.: Yes, that is also possible of course. But here, so close to Abuya. Normally, no.

Abi's role was judged differently. According to most villagers, he was not as learned as Abuya. He was also a more controversial figure. It was no secret, for example, that he had close ties with the police, the military, and intelligence (commonly taken together as *aparat*, the security "apparatus"). During the conflict, defecting GAM fighters reported to the *dayah*, after which Abi requested their pardon. This role was coordinated with the government and the military. Whenever combatants came to the *dayah*, Abi took their weapons, called their families, and guided them on the "right path" (*diberi arah*). These fighters remained unpunished, or so it was said.

Abuya and Abi, it may be clear by now, were fervently opposed to GAM and its goals. According to Abi, the separatist movement comprised a small group of fanatics and a large group of ignorant young men without education. "GAM people are agents of chaos, who fight against a lawful government." When I asked him whether local people might be unhappy with his own role in the conflict, he answered, "If I do not step forward, then where do we go?" He escaped from an attack once. A bomb exploded nearby. It might have been meant for him. "They are terrorists," he stated. "This is why we oppose them. I have never been paid by the government" (*digaji merah-putih*, lit. "red-and-white").

The people of Jurong were generally ambivalent about the association between *dayah* and *aparat*. Many of them sympathized with GAM, and during the 2009 legislative elections a large majority voted for Partai Aceh. However, very little fighting had taken place in the vicinity of the village. Owing to its location—close to the main road, the local police station, and the *dayah*—Jurong was spared much of the violence that was inflicted on the more isolated parts of Aceh Besar, such as the mountainous areas around Lam Teuba and Lam Kabeu, places that were known as GAM hotspots. Many people believed that it was partly because of Abi that soldiers refrained from harassing Jurong and other nearby villages. Once, when fighting did break out in a nearby forest, villagers were able to take refuge in the *dayah*. They were grateful that the war had not completely engulfed them like other places in Aceh. For the rest, they had their own private thoughts.

A greater source of tension was the interference of the *dayah* in "village affairs" (*urusan kampung*). Abuya's family had assumed central positions in the village leadership. Bang Ali acted as *imam*. Abi was the head (*ketua*) of the *teuha peut*. Fachri, another of Abuya's brothers who lived in the village and worked as a contractor, was the village secretary (Sekretaris Desa, "Sekdes"). Discontented villagers thought that they used these positions to gain access to state resources. This was not a strange thought. Villages in Indonesia are entitled to various funds, mostly directed at "development" (*pembangunan*). By controlling Jurong's administration, it was argued, this funding was partly channeled to the *dayah*. At the root of the disagreement lay the question of whether or not the school should be seen as a "part" of Jurong village. The *dayah* compound was located within the official administrative boundaries of the *desa*. However, both villagers and *santri* regarded the *dayah* as a separate social sphere, even if it was connected to the village through proximity, family ties, and religious services. The students had no particular relation with Jurong. *Santri* often came from far away, while *santriwati* were mostly from other villages in the district. Both villagers and students spoke of the village and the *dayah* as different places.

The tension escalated in 2007, after the election of the village head (and one year before my first visit to the village). Ilyas had never wanted to become *geuchik*. He was originally from another subdistrict in Aceh Besar, and it had not been very long since he had married a woman from Jurong and moved to this village. He was taken by surprise when Abuya summoned him to the *dayah* for a private conversation and asked him to stand as a candidate. Other villagers were less surprised, however. Zulkiflar, the previous *geuchik*, was known as a "puppet" (*boneka*) of the *dayah*, and Ilyas's candidacy was seen as a move to replace him with an equally loyal and discrete figure. Ilyas's wife was a full niece of Umi. This, and the fact that he was an outsider, made him an obvious choice. Two other candidates contested the position. Din, a man in his forties, sold rice and *gulai* (a spicy beef stew) in one of the coffee shops on the side of the main road. Miram, a son of my host parents, was in his early thirties and earned his living by transporting people and goods with his pickup truck. However, on the morning of the election (which took place at the *meunasah*), and to the great surprise of the villagers, more than a hundred *santri* came down from the *dayah* to cast their vote. A few hours later, Ilyas had won with more than a hundred votes' difference.

The outcome did not remain undisputed. A small group of villagers requested a meeting with the *camat*. They complained that, although apparently the *santri* were officially registered as inhabitants of Jurong village (Zulkiflar, the previous *geuchik*, had taken care of this), they did not have the right to vote for they were "not part of the Jurong community." The *camat* brushed them off. The elections were legitimate, and nothing could be done about it. One of the protesters summarized the villagers' sentiment for me by stating that, apparently, the *camat* was already "under the foot of Abuya" (*camat sudah di bawah kaki Abuya*).

The election of Ilyas was the apex of what people in Jurong called a "crisis of solidarity" (*masalah kekompakan*). In the course of years, a disruptive rift had emerged between the *kampung* and the *dayah* and, within the *kampung*, between a "*kampung* group" and a "*dayah* group" (*kelompok kampung/dayah*), the latter consisting mainly of Umi's relatives. The conflict was considered by many of my interlocutors as the single most important problem facing Jurong at the time of my stay. Some families were refused religious services, such as *santri* coming to pray at *kenduri*—according to one person, because they were "being tested" (*dites*; i.e., in their loyalty) by the *dayah* leadership. More importantly, the conflict caused strife at every level of village life. It obscured the decision-making process. Some matters were discussed in meetings. Others were not and were decided instead among the *geuchik* and the *teuha peut*. In the meantime, the allocation of government subsidies had become increasingly dependent on shadowy allegiances, machinated, according to many villagers, by Abi. Some families who supported Abi's position in the village leadership were accused of gaining economically from this. On the other hand, not everyone related to Umi supported the *dayah*. Some of Abuya's greatest critics were relatives, who became enmeshed, in turn, in intrafamily conflicts. The situation, in other words, was festering. I once attended a village meeting that was called together to resolve an argument from the previous meeting, and then got almost out of hand. As the atmosphere became heated, a young man sitting next to me whispered in my ear, "Sorry, it is always like this. In Jurong there's a lot of fighting."

Let me give an example of the rows that plagued the village during this period. In the course of 2009, the *geuchik*, together with the village secretary and the *teuha peut*, successfully applied for assistance from a government program for poor village youth. The support came in the form of money, under the condition that this was spent either on seeds (for *sawah* or gardens) or livestock (goats), encouraging beneficiaries to set up their own businesses. Distribution was not publicly discussed. Instead, a private meeting of the *teuha peut* decided that half should be granted to the *pemuda* (village youth), a quarter to the village leadership (the *geuchik*, members of the *teuha peut*, the *imam*, the *kepala lorong*, and the *kepala pemuda*), and a quarter to the *dayah*. Unsurprisingly, this angered many young people, who heard about it only when the subsidies had already been allocated. The *pemuda* also quarreled among themselves. The amount was too small to be divided among all of them, so only ten people were selected. It soon became evident that people close to Abi (rather than the poorest section of the *pemuda*) were given a share. The affair created such tension that unusual forms of reconciliation (*perdamaian*) were needed to normalize relations. The youth representative in the *teuha peut*, for example, used a part of the money allocated to him to organize a trip to the beach for the male youth of Jurong. Apart from soothing his conscience, he did this in the hope that it would end the discord (*fitnah*) resulting from the "problem with the goats."

Caught in between the quarreling parties was the *imam*. Bang Ali was the oldest brother of Abuya and Abi. He was less tied to the *dayah*, making a living by teaching weekly lessons in villages around the district. Bang Ali thought that the conflict was the "biggest problem in Jurong." Instead of a rift between village and *dayah*, however, he spoke of an "Ilyas faction" and a "Miram faction" (*kelompok* Ilyas/Miram)—that is, supporters of the election rivals—thus locating the conflict squarely in the village community. He defended the election of Ilyas, but also acknowledged that the problem was partly his responsibility as a village leader. This was not an easy problem to solve. "People argue behind your back," he said, and villagers were shy to speak straight to the ulama. He hoped that the tensions would ease as time passed.

Generation and the Perception of Moral Authority

During my fieldwork in Jurong, I gradually became aware of a difference between older and younger generations in this "crisis of solidarity." Older villagers often complained that "it had not always been like this." Over the years, the *dayah* had become increasingly affluent. After Abuya and Abi had relocated the female students to the central *dayah* compound, the previously shabby accommodation was replaced, bit by bit, with modern, partly storied concrete buildings, equipped with large communal kitchens. The residences of Abuya and his siblings became larger and larger, until they were the nicest and best furnished in Jurong. As the *dayah* grew, the star of Abuya rose. He received the *bupati* and the Banda Aceh mayor and became less concerned with people in Jurong. For older people this was a problem. The founder, Abu Nazir, had been modest and accessible. He knew every villager personally and cared about their problems. His sons were different. They cared about the *dayah* and (some said very explicitly) about their own personal interests. As community leaders (*tokoh masyarakat* or *tokoh adat*) they had alienated themselves from the village. Younger villagers, in contrast, were generally less outspoken in this regard. They agreed with the importance of mutual trust and social harmony but objected to the principled manner in which their elders framed the problem. Instead, they approached the conflict in a way that was, in their view, more pragmatic, constructive, and suitable to modern times. Let me give a few examples.

Mustafa was a widower in his seventies, who lived together with his unmarried daughter. Born in Keumala (Pidie), he had come to Jurong as a child. He had been a landless farmer all of his life until he became too old to work in the fields. His daughter earned some cash by doing other families' laundry. They were considered to be among the poorest households of the village. When I talked to Mustafa about the *dayah*, he said:

> MUSTAFA: Abu Nazir, ah, I knew him well! He was a good man. He did not accept money from the government. The *bupati* back then was Teuku Bachtiar. Abu Nazir used to say: if he [T. Bachtiar] wants to give us money in the name of the *bupati* then let him bring it. There is a river here, I will throw it all in. But if he wants to give money in his own name I will accept it. . . . In the past, the ulama (*teungku-teungku*) were common people like me. [Now it is] nice and easy but not nice (*enak-enak tapi tidak enak*). Nice and easy for them, but not so nice for the people. . . . We do not know where the money comes from. The *bupati* does not see the difference. Money is money, even if it is the levies taken from pigs (*sampai pajak babi*). Tell me, David, who is the richest man of the village?
>
> DAVID: Teuku Arif?
>
> M: Wrong, it is Abuya, he owns a thousand cows!
>
> D: Is that a reason to have less confidence in the ulama?
>
> M: No, not that. We have to trust them. If we do not trust them it means we have no faith.

Mustafa used to be a member of the *teuha peut*. In the past, he said, they were not paid for this (*digaji*). It was considered normal to serve the village community. "But now I don't care anymore."

Teungku Maimun was in his forties and, for a farmer, relatively well to do. His oldest child was a student in Banda Aceh. Maimun was a nephew of Umi and thus related by blood to Abuya and Abi. After the election of Ilyas, however, he joined the villagers who protested to the *camat*:

> TEUNGKU MAIMUN: When we visited the *camat*, [Abuya and his family] were very angry with me, because we are kin (*saudara*). But I was not afraid, because I know we should do what is right. It is the principles that count. . . . I do not answer to them, I answer to the Creator (*sang pencipta*). . . . Perhaps I'll be less happy here, but more happy there [i.e., in the afterlife; *akhirat*].
>
> DAVID: Did you not consider taking up the matter directly with Abuya?
>
> T.M.: No, there is no use. They are people with lots of knowledge (*ilmu*). Even the *camat* is afraid of Abuya. . . . We are at the bottom. We better just mind our own business.
>
> D.: Does that make you feel bad? (*sakit hati*)
>
> T.M.: No. Why? If you follow what is right then there is nothing to feel bad about.

This kind of ambivalence could be found in many people of his age. A fundamental critique of the worldly interests and engagements of religious authorities was coupled with an equally fundamental refusal to deal with these matters directly. Challenging the *dayah* leaders openly, Teungku Maimun explained, would be to transgress the basic norms that guided the relationship between villagers and the "people with lots of knowledge."

In some cases, this ambivalence led to a near-complete severance of social ties. Teungku Usman was sixty-six years old, a former market trader and father of three adult children. His analysis resulted in one of the sharpest condemnations of the *dayah* leaders I have heard:

> [The *dayah* leaders] are interested in money. If no money is involved, they do not bother. . . . They have gardens, they have rice fields, they even bake cakes [to sell]! But this is not their business. This is the right of the poor. . . . They turn in a proposal for this, a proposal for that [i.e., for government funding]. . . . And they take money from the *kampung*. . . . Actually we do not need to listen anymore. We really do not need them anymore.

Now let me compare Teungku Usman's comment to that of his youngest son. Putra was twenty-two years old. He prayed diligently, and on Thursday nights he usually went to the *dayah* to attend Abuya's *pengajian*.

> PUTRA: The villagers do not respect [the *dayah* leaders] anymore. They say, in secret, that they are no longer ulama. They became businessmen (*towkay*)!

DAVID: If this is true, then why do people still go to the *pengajian*? Why
do you?

P: Because Abuya can still explain the *kitab*. No one knows the *kitab*
better than he does. We do not listen to Abuya, we listen to the *kitab*.
They still have the right to teach. And it is an obligation to search for
knowledge. It would be sinful not to listen to them.

D: And why do people still work together with them in the village, for
example in the *teuha peut*?

P: Because we are professionals.

Just like his father, Putra was ambivalent about the *dayah*. Yet his position
was different. He did not think the ulama had become redundant. They represented a source of religious knowledge and services that remained of crucial
importance for villagers.

I found a similar contrast in other families. Yanah and Muhamad were a
married couple in their fifties, who owned a shop in the local market:

YANAH AND MUHAMAD: There is a problem with the leadership. The
leaders of the *kampung* and the leaders of the *pesantren*. . . . They are
unjust. They don't know *halal* from *haram*. It would be better if they do
not interfere with the affairs of the *kampung*. They already have a job.

DAVID: Do you think this is just a problem in Jurong? Or in other places
as well?

Y/M: No, just here, in Jurong. . . . Other places we don't know about. . . .
Why would we want to know? The important thing is we have this
problem here. Well, maybe in other places too, but we don't know.

Their daughter Cut (twenty-seven, married, one child), in a different, private
conversation, said:

People have doubts about the ulama being pure of heart. [This is a problem because] they are our role models. . . . For example, if the children of
ulama have other interests than teaching, they should pursue other things
and this is no problem. They should still behave well, however, because
they are the children of ulama. So they are different from ordinary people. . . . [On our part] we have to respect the *pesantren*. We can choose
when we want to deepen our own knowledge. At the moment, I am not
ready for this yet. But since in our village the *pesantren* is nearby, we have
to pay them our respect . . . for example by wearing a headscarf when we
pass by that side of the village.

Cut's view may be compared to that of Hafid, her twenty-four-year-old unmarried cousin:

DAVID: Does the crisis of solidarity make it more difficult for you to accept the opinions of the ulama? For example, when they tell the villagers that certain behavior is not allowed?

HAFID: [Reacts with surprise] Of course not! Why? These are the rules of our religion. It is good when they remind the people of this. . . . Of course, different people react differently. . . . These are matters of faith (*iman*) and practice (*ibadah*). But it is good if certain things are forbidden.

Like Putra, Hafid regularly attended Abuya's weekly *pengajian*. On his mobile phone he collected, and regularly listened to, recorded sermons of Aceh's well-known ulama. He agreed with the need for ulama to join politics as a counterweight to established political elites. At the same time, his explanations of the way in which the crisis of solidarity compromised the integrity of Abuya and his family were incisive. For him, this was not a matter of detached analysis but part of a deeply felt internal struggle.

Putra, Cut, and Hafid distinguished, more than their elders, between the "self-evident" traditional authority of the ulama and the divergent, debatable knowledge and values they transferred and represented. Compared to their parents, they regarded the social configuration of Jurong in a more pragmatic, strategic, and individualistic style. The next section elaborates on this contrast by discussing one particular event. I will use this case to illustrate how discursive differences between generations came with particular consequences for the way in which people responded to, and acted upon, lived crises.

The Theft from the Dayah

It was the talk of the village, and perhaps the neighboring villages as well: the theft from the *dayah*. For several nights in a row, three boys from Jurong (one fourteen, the others seventeen years old) had broken into the *dayah* to steal from the communal kitchens. It was Ramadan, the fasting month, so it was quiet in the *dayah*. Most of the students had temporarily returned to their home villages. The boys had sought out *tarawih*, the daily recommended prayers following the mandatory *isya* prayer, as their opportunity to enter the compound unnoticed. Youthful rogues rather than professional criminals, they had planned to collect a number of cooking stoves, take them apart, and sell the components to scrap metal dealers for petty cash. Still, the theft was not small, with the retail value of one stove equaling three days' wages of a day laborer, and the boys taking more than thirty pieces.

Arriving in Jurong on a Saturday afternoon, I was told by villagers that one of the boys had been caught red-handed the evening before, and taken, on personal orders of Abuya, to the local police station. There he had disclosed the identities of his accomplices, who were subsequently lifted from their beds. I was shocked when I heard the names. One of them, Irwan, was a younger brother of my friend Fendi. He was fourteen years old. I knew him as quiet and polite, certainly not as a "criminal."

The next morning, I looked up Fendi, who owned a small shop near the market. He told me that, after coming home late on Friday night, he had found his mother, Cut Nurul, crying. Irwan had just been arrested. His father, Zainuddin, was at the police station. Fendi had immediately jumped on his motorcycle. Entering the police station and seeing his younger brother, he had lost his composure and slapped Irwan hard, right on his ear. His younger brother had shriveled on the spot, and Fendi had lectured him, emphasizing the irresponsibility of not thinking about the consequences, including the shame that this whole affair would cause for his family. Fendi lit a cigarette and looked at me. "I still can't believe he has been so stupid." I asked him whether he knew when Irwan would be released. He shrugged. "No idea. First there has to be a solution."

I went back to the village. Cut Nurul looked distressed. She had hardly slept and suffered severe headaches. She was afraid that Irwan might not come home before Hari Raya Idulfitri, the celebration of the end of the fasting month, commencing next Friday. Zainuddin was not at home. I stayed and tried to comfort her. Later that afternoon I met the *geuchik*. No solution had been reached yet. He said that the boys' families would have to compensate the *dayah* for the damage. It was not just the money, however. The boys would have to feel the consequences of their actions. Their detention was as much a punishment as an incentive for the families to seek a financial solution. According to the *geuchik*, it was up to the police and Abuya to decide how long this would take. I asked, "Do you think the boys will be released before Hari Raya?" He replied, "I don't know. Maybe yes, maybe no, everything is in process." "So what happens if there is no solution?" I asked. "Then they will be taken to court. There is a juvenile court in Jantho [the district capital]. There even is a juvenile prison. But I don't think it will come to that."

Irwan and the other boys were not actually locked behind bars. They were allowed to walk around freely as long as they did not leave the building. Officially, their detention was the decision of the local police chief (Kepala Polisi Sektor, "Kapolsek"). Most villagers, however, assumed that it was Abuya who made the calls. On Monday, Fendi's family invited me for the breaking of the fast. Irwan had now spent three nights at the police station. Cut Nurul was doing better. At the same time, the shamefulness of the situation was sinking in. "I am sad about what Irwan did," she said. "Everyone is talking about it. Everyone knows."

One day later, Zainuddin was among the forty to fifty men assembling at the *meunasah* to perform *isya* and the subsequent *tarawih* prayers (figure 7). Once they had finished and were readying themselves to go home or to the

FIGURE 7. The *meunasah* (communal hall) in Jurong (August 2010). Photo by the author.

coffee shop, the *geuchik* suddenly requested that they stay somewhat longer. The Kapolsek was on his way to the *meunasah* in order to "hand over" the young thieves to the village (*serah terima masyarakat kampung*). The men sat down. There was no attempt to convene other villagers, although a number of people, men and women, also came to witness the event. Fifteen minutes later, a police pickup truck arrived, carrying the three boys, the Kapolsek, and two officers. Not much later Abuya arrived, on foot, chaperoned by a group of *santri*. The boys were told to sit in the middle of the *meunasah* while the men assembled around them in a big circle.

The *geuchik* spoke first. He asked the villagers to accept the hand-over of the boys and to participate in a reconciliation ceremony (*perdamaian*) aimed at restoring (*memperbaharui*, lit. "to renew") the relationship between the *kampung* and the *dayah*. He then read two documents. The first was an "announcement" (*pengumuman*), drafted one and a half years earlier by the village leadership and signed by the *geuchik*, the *teuha peut* (the village council), and the *kepala pemuda* (the head of the village youth). The document stated that, in the case of theft by a village resident, the perpetrator would be subjected to *adat* sanctions (*sangsi adat*), including the obligation to pay damages and, in the case of noncompliance, the risk of being expelled from the village. The second document was drafted earlier that day. It was signed by the "perpetrators" (*pelaku*) and their guardians (*wali*, in all three cases their father), stating that they would compensate the *dayah* for "material and immaterial damage." It also included a provision that, in the case of relapse, the affair would no longer be dealt with informally (*secara adat*) but brought before the court.

Abuya spoke next. Children, he explained, are entrusted temporarily by God into the hands of their parents (*anak adalah titipan Tuhan*). He warned that the behavior of the boys brought shame not just on their families, but also on the village (*buat malu kampung*). He ended his speech by asserting his personal authority. If this happened again, he would not hesitate "to send the perpetrators across the sea," which was understood as a reference to Nusa Kambangan, the infamous, high-security prison-island off the coast of Java. Directing himself to the boys, he threatened, "Your parents would not be able to visit you, because there is no ship to take them there."

Finally, the Kapolsek spoke. He started with a point by point summary of events: how the boys were caught, what goods they had stolen, and what they had done with them. The boys had not been "jailed." Rather, they were held for "general safety" (*untuk keamanan*). It was normal procedure for the perpetrators to be taken into custody until a definite solution was found. Although it was never the intention to keep them longer than a few days, this might be their last chance of reaching a solution "within the community" (*di dalam kampung*). Next time there would be no "exemption" (*dispensasi*). Instead, they would be transferred to the district court in Jantho. The damage, he clarified, amounted to 1,450,000 rupiah (US$155) per family. He continued with a note about education, directing himself to the fathers of the boys. Fathers should take at least an hour each day to talk with their families about "right and wrong." "Why," he said, "do the fathers always enter the house through the front door and the sons through the back door? How can they know what their children are up to?" He ended by declaring that it was the task of the police to "make big things small, and to make small things disappear." On the one hand, this was a reference to the willingness of the police to facilitate an informal solution. On the other hand, the comment seemed to urge people not to blow controversial decisions (such as the detention of the boys) out of proportion.

All this time the boys sat quietly, shoulders bowed, with their faces turned to the ground. After the Kapolsek had finished, the children and their fathers signed the first document. Photos were taken of the boys, further officializing the "hand-over." The meeting ended with a public apology, which is a common element of reconciliation (*perdamaian*) rituals in Aceh. The boys and their fathers went around the *meunasah*, approaching every person present with a greeting (briefly touching the tips of the fingers, then raising one's own hand to the chest) and a spoken apology (Ac. *meuteume ampon*). Once this was finished, everyone left, and the boys were allowed to go home.

One week after the *perdamaian*, I discussed the incident with Abuya. As a community leader, he concerned himself with matters of religious law (*hukum agama*) and *adat* law (*hukum adat* or *hukum kampung*). "Criminality" (*kriminalitas*), like stealing, violent assault, or drug use, should be seen instead as a matter of civil law (*hukum negara*), to be handled by the police rather than the community (*masyarakat*). However, the theft from the *dayah* was an unusual case. When I asked why the theft had been forwarded to the police, he said that it was never his intention to try the boys in court. Rather than "threaten" the boys (*mengancam*; his term), he wanted to prevent the incident from happening again. He emphasized that one of the two older boys had a track record of petty crime. Also, he could not ignore the scale of the theft. When I asked him again whether theft, generally speaking, should be considered a matter of civil law, he said, "No. Not in the case of children under age. In Islam, it is enough to have them pay damages and give them a warning (*peringatan*). This is enough." Thus he suggested that the procedure was one of protection, not punishment.

Abi's stance was more confrontational. "First we ask: how is it possible that children from the village steal." This was a rhetorical question. According to Abi, the blame should be sought with the parents and their own failing education. In the case of the boy with the bad track record, the father was a former thief himself and thus a particularly bad example. In the other two cases, including Irwan, the parents were not sufficiently educated. In his view, the arrest and detention of the boys were not a punishment but a deterrent for the parents (*untuk bikin jera*), encouraging all villagers to put more effort into raising their children. A *perdamaian* alone would not instill sufficient warning. Keeping the case within the confines of the village community might lead people to "think lightly" (*menganggap enteng*) about the issue. Just like Abuya, Abi denied that involving the police would side track *adat* (*di luar qanun*). "We take them to the police to coordinate matters and to make people change their mentality (*berobah pikiran*). That is all."

Villagers were ambiguous about the affair. Few people felt bad for the boys. The arrest was seen as their own fault, and some people thought it was a good warning for other aspiring criminals. No one believed it would be appropriate to keep them locked up for a long time. Most people described the boys as "naughty kids" (*anak nakal*), who probably had not thought very hard about the consequences of their behavior. They believed that the case should be relatively easy to solve, if only the damages were paid. Like Abi, many people pointed at the role of the parents, arguing that they had apparently not looked after their children well enough. Everyone agreed that the incident caused great shame for the boys' families. Some people used the language of shame to denigrate them, especially when particular grudges, such as jealousy or previous feuds, were in play.

At the same time, the theft from the *dayah* was also thought to implicate the community as a whole. Villagers stated that the incident affected the "good name" of their village. This idea of collective shame was a powerful discursive element, which could be used to address a variety of issues, including crime and the violation of religious norms and *adat* (see Kloos 2014b). One villager explained that, if Abuya said that "shame was brought upon the *kampung*," what he really meant was that "shame was brought upon him." This was a pattern. There was a conspicuous parallel, for example, between Abuya's speech during the "hand-over" of the boys and his sermon a few months earlier during *maulid* (the celebration of the birthday of the Prophet). Knowing that many people from other villages would come to listen, he publicly criticized the Jurong community for not showing up at his weekly *pengajian*. What would be thought of him, he asked, if people from his own village did not attend? The next section discusses the contrasting positions in this case of Irwan's father, Zainuddin, and his eldest son, Fendi, in order to elaborate the perceptions of power and morality that lay at the basis of these discourses of shame.

"My Father Is a Good Man but Too Stubborn"

Zainuddin was one of the villagers who complained to the *camat* about the controversial election of Ilyas. Unsurprisingly, this made the incident extra sensitive. What struck me most, however, was the reaction of Fendi, Irwan's older brother. Fendi, twenty-six, was the fourth of Zainuddin and Cut Nurul's five children. I had come to know him as a responsible young man. Working in his uncle's small but successful shop, which became his personal property in early 2010, he earned the largest part of the family's income. Although he had a girlfriend (a student in a *pesantren* near Sibreh), he was not yet thinking seriously about marriage. For now, he was enjoying the respect he had already earned.

Over the years, Fendi gradually assumed responsibility over his family's finances (which meant, for example, that whenever Zainuddin sold a portion of his yield, he let Fendi manage the money). Fendi's sense of responsibility went further, however. For example, in a conflict about irrigation water it was Fendi who represented his family. But in this case things were different. Except for his emotional outburst at the police station on the night of Irwan's arrest, Fendi kept aloof from the affair. He stayed away from the *perdamaian*, even though he knew about it. At first, I thought he felt ashamed. Then I realized there was a different reason, connected to a subtle, largely unarticulated difference of opinion between him and his father about the relationship among family, village, and *dayah*.

Let me start with Zainuddin. After breaking the fast together on Monday night (Irwan was arrested on Friday night), Fendi left the house to reopen his shop. I stayed behind to drink coffee and smoke a couple of cigarettes with Zainuddin. He had just come home from the *sawah*. He seemed tired and weary. The combination of the situation and the fasting month was taking its toll. Once we started talking about Irwan, however, I noticed that he was furious. Zainuddin agreed that Irwan had done a terrible thing. Yet he considered the way in which the situation was handled to be entirely out of proportion. Irwan, he said, was "like all children," which meant that he did "not fully possess reason" (*tidak penuh akal*). "He does not know anything, he does not know what it means to be sinful, he does not think about the long term." As a result, Irwan could not assess the consequences of his actions. He did not know the real value of money. Although Zainuddin stretched the argument (other villagers were less eager to explain the theft as being "without reason"), this view was compatible with a dominant discourse about children and moral responsibility (which is based on the Islamic idea that children reach a state of moral "maturity" after reaching puberty). According to Zainuddin, one could not expect a fourteen-year-old to have fully internalized the difference between right and wrong. This, he said, was both a "universal" and an Islamic principle, found equally in Christian religion (*agama Nasrani*) and human rights ("HAM," Hak Asasi Manusia).

The involvement of the police, Zainuddin predicted, would turn out to be expensive for him and for the families of the other boys. Of course, he said, it was reasonable to pay compensation for the damage caused to the *dayah*. "If I do not have enough money, I will borrow it, or I will sell one of the buffaloes." But this was not the point. The Indonesian police is generally seen as a predatory, unreliable, and costly institution. So why did Abuya not simply solve the case in private, in consultation with the village leadership? Zainuddin thought that he used the incident to retaliate for the conflict over the election of Ilyas. For him, this was just another confirmation of the impoverished status of Abuya as a community leader. By involving the police, Abuya had failed to respect *adat*. His proper role, Zainuddin explained, was to help people, not to be above them.

> We have no education or advanced knowledge (*ilmu tinggi*). We are just farmers. Abuya is an ulama. He is like a guide (*pedoman*). But how can the ulama be guides if they act like this? We may be ignorant people, but we do know *adat*. . . . How can Abuya, who is so great (*hebat*) and rich (*kaya*), and who has gone on hajj how many times, be so careless?

Yet even though Abuya seemed careless, Zainuddin felt utterly powerless to do something about it. He thought that everything he said or did would make the situation worse. At the police station he was all cooperation. Complaining would be useless, for engaging a higher authority would presumably only increase the cost. So instead he chose to keep quiet and consent. Being forced to keep his mouth shut was an extra humiliation. Asked whether he felt ashamed, he answered that "everyone makes mistakes." Still, there was no need for the whole district to know. He turned the argument around. Abuya had not shrunk from putting children in jail. This, he believed, was where the real shame was.

It took a few days before I could speak to Fendi privately. This was un-usual. A week earlier, a text message would have been sufficient for a late-night cigarette behind the house. Not this time, though. Fendi, I rightly guessed, felt trapped. His father, via his mother, had asked him to settle the problem. Fendi had refused. When I asked him why, he said, "Because I get angry too quickly." As we talked longer, however, it turned out that there was another reason: Fendi no longer wanted to take responsibility for a situation in which, he thought, his father was to blame. Fendi agreed that Abuya should not have sent Irwan to the police. He also shared the suspicion that his primary interest was to get back at Zainuddin. In fact, this was the root of the problem. Fendi held his father in high regard, but he also thought that Zainuddin was too in-flexible and not sufficiently pragmatic:

> My father is a good man. He hates injustice (*ketidakadilan*), but he is too stubborn in his opinions (*teguh pendirian*). If he wants to go to Banda Aceh, he will go to Banda Aceh. Whether it rains or whether it storms, he will go. This time it is not different.

In Fendi's view, this attitude was no longer appropriate. In summary, his argument was this: "Today, there is no use in resisting people that are rich and powerful. We will always lose out. This world is a different place compared to the time when my father was young. His reaction to these matters is old-fashioned and not sensible. We should cooperate with them instead of aggra-vating discord." I replied, "But is that not exactly what Zainuddin has done?" Fendi answered, "Yes, but everything would have been easier if he had done so from the start." Gradually, the tone of our conversation changed. I felt irritated and asked Fendi how, if everyone thought like him, people would be able to "stand up against the rich and the powerful." Fendi coolly replied that I was right, but that I should understand that it was important to take into account the interests at stake. Personally, he had "no problem" with Abuya, and he thought that people should "mind their own business" and focus on making a living, rather than make matters worse. Because of his economic position, and because his parents were getting older, Fendi had, in effect, become the "head of the family" (*kepala keluarga*). Nonetheless, he did not feel like taking responsibility for Irwan's mischief. "I am not going to be the one who pays."

This statement was not just about money. Fendi simply did not want to become personally implicated in a vendetta with a powerful figure like Abuya. His argument was complex, however. First of all, he thought it was important for ordinary people to be "close" (*akrab*) with the ulama. Becoming alienated from influential people like Abuya and Abi was not very strategic. In the case of a conflict with Abuya, *santri* might not come to the village to pray at important rituals, such as funeral *kenduri*. With Abi, the situation was different again. Abi controlled the flow of money from the government to the village. Like most other villagers, Fendi thought that this was a problem. Whenever the villagers of Jurong seemed entitled to government subsidies (*bantuan*), part (or all) of the money was redirected to the *dayah*. Yet at the same time Fendi thought that Abi's activities and network created opportunities for the village and its inhabitants. This was a problem of equity. The shady redistribution of government subsidies was felt mostly by the poor, who noticed every year that there was less Raskin. For Fendi the situation was different. "I am independent (*mandiri*). I work, I make sure that my earnings are *halal* and I take care of my family." In other words, there was very little to win and (potentially) a lot to lose in jeopardizing his relationship with the *dayah*.

A fundamental ambiguity thus informed Fendi's position. One way of dealing with this was to distinguish between Abuya and Abi. Abuya, Fendi explained, was a learned and widely respected ulama, who derived much of his income from alms (*sedekah*). Abi was different. He was "not an ulama," as he gained most of his authority from connections with the government, the provincial parliament (Dewan Perwakilan Rakyat Daerah, DPRD), and the security apparatus, rather than religious learning. Both were people to be reckoned with, albeit for different reasons. Another way of reasoning was to put the responsibility of moral judgment in the hands of God. "It is not good to be scornful (*menghinakan*)," Fendi stated. "But you do think this situation is bad," I responded. "Yes, I do. I hate people who are not good. But this is in my heart (*dalam hati*). I feel bad for the poor, but I do not show this too much. There would be little gain." In the end, things would be settled by God. Rather than mentioning Abuya or Abi, he referred to one of their nephews, who was a member of the DPRD. "He has a bad skin disease. Everyone knows this." Fendi explained that, in the Qur'an, there is a story about a particular type of skin disease, which is given to those "who are most hated by God." "My grandfather had a stroke. He prays every day for a cure. And perhaps he will get better. But imagine that, afterwards, he forgets about God. Certainly he will fall ill again! This is the same thing."

Village Politics and the Reconceptualization of Local Leadership

Is the "crisis of solidarity," as I encountered it in Jurong, a result of the "crisis of authority" in Islam? Let me try to answer this question by placing the position of the ulama in a more general context of local leadership in Aceh. In the course of my fieldwork, I observed that many people, and young people in particular, accepted and were comfortable with the idea that the roles and interests of religious leaders, agents of the state, and ordinary villagers overlapped. In Jurong, despite the anger and unease over the way in which the *dayah* appropriated local government funding, Abuya continued to be regarded as an authoritative figure, who was respected for his knowledge and guidance. Rather than a breakdown of religious authority, the "crisis of solidarity" reflected a broad and ongoing contestation over money, power, and moral leadership at the local level. The real problem, then, is that local institutions are vested with insufficient capacity to absorb the social disruptions that are caused by these clashing interests and to resolve conflicts in a way that is morally acceptable to a majority of people (cf. Kloos 2014b).

Let me clarify this point by looking at the position of the village head. The *geuchik* is chosen from among the villagers. He is traditionally an elderly man (though there are also some female village heads in Aceh) who is (reasonably) pious, knowledgeable about *adat,* and sufficiently charismatic to deal with local conflicts. Over the past decades, however, the responsibilities of the *geuchik* have increased. Today, people expect the village head to lobby for government support, to make sure that villagers are properly registered, and to improve the village living environment and infrastructure. Not too long ago, this was largely a matter of *gotong royong,* communal labor. While *gotong royong* remains important today, the *geuchik* is expected to persuade both the local government and the more affluent segments of the population to invest in the village or neighborhood. Community leaders find these expectations increasingly difficult, if not impossible, to fulfill. At the same time, respected and capable people are often unwilling to accept the office, anticipating that they will make enemies rather than friends, regardless of the way in which they would carry out the task.

Ilyas was not the villagers' first choice. He had not lived long enough in Jurong to accumulate the local knowledge necessary to solve problems. He never wanted to become village head and likened Abuya's request to "someone telling you to eat." Unsurprisingly, the situation came down hard on him, especially when there were conflicts about money. The problem with the *pemuda* and the goats made Ilyas feel torn apart by the two factions. As a result, he no longer wanted to be involved in funding proposals that involved large parts of the village population. Although he acknowledged that it was his role to "restore the community" (*buat persatuan*), he complained about the lack of cooperation. Ilyas compared himself to a herder guiding a group of buffaloes. "There are always a few who don't want to listen, who go this way, who go that way." Ultimately, he seemed to be a lonely man, who very much felt a victim of the situation. To a large extent, I think he was right. Ilyas was not seen by his fellow villagers as a bad man. Rather, he felt paralyzed as a leader, and he had neither the charisma nor the necessary support to bring peace to the community.

In Blang Daruet, my other field site, the *geuchik* was a local, who was chosen in a fair election by a majority of the people. There was no *dayah* in Daruet and no "crisis of solidarity." As in Jurong, however, anger, disappointment, and discontent about unequal economic opportunities were directed, albeit not very openly, at the *geuchik*. Like Ilyas, Syahrul was seen as an ineffective leader. People would state, for example, that there was hardly any change during his tenure and that he was not sufficiently "clever" in lobbying (*melobi*) the government. When I asked for concrete examples, people would start about the bad quality of the water, the underdeveloped infrastructure, or the lack of local initiatives for education. I once asked a group of particularly critical women whether this was not the responsibility of the whole community. They reacted slightingly. That would be the world upside down! It was the task of the *geuchik* to lead the community, not the other way around. At the same time, Syahrul was criticized for helping his own family rather than distributing government funding and opportunities justly. Syahrul was not an affluent man, and he was regularly accused of taking public money for private use.

Although many people complained about Syahrul's leadership, it was young people in particular who argued for a more adequate, or "modern," interpretation of local leadership. Take, for example, the analysis of Andri, Blang Daruet's young and energetic village secretary. Andri was an intelligent young man, who put a lot of time and effort into professionalizing the village administration. He produced extensive village reports, reorganized population records, organized village meetings (with neatly typed out invitations and attendance lists), and spent a lot of time in the *camat*'s office promoting Blang Daruet interests. Andri did not, however, seek to replace a traditional leadership system with a bureaucratic one. Although he complained about old-fashioned village leaders, he criticized those who did not accept the authority of neighborhood leaders:

> One of the biggest problems is that people no longer want to accept the decisions of the *geuchik* and the *teuha peut*. . . . According to *adat*, the village leaders are mediators (lit. "between the people," *di antara orang*). . . . The people don't accept this anymore. They want to be right. Today, people bring things straight to court. . . . They are egoistic. When there is a conflict, they want to take everything. They are not interested in the middle road, even though this is the essence of *adat* law (*esensi hukum kampung*).

To some extent, Andri thought, this problem was connected to the tsunami and its aftermath, when there was lot of money in circulation, and conflicts sometimes emerged over the entitlement to aid and problems of inheritance. In his view, this explained, at least partly, why people were "egoistic," and why problems were "difficult to solve."[9] He did not blame a specific group. "It is everyone's fault. No one cares." If people would make an effort, things might change. He pointed to himself. Having only graduated from senior high school, he was not particularly highly educated. He did not have rich parents, and he was not even "fully Acehnese" (his father was from Padang). He did, however, want to know "how everything worked," and he was motivated to make a career out of his attempt to improve the condition of the neighborhood.

The views and strategies of younger people in Jurong were comparable to Andri's. Young people judged, and acted upon, the conflict between the village and the *dayah*, not by drawing on a principled or ideologically coherent approach to traditional religious authority, but by navigating, and finding a balance between, traditional norms and life course strategies. Despite the dubious role of the *dayah* leadership, and the near-complete co-optation by the *dayah* of the village administration, they did not simply dismiss, like some of their elders, the need for "traditional" leadership. Instead, they observed the way in which careers, access to resources, and the establishment of local networks could be reconciled with a moral attachment to the community.

To an extent, this personal navigation of moral authority supports Francis Robinson's statement about a crisis of authority in Islam. However, the material presented in this chapter also complicates some of his conclusions. In both my field sites, young people behaved—more than their parents—as consumers of authority, for example, by investing in particular relationships or networks or by deploying or adapting sources of authority to their own personal concerns, preferences, and situations. Yet the situation as I observed it in Jurong and Blang Daruet also resists the argument that "increasingly every individual's view comes to have the same value as everyone else's" (F. Robinson 2009, 353). Young villagers valued—perhaps even more than their elders—the need for a distinct realm of moral authority, one that was local and that preserved social and religious norms in a context that was recognizable, predictable, and safe.

Conclusion

In Aceh, the position of the ulama, as transmitters of religious knowledge and main bearers of traditional religious authority, has been subject to change. A variety of factors are in play, ranging from the social, political, and cultural transformations associated with the "crisis of authority" in the Muslim world to more place-specific tensions. A crucial factor is the contested alignment of many traditionalist ulama, during the conflict between the Indonesian government and GAM, with the state. I have sought to analyze the changing position of the ulama and their changing relation with the state not by foregrounding formal politics or armed conflict, however, but by focusing on the worries, aspirations, and situations of ordinary people.

Central to this chapter has been the tense relationship between the leaders of Dayah Darul Hidayah, a large traditional boarding school, and the adjacent village of Jurong. The interference of *dayah* leaders in village affairs culminated in widespread allegations of manipulation, favoritism, and abuse of power. Some people saw this so-called crisis of solidarity as the outcome of the abandonment by the ulama of the "common people" (*rakyat*, or *orang kecil*). However, most people expressed a more ambivalent view. Young people in particular argued that the personal connections and supraregional networks of *dayah* leaders constituted an important reservoir of local status and state support. Taking my cue from these responses, in this chapter I have focused on generational dynamics, demonstrating what I regard to be the single most important trend in the reconfiguration of traditional religious authority in Aceh. Young people today are prepared, much more than their elders, to accept and act upon the role of traditionalist ulama as agents of the state. They conceptualize the terms of moral leadership by addressing, and maximizing, the use of state resources in a way that can be seen as both effective and just at the same time. This shift connects to the ways in which people navigate social relations and conflicting interests on the basis of personal assessments of moral responsibility.

Conflict-centered narratives tend to place the Acehnese in a position that is fundamentally opposed to the Indonesian central state. In reality, however, the state caters to the aspirations of many, especially younger people. Influential local figures, such as the leaders of Dayah Darul Hidayah, play a central role in this interaction. This observation has implications for the way in which we frame the everyday constitution of religious agency. Particularly important, I believe, is the simultaneous functioning of the state as a resource and a repertoire for moral action. As I have argued, the gradually expanding state has increased the level of control exerted by formal and informal institutions (such as the *dayah*). Often forgotten, however, is that this process has also increased the agency of ordinary villagers, who make use of the state as they engage in local, morally laden contestations about issues connected to concepts of community, shame, respect, wealth, and punishment. The next chapter further elaborates on these themes in the context of the global Islamic revival and the development of Aceh's post-conflict, post-disaster society.

4

Islamic Scripturalism and Everyday Life after the Disaster

Heaven lies under mother's feet.
—MELI (BLANG DARUET, 2008)

The family is an important site of religious contestation. This chapter examines the interactions between Eri, a young man who became heavily influenced by the scripturalist views commonly associated with the global Islamic revival, and his parents, Ikhsan and Meli. Together with Eri's siblings, they lived in the reconstructed, but still deeply uprooted, tsunami-affected neighborhood of Blang Daruet in Banda Aceh. When I first met Eri, in October 2009, he was twenty-four years old. Earlier, he had spent two years at an Islamic school in Jakarta. There, he felt attracted to the Islamist ideology of PKS (Partai Keadilan Sejahtera, or Justice and Prosperity Party). Back in Aceh, he adopted a strong, "outwardly" directed pious lifestyle, as well as a moralistic attitude toward his family. Eri's ideas about the observance of scriptural norms were accommodated, rather than rejected or fully accepted, by his parents. Their response is a demonstration of the complex relationship between expressions of personal piety and responsibilities toward the family, which in recent years has become an important theme in the anthropology of Islam in Southeast Asia (see, e.g., Fischer 2008; Frisk 2009; Gade 2004; Simon 2014). The goal of this chapter is to illustrate and analyze the flexibility of many ordinary Muslims as they engage with the claims and appeals of normative Islam. As such, it shows a crucial aspect of religious agency in Aceh and the contemporary Muslim world more broadly.

Aceh is often seen as a place where, compared to other parts of Indonesia, the global Islamic revival has not been very influential. This is true, to the extent that the separatist conflict made it difficult for (trans)national, revivalist, or radically Islamist groups to establish themselves in the province.[1] At the same time, such comments tend to reproduce stereotypical discourses of Acehnese exceptionalism, either implying or explicitly stating that the Acehnese are an inherently conservative, inward-looking people who are hostile to outside influences (cf. Kloos 2015b). As I have argued in the previous chapters, Aceh has never been an isolated place. Globalized expressions of Islam have affected society and everyday lives for a long time and in different ways, both in relation to the propagation of outward piety (most notably through the implementation of shari'a law) and in the more personal dimensions of what Francis Robinson termed the "inward turn." My focus on family relations serves to trace the significance of the inward turn for Muslims living in the wake of great social and political upheaval.

More generally, this book speaks to and builds on a body of literature that deals with the effects of the Islamic revival on the lives of ordinary Indonesian Muslims. I will discuss this literature and my specific contribution in more detail in the final section of this chapter. For now, let me single out one remarkable study, which, in researching and writing this book, struck me as both inspiring and problematic at the same time. Andrew Beatty's (2009) intriguing "anthropological memoir," *A Shadow Falls: In the Heart of Java*, describes in detail the imposing presence of a group of Islamic hardliners in a rural village in East Java in the 1990s. It is a personal and emotional argument that the "heart" of Java, with its age-old syncretic and tolerant religious tradition, is on the verge of being swept aside by the inflexible and fanatical side of the Islamic resurgence. While Beatty's book has been rightly praised for its empirical richness, its eye for generational conflicts, and its empathy with the ways in which ordinary villagers try to deal with the transformations taking place within their society, it has also been criticized for reproducing the image of a mythical, "timeless" Javanese identity, thus missing the opportunity to present a nuanced analysis of religious change (see, e.g., Samedi et al. 2010). While I draw inspiration from Beatty's personal engagement and literary style, I also agree to a large extent with this critique. In my view, a solid understanding of the increased prominence of scripturalist attitudes and its impact on local communities requires a more inclusive approach, one that approaches religious agency as a product of social interactions between groups and individuals of different backgrounds and religious persuasions.

I will start by introducing Eri's family and neighborhood and some of the religious debates that were raised within the family after his return to Banda Aceh. I proceed with two stories—one focused on the life and experiences of his father, Ikhsan, and one on his mother, Meli—to demonstrate the ambiguities inherent in these debates. I then move on to a more abstract level of analysis, looking at the impact of Eri's scripturalist repertoire on his parents' perceptions of community, and using money and economic behavior as a prism to make sense of the tangle of everyday concerns, both religious and nonreligious. The final section addresses the relationship between outward piety and inner states of being and, in relation to this, the problematic contrast that has arisen recently within the anthropology of Islam between the pursuit of piety and the trials and tribulations of everyday life. As my analysis shows, a focus on self-perceived moral failure and the factor of age and life phase constitutes an important starting point for theoretical innovation.

Routines and Debates in a Tsunami-Affected Neighborhood

One of my first observations in Blang Daruet concerned the distinction between both "sides" of the neighborhood. The people in the area around the mosque considered themselves "locals" (*asli Daruet*) with descent usually traced through the line of the mother. The majority of people living on the other side of the road were seen (and commonly presented themselves) as "newcomers" (*pendatang*).[2] In general, these people were better educated and wealthier than the *asli Daruet*. Many of them had government jobs. They often rented and did not plan to stay in Blang Daruet for the rest of their lives. In daily conversations, the differences between both areas were presented matter-of-factly, with particular connotations connected to "this side" (*sebelah sini*) and "that side" (*sebelah sana*). Ikhsan and Meli were *pendatang*, and they lived in the "newer" part of the neighborhood. At the same time, they seemed to fit neither one of these categories well.

I came to know Eri and his family in October 2009, when I moved into a house opposite theirs. The first time we met, Meli pointed out where their old house used to be. They built it when they moved to Blang Daruet in 1997. It was made of wood and brick and had five rooms. Before that, they rented a house in Ikhsan's place of birth, another urban *kampung* called Lam Pasai, about fifteen minutes away by motorcycle. The tsunami had annihilated the old house. The only thing that remained of it was a small strip of grubby, overgrown tiles, which used to be part of the bathroom floor. Now there was a small hen house and some washing lines. Next to it was an open, grassy patch, across from which stood their new, concrete house, built in 2006 by World Vision. The house had a sitting room, two bedrooms, a small bathroom, and a kitchenette (most "tsunami-houses" in Banda Aceh look more or less like this). They had been allocated three such houses, built next to each other, because they had six children, including four young adults. However, when the houses were finished they decided to sublet two of them. This meant extra income, but also that their house was a crowded place.

Meli and Ikhsan were usually at home. They did not have paid jobs. Their main source of income was the property they sublet, including the two houses and a shop house in town. In addition, Ikhsan owned some *sawah* land outside the city, which was worked by local people. Twice a year he received a share of the yield, which meant that they rarely needed to buy rice. Finally, there was the kiosk, a small roadside shop built just before my arrival. Here, Meli and Ikhsan sold daily fare to fellow *kampung* dwellers: rice, noodles, vegetables, eggs, coconut, petrol. Every morning, Ikhsan and Meli took their motorcycle to the market to buy new stock. In the morning the children were at school or on campus, except for the youngest, Zakhi, who was four. In the early afternoon Ikhsan often slept, while Meli stayed in the kiosk. Late at night it was the other way around. The kiosk stayed open until eleven at night and became a meeting place. Across the grassy patch, in the houses sublet by Meli and Ikhsan, two young families lived, both consisting of a male civil servant, a housewife (*ibu rumah tangga*), and a small child. In between chores, the women gathered at the kiosk to chat and exchange news. Other people from the neighborhood occasionally hung around. I often sat there, smoking and socializing. A small television showed soap operas, sports, or the news.

Another daily routine was Eri's walk to the mosque. Eri was Ikhsan and Meli's oldest son. After finishing high school in 2005, he was given a chance, together with two friends, to study in a religious boarding school near Jakarta. This was not a typical "traditional" *pesantren* but a *pondok pesantren hafal al-Qur'an*, a place for memorizing the Qur'an. Eri spent two years in this school and managed to memorize about one third of the Qur'an. He then returned to Banda Aceh and enrolled in an undergraduate program at the Faculty of Ethics (Fakultas Adab) of the State Islamic Studies Institute, IAIN (presently National Islamic University [Universitas Islam Negara, UIN]) Ar-Raniry in Banda Aceh. Since his return, he had not missed a single prayer. He made a point, moreover, of performing every prayer in the mosque (which is considered particularly rewarding by most Muslims), going there on foot (a typical *salafi* practice, emulating the Prophet Muhammad and his contemporaries). I soon got used to the ritual of Eri appearing from their house, just before the afternoon or evening *azan*, dressed in a proper "Muslim shirt" (*baju Muslim*) and smart trousers, smiling, on his way to the Blang Daruet mosque. The other family members were less pious in their studies. Santi studied at Serambi, one of Banda Aceh's smaller universities, and hoped to one day become a teacher. Taufik took his undergraduate degree in chemistry at Universitas Syiah Kuala (Unsyiah), Aceh's most prestigious secular university. Anril had dropped out of school and moved from one odd job to the next. Imran was in primary school and Zakhi was still at home. Neither Ikhsan nor Meli had made it to secondary school.

Eri described himself as a thinker. Although he was a friendly, easygoing, and attentive young man, he did not consider himself to be very socially adept. He found it difficult to express himself in front of strangers, especially groups. He dreamed about writing books one day and becoming a "modern Islamic scholar" (*ulama modern*). His favorite author was the Egyptian teacher and scholar Hasan al-Banna (1906–46), known as the founder of the Muslim Brotherhood. Eri was not the typical revivalist proselytizer (*orang dakwah*), however. He was not a talented preacher. He preferred studying at home over religious discussion in small study circles (*usrah*), the characteristic feature of the (revivalist) *tarbiyah* movement to which he felt attracted. In Jakarta, he had been jealous of students with a ready tongue. Although he did some volunteer work for PKS, he saw political activism as a dilemma. He called politics a dirty business but acknowledged that one should commit to compromise in order to change the "system." If a lot of people changed little things, he thought, the system would also be changed. He evoked al-Banna, who believed that instead of creating chaos by destroying the system, activists should focus on the smallest organizational level, one's own family. Here, Islamic norms would have to be reinstituted. That, Eri said, following al-Banna, was the basis of society.

My focus on the ambiguous religious stances of Meli and Ikhsan should not be taken to imply that Eri's views were always clear cut and coherent. In fact, Eri's opinions and aspirations for the future were filled with doubt and insecurity. Although he wished to become a scholar, he found it difficult to understand and explain the ideas of the scholars he read. Once, when I asked him about the most realistic prospect after his studies, he replied that he might end up, like many of his peers at the IAIN, somewhere in the graceless bureaucracy of the Department of Religion. As for proselytizing activities within the family, he was careful. His behavior might easily be judged as haughty or inappropriate. Much of the time, he felt torn between the need to spread the word and the fear of alienating his family.

Some of Eri's messages fell on fertile ground. During my first week in Blang Daruet, I sat with him in front of the kiosk, talking about Islam, politics, and corruption. Eri was talking, I was listening, and Meli cheerfully shouted from inside (apparently overhearing us), "They're all thieves!" Other issues were more contentious. Shari'a law obliges women to wear a headscarf in public. Meli, who had seldom worn a headscarf before the implementation of this regulation, said that it did not bother her much to cover her head while going out. However, like many other women she cared less about it around the house or in the small streets of the *kampung*. A scarf usually lay within reach inside the kiosk but my impression was that she used it as a dust cloth rather than a head covering. Eri had a problem with this. He told her it was wrong, which annoyed her. She agreed with Eri that it was better for women to cover their heads, but she did not believe that one could—or should—change overnight. Like many other women, she argued that this decision should be taken within the heart (*dalam hati*) and not because of someone else. Sincerity, she explained, should precede outer appearance. Otherwise it was meaningless.[3]

Ritual meals (*kenduri*) were another topic of heated discussion. In Aceh, the *kenduri* is the most common way of celebrating or commemorating both happy and sad events. They are held when children are born, when boys are circumcised, or when a new religious school is opened. Scripturalists consider the practice problematic. Funeral *kenduri*—seven- or ten-day-long communal meals facilitating shared mourning of the deceased—are particularly contentious (see chapter 2). Besides the validity of claims about intercession, Eri complained that the extravagance of *kenduri* weighed heavily on the bereaved. Particularly burdensome, he argued, were situations in which the deceased was the breadwinner of the family. To visit and eat in such circumstances constituted a sin. His problem was that, in Aceh, failing to attend a *kenduri* is generally considered as extremely impolite (cf. Birchok 2015, 514). Thus, instead of banning the ritual altogether, Eri agreed to visit as long as the goal was to pray, not to eat. This stance led to an ongoing debate with his parents, who considered not eating to be equally impolite. As a result, Eri came up with creative solutions, such as bringing his own water in a plastic cup to drink on the spot.

For Meli, Eri's admonitions were difficult to accept. She argued that they were "his beliefs," while she had hers. Ikhsan was more susceptible to his son's opinions. When a person dies, he said, Acehnese should organize a *kenduri*, whether they are rich or poor. "But the people who know about Islam, who have studied it, will not eat. They pray, but they do not eat. . . . The verses [i.e., the Qur'an] say that it is forbidden (*haram*) to eat the food in the house of an orphan." He referred to Eri for further explanation. When I asked him whether he agreed with Eri on all points, he answered, "If you ask me if I agree, then I agree. The point is that [unlike Eri] we have not studied it." Ikhsan considered Eri to be far more knowledgeable and saw no use in contradicting him. Regarding the *kenduri*, he avoided some of the sharp edges by taking Eri's arguments utterly literally, concluding that it was only sinful to eat at a place where the breadwinner had died and where the children were still very young. "If children die, small children, or when the people are rich, that is something different. Then it is no problem [to eat there]."

Eri's knowledge remained unquestioned, in the sense that his parents would never ask him directly about the authority of sources, the content of written commentaries, or the exact meaning of analogies. However, there were frictions and debates, some of which remained implicit, and some of which led to open quarrels. Eri never commented directly on his father's behavior, which is unsurprising in the Acehnese context where, as said, fathers and sons develop avoidance relationships. Ikhsan did, however, generally listen to what Eri said. As we shall see, Eri was less reluctant to comment on the behavior of his mother.

In her approach to the cultural construction of the self in Bali, Unni Wikan (1995) made a distinction between "narratives" and "acts" as presenting different, yet equally relevant, sources of analysis. "A feature of narrative is the narrator's freedom to construct a plot, to control fully in what order the reader or listener becomes aware of what happens. . . . Action in and on the world, on the other hand, is constrained by causality and less manipulable with regard to making information available to others" (Wikan 1995, 265). The next two sections use narratives, or "stories" as I prefer to call them (which can be told, retold and adapted to the situation), to focus on two sets of concerns. The first centers on Ikhsan, his mental "condition," and the meanings attached by him to acts of worship. The second centers on Meli, the challenges of motherhood, and the transmission of religious norms. Although it was not always clearly articulated in the context of daily trials and tribulations, Eri and his ideas about Islam constituted an important frame of reference for both of them. While I take these stories seriously as self-representation, I have also tried to interpret them, as Wikan suggests, in the context of a person's need to "respond to the flow of events, create and consume resources, and influence the events and course of social interaction." It is important, in other words, to place the act of telling these stories in a context of "other actions, options, and circumstances," and to view them in relationship with one another, considering that "it is through acts, primarily, rather than narrative that people fashion themselves" (Wikan 1995, 265–66).

A Lost Zeal for Business

Ikhsan had been a trader for many years, dealing in office equipment, furniture, cloth, and many other things. Now, in late 2009, he was tired. Somehow, he had lost his zeal for doing business (*hilang semangat bisnis*).[4] He no longer had the desire to "go out there." When I asked him what had happened, he said, "There is no use. I do not have the daring anymore. The blood has become cold." "Was this before or after the tsunami?" I asked. He replied, "Before the tsunami I still had a business. I sold motor-taxis. I bought them for three million rupiah, I improved them and then I sold them again for four. But now I have just become lazy. I am tired of trying to earn money (*capai cari rezeki*)." For a long time, I thought that the loss of his zeal was connected to the tsunami. In fact, the problem seemed quite clear to me: depression caused by shock. Although Ikhsan and Meli had been very lucky that all of their children had survived, their situation was still horrifying. Ikhsan lost his mother and 125 people on her side of the family alone. The house, including most of their material possessions, was gone. Neighborhoods—both the one Ikhsan grew up in and the one in which they had lived for two decades—had been swept away. Many months later, I still thought that if Ikhsan would go to a psychologist, in Aceh or anywhere else, he would probably be diagnosed with trauma or one or the other mood disorder. Then I learned that the situation was more complex.

Ikhsan and Meli were not from wealthy families. Meli was originally from Sibreh, a market town roughly thirty minutes outside Banda Aceh. Her father died when she was only seven years old, which meant that her mother, who never remarried, had to earn a living when her children were still small. Ikhsan also lost his father at an early age. As a child, he moved to the house of his *pak chik*, his mother's younger brother, who sold office utensils. Ikhsan worked in the shop and discovered a mercantile talent. When he was old enough, he set out for himself, looking for goods to sell. The first real hit was embroidery, used for the decoration of head scarves, which he bought in Bukittingi, West Sumatra. In his mid-twenties, he opened a billiard hall. "That was a really good business. I made a lot of money." When they married, he was trading in furniture, buying in Medan and selling in Banda Aceh.

One day, while I was sitting in the kiosk alone with Ikhsan, he told me a story. He had been a young man, still unmarried, and already quite successful in the furniture business. At a certain moment—this must have been in the 1980s—he agreed to let his sister's husband, who was jobless at the time, manage one of the two shops he owned. For a while, everything went well, but then Ikhsan began to suspect bad intentions. First, he was persuaded by his in-law to invest in a construction project, in which the latter had "good connections." Ikhsan sold some gold and gave him the money. The shops were never built, and his sister's husband made up weak excuses. The money, he said, was "out of his hands." As the conflict dragged on, something peculiar happened. One day, Ikhsan came to the shop unannounced. His brother-in-law had left for Medan to buy goods. On entering, Ikhsan found that one of the drawers in the office was locked. He opened it with a screwdriver and found a small, cylinder-shaped cigarette tin with strange objects in it: a couple of teeth, some hairs, and a little package, which he did not dare open because he suspected that inside might be wrapped a dead child's tongue.[5] When his brother-in-law returned, Ikhsan demanded an explanation. His sister started to cry. At first, her husband said he knew nothing. Finally, when Ikhsan pressured him, he admitted putting the tin in the drawer. He said that he did not intend to hex anyone, but Ikhsan did not believe him. He was convinced that they were using black magic (*ilmu gaib*) to "silence" him. Their plan, he suspected, was to rob him of his business and money, while making sure that "he could not talk back." Ikhsan expelled both of them from the shop.

I probed Ikhsan for more details, curious to know whether he had tried to do something about the spell, but he refused to say more. "We should not talk about it. They died, both of them. They died in the tsunami." It is a sin to say bad things about the dead. Besides, he thought, afterlife would be hard enough on them, because of what they did. He did not want to make it worse. He forgave them both.

I did not think about the story for a while until Meli reminded me of it. We were talking about the past. Meli thought back to the time when Ikhsan was still a smart and energetic businessman. When I asked her to explain his change, she said that the problem lay with his family. When Ikhsan became successful, some relatives became jealous. They had tried to make him "stupid," so he might forfeit his business and allow them to take advantage. They failed, but the consequence was that Ikhsan lost his *semangat*. As Meli told it, Ikhsan's lost zeal was not so much an event. It was a process, which was as difficult for Meli as it was for Ikhsan. Her husband used to be away often. He was always full of ideas and plans. Now he just wanted to stay at home. Meli was worried, because the property they were living off had taken many years to accumulate. The tsunami had robbed her of most of her personal possessions, notably her gold, which had been in the house when they fled from the water. But money was not the only problem. Meli liked her husband more when he still had *semangat*. Building the kiosk had been her idea. Persuading Ikhsan had been difficult. When he gave in, it was a sign of hope. There was still a possibility that things might change.

As it turned out, the bitterness Ikhsan felt about a part of his family was greater than I had previously thought. The drift of his argument was that success causes trouble. As soon as Ikhsan's earnings increased, he became morally responsible for his younger siblings' education and providing starting capital (*modal*) to relatives. He considered this an obligation, but at the same time he experienced the feeling of being abused. "The bugs crawl into your sleeve," he said (Ac. *limpeun dalam sapa baje*, lit. the "centipedes"). "They will surely bite but they cannot be easily removed." His brother-in-law had behaved "like a buffalo lifted from the mud." Instead of being grateful, he had tried to kick him. Ikhsan spoke bitterly about his brother-in-law. He was a "bad person" (*orang jahat*), who did not pray and thought only about money. I asked him again whether he had tried to do something about the spell. Was there no possibility of performing a counter-hex? (*berobat*).[6] He argued that it would be difficult to find a religious specialist with the appropriate skills. The hex was probably complex. There might have been things in his drinks or his food. He did not trust anybody to interfere, as it might be riskier than the spell itself.

This consideration resonated with earlier discussions I had with Ikhsan and Meli. Both of them believed that religious experts in Aceh were no longer as powerful as they used to be. In the days of the war against the Dutch, they stated, almost everyone in Aceh was an *alim*, with many people possessing *keramat* or some kind of supernatural power. That time was long gone. Ikhsan was more convinced about this than Meli, who, perhaps, thought of her mother's skills as a healer (I will come to this). According to Ikhsan, the disappearance of *keramat* was a result of the hypocrisy and insincerity of the ulama. In the past, he proclaimed, someone looking for knowledge would go to the ulama and be taught. Today, it was necessary to bring sugar, coffee, and, especially, money. Although there were still places infused with *keramat* (such as the graves of saints), there were no more "holy people" (*orang keramat*).

Thus, like all others he was left alone with his problems. "It is difficult to find a specialist (*ahli*). What remains is to stay at home and pray."

At this point, connections began to appear between this past, Ikhsan's personal religiosity, and the scripturalism of Eri. Previously, I had asked Ikhsan whether he felt encumbered (*berat*) or sad about the fact that he was less affluent than before. To these questions he seldom answered directly. Instead, he argued that it was important to shut oneself off from such emotions. The important thing was that his children were able to go to school and that his family was not hungry. He tried to avoid stress (*stres*, or *pikiran*) because worrying or brooding "makes people sick." There was a strong religious charge to this thinking: "Everything is in the hands of God." It was more important to think about the future than to worry about the past. For Ikhsan, this meant that earning lots of money had lost its relevance. "I still have the pickup-truck. I can use this for transport. It is easy to earn money that way." He just did not see the real benefit anymore. "The important thing is that we pray."

In such expressions of piety, Eri was a major point of reference. According to Ikhsan, his oldest son was "pious" (*saleh*) and "obedient" (*patuh*). When Eri asked for permission to study in a *pesantren* and learn to memorize the Qur'an, Ikhsan was against it. It took a while before he and Meli were convinced. Now, he applauded his son's determination. People who know the Qur'an, who are able to pray and recite perfectly, "will be protected by God." Personally he was not an *alim*. Perhaps he could have been one had his own father lived longer. Eri's grandfather had been much more knowledgeable. His death meant that Ikhsan was given little time to study. "I never had the opportunity to gain in-depth knowledge . . . I know how to pray. Everyone in Aceh knows how to pray. I know the shorter verses . . . but I never attended the lessons of the teachers (*pengajian teungku-teungku*). I pray, I give *zakat*, I give *sedekah* to orphans, but I do not tell anyone about it. In Islam it should be like that. Only arrogant people say how much *zakat* they give. My wife knows . . . because in Islam, husband and wife should agree."

With little knowledge, and having admitted to many (unholy) temptations in the past, Ikhsan concluded that he was probably "far from heaven." Eri, in contrast, was on his way to becoming an expert. He had the right character. He was interested in learning and not greedy (*seraka*). Ikhsan recounted how, after the tsunami, Eri went around the emergency barracks to teach children how to recite the Qur'an. A foreign nongovernmental organization (NGO) paid him for this, but Eri gave the money to the local mosque. I asked, "Is Eri very different from your other children?" Ikhsan laughed and answered, "Yes, the others certainly would not have a problem accepting the money!" He was glad that Eri was there, reading his books and reminding his family that they should not forget to pray. Like many others, he saw the tsunami as a warning from God. He called it a "test" (*percobaan*) and an "exam" (*ujian*). When

I asked him whether he would like to rebuild his old house, he said, "I am almost sixty years old. I could rebuild everything. A storied house, filled with beautiful things. But I do not know whether God will take it all back. The tsunami was an exam. God wants to see how we deal with it. Now I simply pray."

Heaven Lies under Mother's Feet

For Meli, the situation was diffcrent. She was a decade younger than Ikhsan and did not share his dispiritedness. She worried how long their resources would last. Although they earned some cash with the kiosk, it was clear that it would not cover their long-term expenses. So in response, she took control over her family's wellbeing. She managed the shop and the household. She took care of food, clothes, and medicines. And she urged her husband to somehow recover his motivation.

At the same time, she had her own personal concerns, one of them being Eri. I should begin this story, however, not with him but with her youngest son, Zakhi, and her mother, Hamdiah. Zakhi was four years old and a handful. He was born prematurely, after a seven-month pregnancy. In general, he functioned well. He played. His motor abilities were fine. He was curious and probably smart. But he also found it hard to interact with other children. It was difficult to get through to him. They worried about this. Meli regularly asked for my advice, inquiring how children with behavioral difficulties were dealt with where I came from. In such instances I felt ill at ease. I did not have children, and Meli was an experienced mother. Usually I mumbled something about my nephews and nieces and changed the topic. I never made much of it. But again, things would prove to be more complex.

Hamdiah, Meli's mother, used to work on the *sawah* and at the Sibreh market, where she sold vegetables and clothes. She was a pious woman, strict in observance, and she had sent her children (including Meli) to a religious primary school (a Madrasah Ibtidaiyah Negeri, or MIN). She was also a healer, who could summon the spirits of deceased ulama into her body to cure other people's illnesses. She had learned to use this skill at a very early age. However, after the death of her husband, the spirits stayed away for a long time— according to Meli, because she was too busy taking care of her children and the household. They came back later. I learned about this when we were talking about my visit to another female healer in a place close to Jurong. After explaining my experience, I asked Meli whether she had ever visited a *dukun* (healer or shaman). She said, "No, that is dangerous." I asked, "How is it dangerous?" "Because it is similar to splitting God" (*memperduakan Tuhan*, i.e., polytheism). She added that Eri would become very angry. Then she told me about her mother and called her an *orang berobat* (also "healer," but a term much less associated with magic or *shirk*).[7]

Eri, in his rejection of most supernatural phenomena, disapproved of his grandmother's practices, but he would never confront her directly with his opinions. Meli once told Hamdiah about Eri's thoughts, evoking little response except for the remark that she used Qur'anic verses. According to Meli, this was not even all that relevant. There were "many things" Eri did not believe (*percaya*) or accept (*menerima*) but that were simply a part of the faith and customs of the Acehnese. He visited ritual meals—reluctantly—but never graves. Meli did visit graves. If her son commented on it, she would listen to him, and leave it at that. She had seen her mother cure people, and she did not argue with her son about the details of the rituals. For her, it was no problem that there were different opinions about religion in the house. It was a case of her "old beliefs" (*kepercayaan dulu*) versus Eri's "modern beliefs" (*kepercayaan modern*). She considered herself to be too old to change these things, nor did she really want to.

Eri did not want to force his family, even if he could. He did, however, accuse his mother, for example of not observing the rules of Islam. Her reactions varied. If Eri said that she should cover her head more often, she took note of this and relied on the arguments mentioned earlier. What affected her more were his comments about the way she raised her other children. According to Eri, his mother was too lenient regarding his siblings' being negligent in prayer, not wearing decent clothes, keeping bad company, coming home too late, being lazy with homework, being naughty or disobedient, and so on. For all this misbehavior, he blamed her personally, reminding her that children are born blank slates (*bersih*, "clean," or *putih*, "white"). In his view, sins accumulate when children grow up and discover the temptations of life (*nafsu*). It is the parents' task to minimize the risk by way of discipline and punishment. Meli did not disagree with this. She also thought that parents were, at least partly, responsible for their children's behavior ("children do not ask to be born") and for teaching them right and wrong. In Aceh, the common contention is that children become moral beings when they reach puberty. This, however, allows for ample flexibility. According to Meli, it could not be predicted when, exactly, a child becomes responsible for his or her own actions. She also held a more sophisticated argument against her son. If what Eri said was really true, namely that Meli was to blame (*bersalah*) whenever her children made mistakes or committed sins, this would mean that *her* parents were to blame as well, and *their* parents, and *their* parents, and so on. Surely, this made little sense!

After this conversation, I viewed rather differently her concerns about Zakhi. In many ways, Zakhi behaved in a "bad way." If he wanted attention, he shouted and made scenes. Sometimes he became aggressive. He wanted to play with other children but scared them away with his rough games. Although his family dealt with him patiently and without making much of a fuss, I realized that Meli's insecurity was connected to the silent battle she was fighting with her oldest son. Although she was an experienced mother of six, Eri's criticism contributed to her doubts and worries. She asked herself whether she was doing the right thing. She argued that she had always sent her children to school and religious lessons (*ngaji*). She had helped them with their homework and taught them how to write. What more could she do? If they refused to pray, how was that her fault? Eri told her to be strict, but how could she force Anril, her unpredictable twenty-two-year-old son, to pray five times a day? Later, in a more defiant moment, she told me that "ultimately, everyone is different." Eri was always at home, studying. Anril left early and came home late, if he came home at all. She did not know what he was doing all day, but she felt that, as long as nothing bad happened, there was little she could or should do about it. With Zakhi, it was different again. It seemed that he did not listen to anything at all. To what extent should she let herself be affected by Eri's views? There was no straightforward answer to this question. She simply did not know.

At the basis of the conflict between Meli and her son lay a fundamentally different conception of morality. For Meli, the meaning of sinning and immoral behavior depended for a large part on the person within. Differences in personal character mattered to her in the sense of how people should be treated and judged. For parents, providing a moral framework was an obligation, but there was not a single model for raising all of her children. In Aceh, a phrase commonly used by religious teachers is that children are "entrusted" by God (*titipan Tuhan*), temporarily, to their parents. Meli and Eri both referred to this phrase, but they explained it differently. Meli said, "All of us have sins (*dosa*) and all of us have to repent (*minta ampun*). Look at Ikhsan. In the past, he often neglected his prayers. Now he prays. Now he repents. This is a big change." I interpreted these words as a claim that moral improvement was a continuous but unpredictable process. For Eri, the view that people were born "clean," without sins, meant that religious life was primarily a matter of controlling the inevitable damage, which could be done only through strict discipline and punishment.

Meli did not simply endure Eri's comments. In her view, an important moral principle overlooked by him was the obligation to respect and obey one's parents. Like Ikhsan, she admired her son for his knowledge. But she also made it clear to him that he should air his opinions tactfully, without hurting people's feelings. For her, there was no excuse for treating one's family disrespectfully, even if they failed to observe certain religious duties. Parents, she said, have the right to be esteemed (*dihargai*), respected (*dihormati*), and obeyed (*dipatuhi*). She made a distinction, moreover, between fathers and mothers. Respect for mothers was especially important.[8] "Heaven," she said quoting a well-known hadith, "lies under mother's feet" (*surga dibawa telapa kaki ibu*).

Like Ikhsan, Meli considered herself to be far from perfect. She could be harsh and disobedient toward her own mother, for which she asked God's forgiveness.[9] She was also a pious woman. She performed her prayers, and on Thursday night she recited the Qur'an. When I asked her how she could do it all, combining her household, the kiosk, and her own religious duties, she answered with an ambiguous *sedang-sedang* ("sufficiently"). It was a balancing act. "There is this world to think about and there is the next," she said. She compared it to steering a middle course and avoiding extremes. "It is not necessary to be rich and it is not necessary to be poor." I think she found her son to be too extreme. Personally, she thought of herself as "just an ordinary person."

These stories, told by Meli and Ikhsan as they reflected on their own lives, were informed by a variety of immediate worries and concerns, or as Wikan (1995, 266) termed it in the spirit of Bourdieu, by a "world of urgency and necessity." One of the "shared compelling concerns" (Barth 1993, 342–43) that feature strongly in these narratives are age and the need (and difficulty) to satisfy the demands and expectations associated with subsequent life stages. The stories give a rich insight into the ways in which people in Aceh frame religious practices and changing moral commitments in terms of a lifelong process of ethical formation. As I show in the next section, these representations of inner emotional and spiritual lives and attempts to "work ethically" on the self (Zigon 2008) must be analyzed not as isolated processes but as contingent, emerging in conjunction with the sense of a life unfolding and with shifting social and economic concerns.

Money, Piety, and Senses of Community

The Islamic concept of fate—*takdir*—permeates everyday language in Aceh. Most people believe that crucial events in life, such as birth, marriage, and death, are predestined by God. Big and small disasters (the tsunami, a minor traffic accident) are commonly framed in terms of *takdiran*. A closely related concept is *rezeki*. Not easily translated, this may refer to livelihood, a gift (children, for example), or, indeed but not often, "luck." *Rezeki* is always a gift of God to individual Muslims. It does not come for nothing. People need to act (work, pray, carry out good works) in order to receive *rezeki*. A common phrase, *mencari rezeki*, may be translated literally as "to look for *rezeki*." In practice, it often means "to earn money" or "to hope for (divine) rewards." *Rezeki*, as a gift blessed by God, is always good. But if there are good rewards, there are also bad rewards. For instance, according to Ikhsan, many people were involved in "bad money," such as money from corruption. In late 2010, the most conspicuous corruption case in Indonesia—featuring in the news for months—revolved around an alleged tax embezzler called Gayus Tambunan. Like most people I knew, Ikhsan and his family were indignant. But they also

SCRIPTURALISM AND EVERYDAY LIFE 119

thought it was funny, and a cause for amazement, that an ordinary civil servant was smart enough to trick the government and channel away billions of rupiah. Proper disgust was reserved, instead, for local, more visible figures. A popular target in Blang Daruet was the *geuchik*, Syahrul, who was elected by an overwhelming majority a few years earlier, but subsequently accused of using community funds for private ends. Another source of contempt was the slush money and bribes demanded on a regular basis by local government officials and the police.

Ikhsan occasionally talked about the bad money he had earned in the past. He had closed his billiard hall two years after the opening because his mother had kept complaining about the sins it invited (alcohol, gambling, prostitution). "Even if I was not involved in these things myself," he explained, "the money I got from it was bad, so it was also my sin." Interestingly, Ikhsan connected his present lethargy to this idea of bad money. Each time he told me about his "lost zeal," he said that "actually it is easy to make a lot of money." His point was that, for him, it had lost its meaning. What he worried about, in this stage of his life, was to improve morally rather than materially. "We have to think about how to become a better person. We have to choose the right path, one that is consistent with our religion." In part, this meant earning "good" or "clean" money.

The tsunami was another important reference point for discussions about morality and materiality. For Ikhsan, the disaster had made shockingly visible how wealth—money, clothes, cars, houses—could disappear in a flash. "When the tsunami happened, money did not matter at all. God does not look at our feathers." It was a democratic disaster, in every aspect a pure manifestation of God's power. Afterwards, he became more concerned about his daily religious duties. A reinvigorated religious diligence was born out of God's "warning" (*peringatan*) and out of the gratitude he felt for the lives not lost. Everything could be taken away suddenly, Ikhsan said, but this is only because everything was given first. People work and make money, but ultimately everything depends on "what God grants us." At the same time, talking about the disaster included a temptation of ascribing changes exclusively to it. The magnitude of the tsunami made it into a pervasive container discourse, a convenient tool for people to explain and define complex events and phenomena as a consequence of fate.

The fact that the tsunami offered a clear-cut religious repertoire for dealing with questions about material wealth and abstract moral values meant that sometimes it obscured more than it revealed. This becomes clear from Ikhsan's own interpretation of his lost zeal. The first time he told me about his bewitchment, he cut our conversation short at the moment I became inquisitive about the relationship with this family. He continued with an abstract discussion of the relationship between rich and poor. The problem, he said, was that people become "arrogant" (*sombong*). This is indeed an important register. In Aceh, arrogance is seen as a major vice. In Daruet, a local story was told whenever people wanted to explain how arrogance would always come back to you. In short, the story went like this: Once, in a time not too long ago, a respected, locally born resident of Blang Daruet amassed a great fortune. He built a large house and bought a car. He was very rich. But then he became *sombong* and started to neglect the other, less fortunate people in the *kampung*. Confronted by *kampung* elders, he acted haughtily and showed no remorse. Ultimately, the people turned against him by ignoring him in every sphere of life. Once he realized that he could not bear this collective punishment, he sold his house and left the *kampung* in which he was born.

In Aceh, moralizing stories about pride and arrogance are almost always framed in religious discourse. This also works the other way around. For example, to be considered *alim* (knowledgeable in Islam), one cannot show signs of arrogance. Religious knowledge (*ilmu*) implies an understanding of the world in which people are merely visitors. Their worldly possessions are worthless in the face of eternity. To explain this, Ikhsan used the following analogy: When the *sawah* is watered (wealth), the stalks shoot up (arrogance). But as soon as these stalks develop fruit (knowledge), their heads will hang down, looking back to the ground (modesty). Sometimes it happens that the stalks do not carry fruit and remain empty. They will stand upright, proudly, but will be of no use.

Why did Ikhsan, in this first cautious exchange about his past, connect the stories of his bewitchment and his lost zeal to a moral lesson about arrogance? It was not until much later that I realized that, in these stories, Ikhsan was actually reflecting—implicitly—on his own social position within the community. As I have explained, a sharp social distinction was made in Daruet between *pendatang* (newcomers) and *orang asli* (original inhabitants). However, it seemed that Meli and Ikhsan belonged in both groups at once. They had lived in Daruet for so long that they were recognized as *kampung* elders. Unlike most newcomers, they participated in *gotong royong* (communal work), and Ikhsan was commonly invited to *kampung* meetings. However, I also noticed—frequenting these meetings myself—that his visits were mostly for the sake of formality. He never said anything. The invitations were a matter of courtesy. When I asked him to what extent he felt like a newcomer, he said, "Actually, we are all brothers (*saudara*), but in terms of the development of the *kampung*, we are regarded differently." For example, when government-sponsored food was distributed in the first months after the tsunami, they were not informed. This was typical, he explained. "On this side of the *kampung*, we are like the stepchildren (*anak tiri*). . . . On that side, they are the real children (*anak kandung*). If there are benefits, we get nothing, or at least we are not told. Over there they are all the *geuchik*'s family."

Apart from his ceremonious role at meetings, and occasionally in the kiosk, Ikhsan did not engage much with the *asli Daruet*. He prayed at the neighborhood mosque on Friday, but this was a very mixed affair. In fact, the majority of people at the Friday prayer were *pendatang*. The central meeting place for *asli Daruet* men was the neighborhood coffee shop (*kedai kampung*). For many *pendatang*, however, the *kedai* was a no-go place frequented by "coarse" (*kasar*), "lazy" (*malas*), or "slack" (*lalai*) people. In the *kedai*, they stated, jobless men came to drink coffee, smoke, play games, and escape from the mosque, their wives, and their dead-end situations. People gathering in the *kedai*—this was the stereotype—neither worked nor prayed. Ikhsan had no salaried job. He was not a civil servant, did not have a high level of education, and was not rich. Still, he would never consider visiting the *kedai*. He was not *asli Daruet*, had some property, and sent his children to university (the definite marker of social mobility). All of this set him apart from the Daruet community of men. On the other hand, however, the *pendatang* were hardly a "community," and even if they were, Ikhsan would probably not have a great feeling of belonging. This was an issue of class and moral distinction. According to Ikhsan, all civil servants were essentially "corrupt" because they profited from the "bad money" (*uang haram*) that kept the system going. They were "material for hell" (*isi neraka*). Although he said this in calm consideration, and not in some kind of angry outburst, this was an emotional argument, rooted in a particular conception of social justice. For Ikhsan, the relative wealth of civil servants constituted a fundamental injustice.

It is in this emotional segment, in which perceptions of belonging, shifting religiosity, and social status intersected, that Ikhsan framed his attraction to the abstract conception of community inherent to the globalized Islamism advocated by Eri. His son stood for clear-cut distinctions between good and bad as well as an uncompromised and individualized moral responsibility. His pious diligence resonated strongly with the emotional trouble Ikhsan found himself in at this point of his life. The story about his lost zeal and the bewitchment is revealing. Born and raised in an urban milieu, by an uncle who cared little about the lessons of the ulama and who nurtured his mercantile spirit, Ikhsan felt no inclination whatsoever to have a religious expert deal with the forces of black magic. For all of his problems, the solution was to stay at home and pray. For Meli, the issue of moral responsibility was equally important, but she framed it quite differently. Let me illustrate this by elaborating on her relationship with her mother.

Hamdiah's skills as a healer were recognized long ago, when Meli was still a girl and Hamdiah's husband was still alive. It started with a possession (in the words of Meli, *ulama-ulama zaman masuk*; "ulama from the past entered [her body]"). When people learned about it, they came to ask for help, which Hamdiah provided if she could. After her husband's death, however, she became so absorbed in the care of her family that it was no longer possible to open herself to the spirits (which took long and regular night-time prayers and recitation).

They came back, however, when her children were adults. It happened suddenly and unexpectedly. Meli was at home (in Lam Pasai) when a relative visited and said that something strange had happened to Hamdiah. They drove to Sibreh, and Meli found her mother in a confused state. She had been brought home by people from the market, who explained that she had started to behave strangely. People from the village assembled and said that she was possessed (*dimasukkin*). Others said that she had become crazy (*gila*, *sakit jiwa*) and should be taken to a hospital. In the meantime, Hamdiah had escaped the discussion by climbing onto the roof. Later, she was examined by a doctor but not diagnosed. After spending two nights in the hospital she was sent home. She recovered slowly. She maintained that she was not crazy but had been possessed by seven saints (*auliya*).[10] She started to help people with small illnesses again, first within the family, later more widely in the area.

Meli did not know why things had happened in the way they had, except that her mother had a "pure heart" (*hati suci*). Hamdiah had devoted her life to the honest purpose of making a living (*cari rezeki*) and praying (*berdoa*). She was not distracted by temptations (*nafsu*). The work she did (selling vegetables) was clean (*bersih*). This must have made her into a suitable person for spirits to enter her body. She mentioned another reason as well. In 2007, Hamdiah had performed the hajj, the pilgrimage to Mecca. As she was just an ordinary saleswoman from the market, she had had to abstain from luxuries for many years, eating less to save enough money. I asked Meli whether she thought she would ever be able to do the same. She answered that, as a Muslim, the desire was strong, but there was never enough money or any chance to save. It was also a matter of priorities. "Our children are studying. There is no money left for anything else."[11]

In the prime of her life, Meli was responsible, virtually alone, for raising a large family. Confronted with her husband's inertia, she decided to take control of her family's daily life. For this, she paid a toll. Meli was permanently tired and often ill. She worried about their financial situation, Anril's dubious friends, and Zakhi's cognitive development. In addition, she felt fundamentally insecure about her personal obligations to her family and to God. In this phase of her life, Eri's comments were not particularly helpful. Instead of carrying resonance, the nature and inflexibility of Eri's reproaches required another balancing act. As I have tried to show, money and material wealth are partly a religious concern, expressed in a moral and cultural vocabulary of cleanliness, purity, and sacrifice. In the case of Ikhsan, who felt detached from the various parallel communities—his family, his neighborhood, the professional community of traders—of which he was once part, this vocabulary was enriched by the abstract scripturalist discourse brought home by Eri. Meli did not experience this estrangement. Her sense of community was more solidly built around her family (in Blang Daruet and in Sibreh) and the hyperlocality of their side of the neighborhood. For her, Islamic scripturalism was not a solution for everyday concerns.

Why did Ikhsan and Meli respond to Eri's admonitions in the ways they did? Why was Ikhsan more receptive than his wife? Are gender or class decisive factors? How much did their personal characters weigh in? Should we conceive of their moral reflections as a struggle about abstract religious ideas, as a process through which they emplaced themselves in the moral communities of Blang Daruet and Aceh, or both? Clearly, these were all important factors. As I have shown in this section, concerns related to social mobility, belonging, and gendered responsibilities and commitments to family and local community are crucial aspects of the increasing purchase of, and resistance to, an "objectified" Islam. At the same time, the case of Eri and his parents provides a warning against the temptation to collapse differences in religious belief or ritual engagement into separate categories of class, gender, or locality. What emerges very strongly from the material presented in this chapter is how life phase and intergenerational interactions are forces that drive religious experience, changing perspectives on faith, and religious commitment. The final section elaborates on this point and draws out some of its theoretical implications.

Age, Life Phase, and the Inward Turn

A focus on subjectivity and the self has become an important area of innovation within the anthropology of Islam. Scholars such as Lara Deeb (2006), Charles Hirschkind (2006), and Saba Mahmood (2005) have challenged the previously dominant, liberal-secular tendency to view pious morality either as "obedience" or as "resistance" against formal religious and political structures and institutions. Instead, they have brought back into the debate other types of behavior, including moral judgment, ethical reasoning, bodily discipline, and the cultivation of inner spirituality and the senses as categories of deliberate action and choice, implying modes of agency that much of the earlier literature on Islam had failed to take into account. While these studies offer important, indeed necessary, critiques of artificial dichotomies, such as submission versus resistance, orthodoxy versus secularism, and indoctrination versus individual assertion, they also focus on a minority of pious Muslims who distinguish themselves from other Muslims on the basis of their religious lifestyles, the cultivation of religious virtues, and (in many but not all cases) proselytization. The result is a biased picture, in which reflection on the self is strongly associated with "outward" piety and activism.

This debate is very relevant for the study of contemporary Aceh. As Michael Feener (2013) and Reza Idria (2015b) have shown, the idea that outward piety and the disciplining of bodies serve to change inner selves is central to the implementation of Islamic law in the province. "Following a model of moral pedagogy well established in Islamic traditions, but ultimately reaching back to Aristotle, the architects of Aceh's contemporary Islamic legal system see the enforcement of good habits of deportment as facilitating the eventual inward transformation of individuals" (Idria 2015b, 176–77). Indeed, as Saba Mahmood (2005) in particular has shown, the pursuit of (inner) faith through bodily practice (and its propagation) is an important feature of the global Islamic revival. It is important, however, not to conflate this view of the relationship between outward practices and inner states with the making of Muslim subjectivities generally. Part of the problem is what Samuli Schielke (2009a, 163) called "the central blind spot of an anthropology of morality inspired by Aristotelian ethics." The idea that pious practices are constitutive of religious subjects—central to the work of Asad (1993) and those inspired by it—wrongfully assumes "a fairly unified and clear disposition of the subject" (Schielke 2009a, 163–64). Human subjects, Schielke argues, are not usually shaped coherently on the basis of one particular moral tradition. Other frameworks, or "grand schemes," including economic growth and romantic love, interact with people's religious sensibilities (Schielke 2015). "What we need, then, are better narratives of exactly how powerful discourses work in practice and of what powerful discourses there are out there anyway" (Schielke 2010, 9).

This is certainly true, and Schielke's own work on Egypt, analyzing a variety of everyday moral engagements, subversive attitudes, and forms of ambivalence (Schielke 2009a, b, 2010, 2015), has helped to inspire an important trend that has used grounded ethnography to debunk the widespread view of the "Islamic revival" as a pervasive, uniform, and progressive force. In a rather brilliant book on Chitral, Magnus Marsden (2005) argues that local forms of Islamic faith, religious debate, and self-understanding are very much at the center of everyday village life in Pakistan's Northwest Frontier, interacting in complex but flexible ways with the normative models of radical Islamists (the Pakistani Taliban). A decade earlier, Michael Peletz (1997) responded to the overwhelming attention in the literature on Malaysia for expressions of political Islam. He showed that, outside *dakwah* circles (concentrated in urban contexts), a great deal of ambivalence, if not plain hostility, existed with ordinary Muslims vis-à-vis religious activists and formal Islamic institutions, thus challenging the master narrative that had arisen around the allegedly rapid, unilineal, and unidirectional "Islamization" of Malaysia.

By showing and analyzing how different normative styles are experienced, performed, embodied, negotiated, incorporated, and resisted by ordinary Muslims, these authors demonstrate that moral ideas and practices are characterized not by a simple choice between Islamic "piety" and local traditions or alternative moral frameworks, but by ambiguity, changeable and flexible patterns of behavior, and deeply felt ambivalence. In my view, this critique is both valuable and problematic. The focus on "ambivalence" and "incoherence" offsets the totalizing tendencies in the study of Islam. The cited works prove that ethical formation is often both driven and complicated by local beliefs and traditions, uncertainty about the "right" path or interpretation, and by nonreligious as much as religious concerns and commitments. However, as Daan Beekers and I argue in more detail elsewhere (Kloos and Beekers 2018), the attempt to substitute the focus on pious practice with a focus on the "changing and often contradictory quandaries of everyday life" (Marsden and Retsikas 2012, 8) holds the risk of creating a false separation between the cultivation of religious ideals on the one hand and the incoherences and inconsistencies of "everyday Islam" or "lived Islam" on the other.

The important challenge is to design conceptual and interpretative frameworks that allow us to explore the dynamic relationship between religious commitment and the unruly reality of, and fragmentation of, everyday lives. One way forward is to take seriously senses of moral failure as a factor of ethical formation (cf. Beekers and Kloos 2018). The next chapter on sinning will engage more explicitly with this question. Here, I want to concentrate on the equally important, ongoing impact of the "inward turn" (F. Robinson 2008, 271–73)—understood as a historically contingent process that continues into the present—on individual religiosities and their relationship to the shifting forces of normative Islam.[12] In this chapter, I have approached this question by centralizing the factors of age and generational tension as shaping both perceptions of community and personal processes of ethical improvement. Let me elaborate on this by discussing some of the major trends in the study of Islam in Indonesia and the specific contribution of this chapter, as well as this book more generally.

In the 1980s and 1990s, scholars began to take note of—and seek explanations for—the "outward" signs of the global Islamic revival in Indonesia. Robert Hefner (1997, 5) neatly summarized the trend:

> Mosques have proliferated in towns and villages; religious schools and devotional programs have expanded; a vast market in Islamic books, magazines, and newspapers has developed; and, very important, a well-educated Muslim middle class has begun to raise questions about characteristically modern concerns, including the role and rights of women, the challenge of pluralism, the merits of market economies, and, most generally, the proper relationship of religion to state.

To explain the increasing prominence of Islam in the public sphere, some scholars have investigated the connections among economic growth, urbanization, the rise of the urban middle class, and political reconfigurations (see, e.g., Hadiz and Khoo Boo Teik 2011; Hasan 2013; Hefner 2000; Künkler and Stepan

2013; Liddle 1996; Sidel 2006). An important development in this regard was the turn to Islam, in the early 1990s, by the New Order (Hefner 1993). Others have emphasized the growing influence on Indonesian Muslims of transnational Islamic organizations and religious networks (Bubalo and Fealy 2005; van Bruinessen 2013a). This book builds in particular on the studies that have explored the relationship between the Islamic revival and the lives of ordinary Indonesian Muslims. These analyses, focusing on changing religious practices, conversion, and local contestations in different parts of Indonesia, date from the 1980s and early 1990s (see, e.g., Bowen 1993; Cederroth 1981, 1991; Hefner 1985, 1986, 1987). They were followed by several other studies of religious transformation, mainly in rural (East and Central) Java (see, e.g., Beatty 1999; Headly 2004; Hyung-Jun Kim 1996; Jamhari 2000; Pranowo 1991). In more recent years, anthropologists have shifted the focus from rural societies to the aspirations and moral anxieties of the lower to upper urban middle class (see, e.g., Fealy and White 2008; Hasan 2017; Hefner 2010; Hoesterey 2015; Jones 2010; Rudnyckyj 2010; Simon 2014; cf. Fischer 2008; Frisk 2009; Sloane 1999 on [sub-]urban Kuala Lumpur), adding significantly to our understanding of contemporary religious authority, the relationship among faith, consumption, and technology, and the ethical modes contingent on urban and metropolitan religious economies.

The Islamic revival, like all major social transformations, is affected by class. There is a strong suggestion in the more recent literature that the Islamic norms and forms of piety expressed by the representatives of the urban middle classes contrast with the religiosity of the majority of "traditional," "moderate," or "syncretistic" Indonesian Muslims. This construction and experience of socioeconomic distinctions, which is rooted in a long tradition of Weberian anthropology concerned with the relation between Islamic scripturalist reformism and modernity (see Soares and Osella 2009, 2–5) is—apart from some conspicuous exceptions (Fischer 2008; Rudnyckyj 2010)—not often critically examined. Ikhsan's upbringing as a trader in an urban area and Meli's youth in a village in Aceh Besar certainly seem relevant when it comes to explaining their divergent religious outlooks. However, in my view it is not enough to see them simply as representatives of a particular class with relatively fixed or idiosyncratic attitudes toward Islam and its place in society. This would ascribe undue credibility to totalizing concepts of "Islamization" grounded in theories of globalization, class mobility, and the "objectification" of Islam (cf. Peletz 2011, 2013). More importantly, it would negate the extent to which Meli and Ikhsan framed their beliefs, dilemmas, and changing religious engagements as contingent on the different concerns and challenges they saw themselves confronted with in present and earlier phases of their lives.

A similar problem occurs when we advance gender to explain the "reach" of the Islamic revival among individual Muslims. Like the turn to urban settings and lifestyles, gender (and the subjectivities of Muslim women in particular) constitutes an important focal point with regard to the study of the Islamic revival and its impact on everyday lives in Indonesia (see, e.g., Afrianty 2015b; Brenner 1996; Lindquist 2009; K. Robinson 2008; Smith-Hefner 2005, 2007). However, as I have argued in more detail elsewhere—with regard to the study of female Islamic authority and building on the insights of Sherry Ortner (1996)—the salience of gender should not be taken for granted (Kloos 2016; cf. Kloos and Künkler 2016). Although Eri's scripturalist piety resonated more with his father than with his mother, this is not to say that Ikhsan followed his son in every practice and opinion, nor that Meli's objections against Eri's moralizing attitude were based mainly or entirely on her roles and social position as a woman. It would be a serious mistake, moreover, to think that the Islamic revival is an exclusively male affair (Mahmood 2005), a warning that seems particularly relevant in the case of Aceh (Afrianty 2015a; Großmann 2015; Jauhola 2013; Kloos 2014b; Srimulyani 2015). In sum, I contend that a rigid foregrounding of class- or gender-based analyses contains a risk of obscuring the religious agencies involved when individual Muslims interact with the forces of normative Islam. In my view, ethical formation generally, and the factors of age and life phase in particular, constitute an unduly neglected aspect of the construction of Muslim subjectivities.

In recent years, the relationship in Indonesia between outward piety and the cultivation of "inner" religious experiences and faith has become a subject of close scrutiny. Works by Julia Day Howell (2001, 2008, 2010; cf. van Bruinessen and Howell 2007) and James Hoesterey (2015), about the place within the Islamic revival of urban Sufism and its search for "inner" meaning and experience, complicates the dominant characterization of the Islamic revival as a predominantly scripturalist trend. Other important work includes analyses of the social and cultural construction of Islamic sanctity through supplication rituals in West Java (Millie 2009), the perceived meaning of outer signs of faith and activism (such as *dakwah* oratory) for people's inner wellbeing (Millie 2012), the management by ordinary believers of "tensions between seemingly conflicting yet simultaneously culturally celebrated visions of moral selfhood" (Simon 2014, 1), and the centrality of "the educative, lived, and psychological aspects" of specific practices, such as Qur'anic recitation, in ordinary Muslims' "personal projects of piety" (Gade 2004, 25). Clearly, religious modes of inner investigation are important to political activists, Islamic intellectuals, and ordinary Muslims alike.

Anna Gade's work, which addresses the "lack of adequate theory to explain why people undertake long-term, voluntary projects in the practice of religious piety such as the memorization and improved reading and recitation of the Qur'ān" (Gade 2004, 48), is particularly relevant for my broader argument. In contrast to the (Aristotelian) focus on the disciplining of bodies, she centralizes the "escalating" effects of affective engagements with the Qur'an. Once her interlocutors started to become involved in this particular practice, she explains, they found it difficult to stop. The reason for this was not that the practice of reading the Qur'an was changing their religious selves, but rather that they encountered within themselves a drive, or desire, to carry on and deepen their relationship with the Qur'an and, as such, with God. Gade applies the Geertzian notion of religious "moods and motivations" as being "not merely an effect but also a cause of religious resurgence" in Indonesia in the 1990s (Gade 2004, 48–51). This is both a psychological and a social process. Rather than a "technology of the self," the practice of memorizing and reciting the Qur'an should be understood as a way for Muslims to become recognized as "preservers" (*hafiz*, pl. *hafaz*) of Islamic tradition, thus increasing their social statuses (Gade 2004, 60).

The stories of Meli and Ikhsan resonate with the work of Gade to the extent that both of them spoke about their personal religious lives as a process, containing (or perhaps rather revealing) a deeper reason or requirement behind the choice to observe—or not to observe—Islamic rituals in a more strict or literalist fashion. In Ikhsan's case, damaged social relations led to a shifting image of the self, making a renewed and more direct relationship to God—as promised by Eri's scripturalist messages—an attractive option for him personally. For Meli, however, Eri's commands about outward behavior were a matter of different ("inner") beliefs. While Gade focuses on constructing a general theoretical framework for understanding Muslims' engagements with ritual, this chapter presents Meli and Ikhwan's affective religious commitments as a feature of their individual religious agencies. More than Gade, then, I am concerned with the relationship between personal processes of ethical improvement and the social and political contexts in which these processes take shape.

Personal attachments to religious ideas and practices go beyond affective engagements with texts and specific rituals. They are also a result of the shifting relationships between ordinary Muslims and state and religious authorities, as expressed in the negotiations that take place at the hyperlocal levels of family and local community. When it came to explaining, through particular stories, their reflections on, and partial incorporation of, their son's scripturalist discourse, both Ikhsan and Meli cited life phase as a crucial factor. For Ikhsan, Islamic revivalist discourse served as an inspiration for a strengthened engagement with prayer and divine interdictions. For Meli, Eri's claims led to friction, solidifying her contention that personal beliefs and customary religious practices should be respected, not necessarily questioned or changed. The perception of different life stages came with different, sometimes mutually exclusive, expressions of the relationship between outward behavior and the development of inner religious lives. The concept of religious agency is useful, because it brings into focus the ways in which this relationship is, simultaneously, rooted in Islamic scriptural and practical traditions and contingent on personal histories and projects of ethical improvement.

Conclusion

The case of Eri and his family demonstrates that the idea of living strictly according to Islamic scriptural rules and admonitions is not a coherent theological or epistemological "package" to be either accepted or rejected. By this I do not mean to say that theological arguments are unimportant, but rather that they exert a different appeal to different people and at different moments in their lives. An exclusive focus on revivalist groups or politics may suggest that people either join in with the global, progressive mode of scripturalist reform or stay behind in their traditionalist and more "flexible" mode of local beliefs and practices, but seldom both. This is to deny the fact that, often, people are not quite certain what they should and should not believe, how to live their lives in a good way, or how to change their moral selves for the better.

In my analysis, I have looked beyond (overly rigid) class- and gender-based models to deconstruct the process that has been termed conveniently, but also rather imprecisely, "Islamization." An objectified conception of religious practice seems to have taken root, indeed, among many ordinary Muslims, in Aceh and in other places in Indonesia and the Muslim world (see, e.g., Ricklefs 2012). However, and this is a crucial adjustment to conventional analyses of the Islamic revival, this objectified Islam is placed by many people, implicitly or explicitly, in a broader context of personalized, life-long, and cumulative processes of ethical improvement. I see this development—the formation of a personalized religious agency—as the most important trend undergirding religiosity in Aceh today.

If ethical formation is deeply personal, it does not mean that it is necessarily very pleasant or "liberating" (cf. Mahmood 2005). In fact, the confrontations within the family reflected a fundamental discomfort, related to the fact that a scripturalist approach to everyday morality, as based on a fixed standard that is transferable but also inflexible, seems to neglect, or misread, the different ways in which individuals of different ages interpret the qualities of a good life. Very few people in Aceh question the authority of the Qur'an and the hadith, or the words, examples, and comments of those who are knowledgeable in interpreting these texts. This is not the issue at hand. Rather, my point is that a certain agentive mode is vested in the connection between ethical formation and the sense of an individual life unfolding, even if this unfolding takes place in ways that are experienced as unpredictable, often hard, and sometimes quite disappointing. The process of living ethically should be seen as simultaneously conscious, responsible, and reflexive, and a source of doubt, uncertainty, and failure. Religious agency, and the idea of a personalized process of ethical improvement, functions as a practical alternative to the contestations over power that define the struggle for the definition of orthodoxy and the perception of correct, incorrect, and punishable behavior. It is this tension, between the contested spheres of morality and power, to which I turn in the final chapter.

5

Becoming Better Muslims

SINNING, REPENTANCE, IMPROVEMENT

Perhaps, because I did not know, I can be forgiven.
—RAHMAT (JURONG, 2010)

In this chapter I discuss the lives, religious ideas, and practices of four individuals to investigate how they dealt, in the context of Aceh's post-conflict and post-tsunami society, with their own perceived sins. I choose this focus to gain a closer understanding of what it means for people to engage in "ordinary ethics," that is, in the ordinary as being "intrinsically ethical" and in ethics as being "intrinsically ordinary" (Lambek 2010b, 3). Sinfulness is regarded by most Acehnese as a social vice and a very personal concern at the same time. As I will show, the ways in which people in Aceh deal with the problem of sinning provides crucial insights into the connections among personal behavior, morality, and formal disciplining, including the current implementation of shari'a law.

It its emphasis on these relationships, this chapter answers explicitly to the calls of scholars such as Michael Lambek (2000, 309–10), Magnus Marsden (2005, 26), and Anna Gade (2004, 48–49) to think beyond conceptual frameworks that treat Islam (or religion generally) primarily as a disciplinary order. Although sinfulness seems to be preeminently a matter of discipline, I contend that even the basic concern of dealing with bad behavior is, at the level of lived experiences, marked by considerable measures of flexibility and creativeness. These sensibilities, in turn, influence the ways in which people approach the moral frameworks formulated by state and religious authorities and the organization of these frameworks in legal and political institutions. The chapter demonstrates that the generally recognized responsibility to reduce personal sinfulness offers space for interpretation and action as much as it restricts personal choices and decisions. As such, it shows another crucial dimension of religious agency in Aceh, namely the role of (self-)perceived moral failure in processes of ethical formation.

At first sight, the ethnographic cases that follow seem to have very little in common. Rahmat was an elderly man in Jurong. Yani was a young unmarried woman in Blang Daruet. Aris and Indra were two young men who ran a barbershop in a Banda Aceh neighborhood. Yet what drives the comparison is not the differences but a similarity. In recent years, it has been extensively argued that postwar and post-tsunami Aceh is undergoing a fundamental transformation. These cases demonstrate that there are also important continuities at work in the way in which ordinary Acehnese lead their daily lives and try to be, or become, better Muslims.

The next section offers a brief discussion of public discourses about sinning in the context of state shari'a implementation. I proceed by discussing, in more detail, the lives, thoughts, and practices of Rahmat, Yani, Aris, and Indra. I use these cases to demonstrate different aspects of the problem of sinfulness, constructed both as a social problem and as an integral part of individual ethical formation. Rahmat's story shows the importance of age, regret, and the increasing awareness of past sins. The section on Yani dissects the relationship between social pressure and personal responsibility. The case of Aris and Indra, finally, looks at perceptions of success, temptation, and pious conversion. I conclude by connecting these cases to a general analysis of the relationship between the officialization of Islam and personal projects of ethical improvement.

Sinning, Shari'a, and the Moral Pressures of the Postwar, Post-tsunami Moment

As I have argued, people in Aceh are used to framing religious practices and expressions in terms of a life-long, personal "project." A good example is the way in which Ramadan is experienced. During the holy month, many of my interlocutors in Jurong and Blang Daruet engaged in the (recommended) *tarawih* prayers following on *isya* (the last of the mandatory prayers). During the first days of Ramadan, nearly everyone joined in. Numbers then steadily declined as the month progressed, only for the mosques and village prayer halls to fill up again on the last day. Some people commented on this by complaining that their fellow villagers (especially the younger ones) were "lazy." A much more common reaction, however, was that *tarawih* is a practice to "get accustomed to" (*membiasakan diri*). Thus, many young people actively counted and remembered the total number of days they joined in and completed the ritual, in present and previous years. Their main argument was that, rather than trying to be perfect, it was important to increase the number each year, or at least to have this intention. As I will show, this consideration is illustrative of a widely shared, flexible, and deeply personalized ethical mode that informs the ways in which people in Aceh approach the problem of "bad"—including sinful or otherwise morally reprehensible—behavior.

When talking about their moral obligations and failures, my interlocutors often mentioned the "exam" (*ujian*) each Muslim is subjected to after entering the "world of the grave" (*alam barzakh*). This is essentially a test of faith, carried out by the angels Munkar and Nakir, who follow each person in life and note down their good and bad deeds. The exam consists of five questions: Who is your God? Who is your Prophet? What is your Book? Where is your *kiblat*? Who are your Brothers and Sisters? After crossing the *barzakh*, the deceased move on to the afterlife (*akhirat*). Ideas about what happens next vary. Many people think that, even though every adult Muslim who dies will be punished (*disiksa*, "tortured") on the basis of his or her record, ultimately everyone will go to heaven. Others think that this record decides whether someone will go to heaven or hell. Finally, there are many positions in between. Thus, I heard people explain that there is a period in the afterlife when "bad" people are tortured, and "good" people wait, until the Day of Judgment (*Hari Kiamat*) arrives to bring the final verdict (cf. Bowen 1993, 251–72). What most people agree on is that sins committed during one's life have serious consequences and that this is something to be concerned about.

Most Acehnese believe that uncontrolled sinfulness has destructive effects not only on the sinner him- or herself, but also on the harmony and integrity of the Islamic community (*umma*). At the same time, the consequences of sinfulness may be mitigated by accumulating (religious and other) knowledge, changing everyday conduct and routines, or developing one's sense of moral responsibility. Three main channels for this mitigation may be distinguished. First, many people think that God judges the behavior of humans not only on the basis of what they do wrong, but also on the basis of what they do right. Thus, the accumulation of sins (*dosa*) during one's life has meaning only in relation to the simultaneous accumulation of divine rewards (*pahala*) acquired by performing good deeds or practices. The second channel bears on the possibility for Muslims to ask for God's mercy (*ampun*) through practices of repentance (*bertobat*) or by asking God directly for forgiveness (*minta ampun*). Third, people commonly emphasize the importance of (good) intentions (*niat*). In other words, they rarely see committed sins as isolated facts, but always in the context of a lifelong process. When they feel the need to judge the behavior of themselves or of others, they take into account the future as much as the past and the present. As I will show, this observation is very relevant in order to understand the construction and the impact of public discourses about sinfulness and public morality.

The proposition that the Acehnese are a particularly pious people is a central element of the post-conflict, post-tsunami dynamic. The destructive force of the tsunami and the widely disseminated idea that Aceh should be built "from the ground up" implied ideals not only of physical and social reconstruction but also of spiritual renewal (see Daly, Feener, and Reid 2012; Feener 2013; Samuels 2012a). As Annemarie Samuels (2015a) has shown, discourses and practices of post-tsunami reconstruction were based on two very different, but intertwined and mutually reinforcing, "improvement narratives," one centered on socioeconomic development, and one centered on concepts of moral and religious improvement. The implementation of shari'a law resonates, to some extent, with these concerns. The disaster helped to "re-energize the work of state Shari'a institutions which had only a minimal impact on society during the first years of the twenty-first century" (Feener 2013, 2). At the same time, it should be emphasized that the shari'a revival is by no means a unilineal, or even a very coherent, development. It is driven by several, partly contradictory processes, including the determination of government officials to create and enforce new laws concerning public morality and public "order" more generally, the tendency of some activist groups and local actors to take the law into their own hands, and the struggle for power by changing alliances of political and religious leaders since the 1999 law on provincial autonomy.

Before elaborating further on these different processes, let me briefly explain the basic framework of the shari'a legal system. In Indonesia, Islamic law applies nationally in two domains, namely family law and the financial sector (Salim and Azra 2003, 11–13). Domains pertaining to public behavior, including criminal law and the ideological basis for the nation and the government, are not formally a religious concern, at least not at the national level. What sets Aceh apart, then, is that it is the only province that is allowed, as a consequence of Law No. 44/1999 on the "Special Status of the Province of Aceh Special Region" and Law No. 18/2001 on the "Special Autonomy of the Province of Nanggroe Aceh Darussalam," to implement shari'a law in exactly these two domains.

This is not to say that Aceh is an entirely odd case. Since the late 1980s, the Indonesian state has become more accommodative toward the forces of political Islam and the call to strengthen Islamic laws and regulations. Expressions of this include the formalization of a corpus of Islamic laws in 1990 (Nurlaelawati 2010) as well as the increasingly conservative and activist stance, especially in the democratic era, on the part of the state-sponsored Council of Ulama (Majelis Ulama Indonesia, MUI) (Nur Ichwan 2013; Olle 2009; Sirry 2013). "Shari'a-inspired" regional bylaws (Peraturan Daerah, or Perda) have been implemented in many other provinces and districts, even if these are not formally categorized as "shari'a" (Bowen 2013; Buehler 2013, 2016; Bush 2008; Parsons and Mietzner 2009).

The implementation of shari'a law in Aceh was initiated in 2002–2003, when Governor Abdullah Puteh issued a series of bylaws (*qanun*) pertaining to a new system of Islamic courts (Mahkamah Syariah) and the regulation of belief (*aqida*), worship (*ibadah*), and symbols (*syiar*), including specific regulations on dress, intoxicants (*khamr*), gambling (*maisir*), and illicit relations between men and women (*khalwat* and *zina*). Penalties for the transgression of these laws include both fines and corporal punishment (in the form of public canings). These regulations led, in turn, to the establishment of several new institutions tasked with drafting, socializing, and enforcing them. Besides the shari'a courts and the provincial branch of the Ulama Council (Majelis Permusyawaratan Ulama, MPU), the shari'a bureaucracy consists of a State Shari'a Agency (Dinas Syariat Islam) and a shari'a police force (Wilayatul Hisbah, WH). (For an extensive analysis of these laws and institutions, and their histories, see Feener 2013.) After the tsunami and the signing of the peace agreement, the status of the shari'a legal system was further strengthened as an element of the 2006 Law on the Governing of Aceh (LoGA). In 2014, a new, so-called comprehensive Islamic criminal law (Qanun Jinayat) was introduced, conspicuous elements of which include the criminalization of homosexuality, the obligation for non-Muslims to comply with shari'a law in public spaces, and much more severe punishments (including a maximum punishment of a hundred strokes of the cane for adultery and same-sex sex acts).

While most people in Aceh seem to agree that the state has a role in upholding public morality, deep divisions exist with regard to the nature of the law, its content and interpretation, and the processes through which Islamic regulations should be drafted, implemented, and enforced. It should come as no surprise, therefore, that the process is strongly contested (see Feener, Kloos, and Samuels 2015; Idria 2015a, b; Nur Ichwan 2015). On the part of formal politics, a key example of contestation and ambiguity is the history of the Qanun Jinayat. An early version of this law was passed in 2009 by the outgoing provincial parliament, in which the Aceh Party (Partai Aceh, PA) was not yet represented. The law raised fierce resistance, especially because of the excessive punishments it prescribed (including the stoning to death of convicted adulterers). Governor Irwandi Yusuf refused to sign it, thus preventing the law from coming into effect.[1] A redrafted version (without the stoning) was ratified a few years later by Governor Zaini Abdullah, who announced that it would not be enforced until mid-2015. Both the number of court cases dealing with breaches of Islamic criminal law and the severity of the punishments handed down has increased significantly since then.[2] At the same time, it should be noted that different stances toward shari'a have developed within the Aceh Party, and that the implementation and enforcement of shari'a(-inspired) regulations has depended in many cases on the ideas, interests, priorities, religious zeal, and whims of local (district and subdistrict level) administrators.[3]

Strong objections have been raised, at all levels of society, against the tendency of shariʻa laws and institutions to target women rather than men and poor people rather than the elite. Women's rights organizations, including several prominent Islamic women's organizations and some female religious leaders, have spoken out strongly, not so much against the implementation of shariʻa as such, but against the ways in which the current system singles out women by regulating dress and women's sexuality (Afrianty 2015b; Großmann 2015; Jauhola 2013; Kloos 2016; Srimulyani 2015). During their patrols of public areas (popularly known as *razia*, "raids"), officers of the shariʻa police (WH) check whether people's behavior and general appearance conforms to shariʻa regulations. In practice, this mostly comes down to stopping and lecturing women who do not wear a headscarf and apprehending couples thought to be engaging in illicit "proximity" (*khalwat*).[4] Adding to the perception of injustice, the spaces patrolled by the shariʻa police tend to be the domain of lower classes rather than the rich.[5] The reputation of the WH has been seriously damaged, moreover, as the result of the behavior of some of its staff. A particularly shocking case, which was widely covered in the local press, concerned the conviction of three WH officers for raping a young girl in police custody in Langsa in early 2010. The WH, like the police more generally, was actively disliked, if not outright hated, by the majority of my interlocutors.

Another set of contestations revolves around the question of deviancy. As Moch Nur Ichwan (2015, 221) has argued, the implementation of shariʻa law has led to the "marginalisation of non-Sharia oriented Muslim groups, such as Sufi and other groups considered as being deviant," as well as the "resurfacing of a confrontation between Sufi *ulama* and Sharia *ulama* in Aceh." The outcome is ambiguous, however. It seems that at least some Sufi leaders, who are regarded as dangerous heretics by their adversaries, have gained a new following in the wake of encroaching scripturalist and legalist interpretations. Another issue that has attracted attention, in Aceh and beyond, is the crackdown on social deviants, including Aceh's lively community of punkers. Although punkers themselves have objected against the view that their lifestyles conflict with Islam, police and administrators have employed shariʻa-based discourses to criminalize, prosecute and "reeducate" Acehnese youth with alternative tastes and lifestyles, arguing that they constitute a danger to public morality, family ideals, and Aceh's moral order more generally. The ideal of transforming society on the basis of shariʻa has met with various expressions of "cultural resistance" (Idria 2015a), however, including "what might be described as the Punk Ethic of rebellion against established social norms and its sharp critiques against perceived hypocrisy" (Idria 2015b, 183).

A particularly sensitive aspect of shariʻa implementation is the perceived relationship with vigilante violence (or "street justice"). While government officials have argued that shariʻa should be seen as a form of protection against, rather than an encouragement of, vigilantes (Feener 2013, 243), human rights advocates have stated the contrary (HRW 2010, ICG 2006). Vigilantism is indeed a serious problem in Aceh (see Feener 2013, 240–43; Kloos 2014b; Mahdi Syihab 2010; Newman 2009; Otto and Otto 2015; Siapno 2002, 36–39). However, as I have argued extensively elsewhere, we should be careful not to place public morality–related violence exclusively, or even primarily, within the framework of state shari'a. This kind of violence has a history in Aceh and is often legitimized on the basis of local customs (*adat*) and the need to protect the "good name" of villages or neighborhoods rather than shari'a. Community leaders usually reject the use of violence. Their inability, in specific cases, to prevent or act against it must be viewed in the context of a broader crisis of moral authority, in Aceh and in post-authoritarian Indonesia more generally (Kloos 2014b; cf. Kloos and Berenschot 2016).

Instead of reifying the implementation of shari'a, we should be sensitive to the relationship between religious disciplining and the complexities of Aceh's post-conflict, post-disaster society. The Acehnese are confronted, on a daily basis and through different media such as political speeches, newspaper articles, and religious sermons, with the suggestion of a "collective failure" to uphold an acceptable moral standard, befitting their history and their name. Perceptions of the separatist conflict as a source of chaos (*kacau*) and discord (*fitnah*), and the tsunami as a divine "punishment" (*hukuman*), "warning" (*peringatan*), "exam" (*ujian*), or "challenge" (*percobaan*), have invigorated this discourse (see Samuels 2015a). Nonetheless, lively debate has taken place within its boundaries. Most of my interlocutors expressed a combination of enthusiasm and anxiety in relation to the idea of Aceh "opening up" to the outside world, the latter including such diverse elements as aid workers and NGOs, domestic and foreign investment, religious teachers, missionaries, researchers, tourists, and alleged "terrorists" (see Kloos 2015b), as well as the more intangible forces of globalization and "Westernization." The past decade has been marked by a " 'climate' of uncertainty and confusion, political change, imaginations and aspirations, possibilities and anxieties" (Samuels 2015b, 234). In the following three sections, I explore how four individuals—Rahmat, Yani, Aris, and Indra—judged and dealt with their own behavior in this context of uncertainty and contestation.

Early Life Discipline, Older Age Consciousness: The Repentance of Rahmat

Under the house, between the thick wooden poles, stood one of the relics of Rahmat's life: an old and dusty yellow Vespa motorcycle built in 1959. Rahmat had bought it from his boss, in the late 1960s, not long after he had moved from Pidie to Banda Aceh to work as a trader in the market. It was not until the late 1980s that he replaced it with a newer model, which he still used in 2010 to commute to the market and the gardens. Still, he would never get rid of that first one. It stood there motionless, and its battery was dead. But if necessary, Rahmat claimed, it would still start (*masih hidup*, "It still works!"). Standing in a dark dusty corner, covered with cloth, it was not a conspicuous object, and I might never have noticed it, were it not for the fact that Rahmat often mentioned it when he talked about the past. There were not many motorcycles around in Banda Aceh in the 1960s, and fewer cars. For Rahmat, who came from a poor family, to become the owner of that Vespa was a significant achievement. At the same time, it symbolized the relationship with his boss, whom he referred to with the (markedly Chinese) term *towkay*. This relationship lasted almost half a century, until the *towkay*'s death in the late 1990s. Thus, the motorcycle stood there as a quiet demonstration of Rahmat's past.

Rahmat, born in 1944 in a village in Pidie to a family with four children, described his youth as "very tough." He remembered periods during which there was no rice but only fruits to eat. His parents were landless farmers. To earn cash, his father sold coarse earthen kitchenware manufactured by his mother. They collected the clay themselves and sold the pots and plates in the vicinity, at markets and in villages. Rahmat dropped out of primary school at an early age. When he was twelve years old, he was told by a maternal relative to follow him to Sigli, where the man traded in sugar and ran a distribution center for government rations. It was the start of a long-lasting relationship, and Rahmat quickly succeeded in earning the *towkay*'s trust. For a few years, Rahmat was allowed to stay in the village (instead of sleeping in the shop with the older workers), and he was given a bicycle to ride every day to Sigli. After ten years, he was ordered by the *towkay* to his newly opened cloth shop in Banda Aceh, where Rahmat would work for the next three decades.

Rahmat met his wife Nurianti at the market in Banda Aceh. Nurianti, who was two years younger, came from Jurong. Her family was relatively well off, at least compared to most other villagers. Her father had been involved in a short military career that had taken him to North Sumatra during the Revolution. After that, he returned to Jurong and became a tailor. Nurianti was one of the few girls in the subdistrict who went to Banda Aceh to study. She wanted to become a teacher. In Banda Aceh, she lived in the house of her uncle, who had become a wealthy man. When her uncle decided to move to Jakarta and asked her to come along, Nurianti declined. Instead, she moved into a boarding house for girls. It was during this period that she ran into Rahmat. They married in 1968, after Nurianti had finished her studies, moved back to Jurong, and found a job as a teacher in the local primary school. Rahmat moved in with her family. A few years later, they built their own house next to the old family home.

In 2008, Nurianti and Rahmat had been married for thirty-eight years and had had five children. In that year, they performed the pilgrimage to Mecca (hajj). Until that moment, neither Nurianti nor Rahmat had ever traveled beyond Medan. Both of them experienced the hajj as a pivotal moment in their lives. They loved to tell the story, in which they concentrated as much on the eccentricities of Saudi Arabian society (its wealth, its crowdedness, its thieves) as the different rites constituting the pilgrimage. Both of them expressed the feeling that the hajj signified the end of a life phase, marking the beginning of their old age. Having completed the last of the five pillars (*rukun Islam*), they felt that they had entered a period of reflection. The hajj, Rahmat said, "is like a lid on my life." It coincided with what he called the "maximum age" for Muslims, sixty-three, the age at which the Prophet died. From now onward, every year was "extra." This meant, in practice, that he should be "extra grateful" and "extra diligent in worship." More specifically, it signified for him a period of repentance (*bertobat*).

To understand the emotional roots and implications of this shift, it is useful to give a brief impression of Rahmat's daily routines, as I observed them in this phase of his life. Rahmat was indeed diligent in prayer, usually performing the five mandatory daily prayers (*salat*) at home. He woke up early every morning at the sound of the *azan* (the call to prayer) to carry out the dawn prayer (*subuh*). After prayer he ate breakfast, usually comprising the leftovers from the previous day's dinner. He usually worked in the vegetable garden in the morning. He came back for lunch and midday prayers (*zuhur*), after which he rested or slept. Sometimes he went out again before returning for afternoon prayers (*asar*). He rarely left the village. On market days (Monday and Friday) he went to the nearby market to buy fish. On Friday, he prayed in the market mosque. Sometimes, if their youngest son felt like driving, they went on family visits. Rahmat liked to go on trips, but not alone. They had an old car, which he never drove. In the village, he mostly kept to the house. He rarely visited the shops or the coffeehouses, except for buying his daily ration of cigarettes. After the sunset (*magrib*) prayer, he spent about half an hour performing *dhikr* (devotional chanting). After the evening prayer (*isya*) he liked to watch television.

Rahmat often referred to the proximity of death, and the need to prepare for the afterlife (*akhirat*). The main purpose of old age, he said, was to ask for forgiveness (*minta ampun*) and repent (*bertobat*). Islamic repentance rituals take multiple forms, but the most routinely practiced is the standard inclusion of repentance in the daily prayers. For Muslims worldwide, *salat* is imbued with a variety of meanings, a phenomenon that, as John Bowen explained, is less the result of pluralism than of the fundamental absence within the ritual itself of a "single symbolic or iconic code" (Bowen 1989, 615). For most Acehnese I came to know, the essence of *salat* lay in the individual's concentration on their personal relationship with God. Thus, young Acehnese were taught that the bodily performance (the exact movements, the careful pronouncement of the Arabic) was closely connected to the attempt to clear one's head of any thought other than that of God, a state of mind referred to as *khusyuk*. Muslims may choose to repent as a part of any prayer by uttering a formula in which they ask God for His forgiveness, either for their own sins or for those of others. Most people believed that the better one succeeded in establishing a state of *khusyuk*, the more directly the prayer, including the request for forgiveness, was heard by God.

Repentance through worship is not the only way in which Acehnese Muslims deal with their sins. Another channel is to compensate for bad behavior by collecting *pahala*, or divine rewards for "good" behavior. According to Nurianti, there were many ways to do this, including visiting the sick, people who had given birth, or places where a disaster had happened. "All these places we have to go to. All of this brings us *pahala*." Most prominent, however, was visiting funeral *kenduri*. For her, this practice was as much a matter of accumulating divine rewards as it was a social obligation. She went more often now than in the past. This was partly because she had more time after her retirement. There was no doubt, however, that her invigorated keenness to visit funeral *kenduri* was also connected to her advanced age and the thought that death was approaching.

Like his wife, Rahmat connected conceptions of ritual, knowledge, and faith to concerns of life phase and death. He was not afraid of death. I asked him, "So do you feel you have sufficient knowledge, you know, for the exam of the angels? (*ujian malaikat*)." He answered that he did not worry, because the "knowledge of life" (*ilmu kehidupan*) was surely enough. He explained, "We Muslims, we must pray. We must fast. And we must not take what belongs to others." When a Muslim is conscious (*sadar*) of this, the answers to the angels' questions will appear as a matter of course. For Rahmat, this faith explained why, ultimately, the "knowledge of life" was more important than the "higher [religious] knowledge" (*ilmu tinggi*) taught in the *pesantren*. This did not mean that he regarded this higher knowledge as useless, but that, at his age, it was becoming less and less relevant for him personally.

He focused on the virtues contained in daily routines. For him, the significance of *salat* lay partly in the fact that it was rehearsed. Prayer, he explained, "is like *sepor*" (a term referring to an old-fashioned Dutch word for gymnastics). "[It is] like a morning-run, it is all about practice (*latihan*)." This was the reason, he argued, that *salat* should be taught to children when they are young. This way, upholding the daily routine should not be difficult or challenging. If one prays regularly from an early age, he explained, a "little clock" is developed inside. The clock makes sure that if a prayer is skipped, a person will feel uncomfortable. Religious duties, such as *salat* and the fast, are doubly charged. They have a function in dealing with sins, but at the same time it is considered sinful when they are not (or not adequately) performed. Rahmat stressed the importance of *salat*, emphasizing that it was not just an abstract religious obligation. The bodily discipline associated with the faithful performance of the ritual constituted for him a physical defense mechanism against the workings of the devil. This was also the reason that he thought it was crucial to pray as soon as the *azan* sounded. "If you do not pray directly after *azan*, you will make the work of the devil easier. . . . The devil will make you lazy."

Rahmat thought that prayer also had a disciplining effect on other (worldly) activities. He made sure I understood, however, that this was not the *function* of the *salat*. When I suggested once, rather carelessly, that perhaps the *salat* could be seen as a kind of disciplinary training for life as a whole, he immediately corrected me. The *salat*, he said, is an isolated practice, in which only the thought of God mattered. At the same time, he acknowledged the effect. "If you are disciplined in the *salat*, you will also be more disciplined in life." The key term for him was *tenang*, which in this context may be translated as "composure," but also as "calmness," or "self-control." He connected the practice of *salat* to key challenges of life, such as making a living and preventing conflict. "If people pray, there will not be chaos. The same goes for one's earnings (*rezeki*)."

One day, when Rahmat had talked long about his life and his youth in Pidie, I asked him what worried him most at this stage of his life. He took a long puff from his cigarette, and thought for a while. Finally he said:

> What is there still to worry about? Earning money? If you do not go anywhere, then what money is there to find? . . . Now my children sometimes give me some money. In the past I gave it to them, now they give it to me. . . . I cannot work anymore. My lungs hurt. But I cannot stand doing nothing either. If I do not go to the gardens for a while, I am reminded of this. If only for once I do not go, I won't feel good. . . . If there was still some money left, I would like to go there again, one more time, you know, to Mecca. That is a thought that makes me happy (*senang*).

When I asked him whether he had any regrets, and whether he would change anything about his life, if this were possible, he answered, without thinking, "The things I neglected in the past." He continued, "It is only now that I think about these things . . . now I am close to death." When I asked him for an example, he followed with a long reflection, filled with regret, about his short-temperedness and the damage he believed he had inflicted because of this. Rahmat, according to his own judgment, had been angry too often, and for too little reason. In fact, he believed that he would still be like that if he did not actively limit his movements. It was only now, after many months, that

I started to understand why Rahmat no longer wished to sit with the other men at the *pos jaga* (the conflict-era "checkpoint" at the entrance of the *kampung*), or at the coffee shop where he went every day to buy his cigarettes. "If I sit there, people might say things, and I might react, and people will get angry, and I will get angry. . . . This is why I am careful now. In the past, I made many people angry, and what to think of my time in Banda [Aceh] with all those haughty people there! It was difficult to control myself."

Rahmat's emphasis on self-control influenced his attitude toward public morality. As in many other villages, privacy in Jurong was curtailed by occasional acts of vigilantism, carried out by young, unmarried males (usually designated as the *pemuda kampung*, "village youth") seeking to protect the "good name" (*nama baik*) of the village.[6] According to Rahmat, the *pemuda* were short-tempered. Once, when a young couple was accused of *khalwat* and publicly (and forcefully) "cleansed" with water from the *meunasah* (see Kloos 2014b, 79–81), he concluded that the *pemuda* had gone "mad" (*gila*).

Rahmat's regrets about his own tempers caused more than a change in daily routines. They were the main incentive for his repentance. Here, the emotional focal point lay in his difficult relationship with his father, which for Rahmat had been characterized by anger, guilt, and disappointment. His anger was rooted in his early youth and the unfairness in the way he and his siblings had been treated as children. Tensions became more serious when Rahmat got older and his father failed to bring home enough money, either because he earned too little or because of his habit of gambling away the little he had. Later, after Rahmat had left his village, anger was complemented by feelings of guilt. In subsequent years, he visited his parents a few times per year. He gave his father a bicycle, so he could stop carrying around earthenware and sell fish in neighboring villages instead. But the meetings were often tense, and he regularly lost his patience with his father and his failures in providing proper care for his family.

These encounters as Rahmat described them were almost incredible to me. In rural Aceh Besar (but Siegel [1969] described a similar situation for Pidie in the 1960s), fathers and sons develop avoidance relationships, in which emotions are concealed and physical proximity is to a large extent avoided. In all the father-son relationships I observed in Jurong, this seemed to be the norm. In addition, regardless of gender, openly issuing reprimands or admonitions to parents is considered very shameful behavior in Aceh. In that sense, perhaps, it is not strange that the memories returned to Rahmat with a vengeance. "In the past, I was often angry with my father. I did not know I should not do this. It is only now that I think about it and that I hear about the need to repent, in the mosque, in the sermons. It is only now that I ask for forgiveness." I asked, "Is it just your own wrongdoings that you repent for, or do you ask forgiveness for your father too, like you said before?" He answered:

That is just the same. What he did was not right and so I ask for mercy. But it is also my sin. In Islam, it is a very grave sin if you become angry with your parents. This is what I regret now, all the more when I listen to the imam when he talks about the need to repent. Perhaps, because I did not know, I can be forgiven. I said those things to my father and it is a great sin indeed. I have only just become conscious.

Although Rahmat emphasized his willingness to repent and his relationship to God, there was a discomfort, or uncertainty, regarding the possibility of mitigating particular sins, which I found specific to older people like him.

Importantly, the problem of sinfulness had not always meant the same to Rahmat throughout his life. He did talk about particular rituals (such as prayer) in terms of being a prerequisite for a good life. However, this was only part of the story. Prayer, in his view, was a condition for faith to take root. But inner enrichment—which was closely related to faith, but, interestingly, built on failure and discomfort as much as self-discipline—came only with age. In the next section, I turn to the life and thoughts of Yani, a young, unmarried woman in Banda Aceh. Although I focus again on sinning, Yani's story shows a different perspective. If Rahmat emphasized the need to cultivate a form of inner spirituality, Yani linked her inner struggles more explicitly to the contentious and sensitive process of developing a moral responsibility in the midst of social and physical reconstruction.

The Responsibilities of Yani

When I first met her, Yani was twenty-nine years old. She presented herself as an open-minded and "modern" (*modern*) woman. She talked freely about contentious issues, such as religious freedom, public morality, or the relationship between unmarried men and women. She liked to know what was going on in Jakarta—in terms of news, fashion, trends, and scandals—but if I asked her whether she felt more Indonesian or Acehnese she said, "Aceh, of course!" (*Acehlah!*). At the same time, she was ambivalent about the supposed responsibilities connected to being an Acehnese woman. Yani lived in Blang Daruet, and her family had been devastated by the tsunami. Her mother and three sisters had lost their lives. Of the immediate family, only her father and a younger brother survived. In 2006, they received two adjacent tsunami houses. Yani lived alone in one of them. The other was shared by her father, her brother, her father's second wife (whom he married in 2007), and the wife's young son from an earlier marriage.

Yani was born in a neighboring *kampung*, which was her mother's. When she was five years old, the family moved to Daruet to build a house on a plot of land owned by Yani's paternal grandfather. Her mother was a teacher at a primary school. Her father was a clerk at the civil court. For nine years (1992–2001), he was village head (*geuchik*) of Daruet. This was rather remarkable. Although the office of *geuchik* was highly unpopular in times of conflict, it was still unusual for a "newcomer" to be elected. He had resigned, however, after fellow villagers accused him of corruption. After finishing high school, Yani attended a vocational college and obtained a diploma in education. Although her family had the means to pay for university, she had no ambition to pursue a degree. In 2009, she worked four mornings per week at the administrative office of Daruet (the Kantor Kepala Desa), doing clerical work on the terms of a poorly paid apprenticeship (*honor*).

Yani was not married, even though most Acehnese women marry in their late teens or early twenties. She still expected to get married one day, but apparently there was no need for her to hurry. She did have clear ideas about marriage, however. She demanded a man with a good character (*sifat baik*), polite in his speech, who would treat her well. He should not be lazy and should earn enough money. Finally, she wished for someone who was comfortable around her. She valued her independence and expected to be able to keep earning her own income. But she also said she would not be rigid. If her future husband demanded that she stay at home to care for the house and the children, she would try to seek a compromise. Also, she argued that, for women, there was always the option of influencing a husband through "talking shrewdly" (*ngomong pintar*).

As I came to know her better, I was increasingly impressed by Yani's self-confidence with regard to marriage, economic (in)dependence, and the future. There was, however, a material dimension to this self-confidence. Yani had inherited land from her mother. I had never cared to ask its worth. When she told me, eventually, I was perplexed. It turned out that, well disguised by their modest lifestyle, Yani and her brother had at their disposal a gigantic capital of up to two billion rupiah (US$215,000). Although the possession of this plot seemed to warrant financial independence, it would be a mistake to reduce Yani's self-confidence to economic power alone. Her self-conscious engagements in ritual and social positioning were equally important building blocks of the moral order she designed for herself and that she used to legitimize her actions and future aspirations.

Yani was serious about her ritual obligations. She cared little, however, about outward appearances and even less about people telling her what to do. A male acquaintance once told her that he was interested in marrying her. Yani did not agree immediately, but dated him for a while so they could get to know one another. Other people told her that the young man's parents were "very religious" (*kuat beragama*). Her boyfriend agreed and warned that, when she met his parents, she should dress differently. I should mention that Yani was not generally very conservative in the way she dressed. Since the implementation of shari'a law, she always wore a headscarf when going out, but she refused to change her habit of wearing tight pants or leggings, as well as high-heeled shoes. In the end, she never got to the point of meeting his parents. The problem started with their refusal to either approve or disapprove of her boyfriend's plans, something that, according to Yani, was the result of people "talking badly" about her. A bigger issue, however, was the attitude of her boyfriend. The only thing he did to improve the situation was to tell her that things needed time. Yani was frustrated by his unwillingness to confront his parents and defend her. She ended the relationship. "It is always like this," she said. "People want to tell me what to do. Neighbors, distant friends, family members. They comment on my clothes, my headscarf. This happens almost every day." It annoyed her, especially when it concerned people who, she thought, were not particularly strict about religious duties themselves. She called them "hypocrites" (*munafik*).

She was ambivalent, however, with regard to the need to defend public morality. She considered religion to be a "private matter" (*usaha pribadi*), claiming that there was a certain amount of personal space she would defend. An older man who lived on her street occasionally reprimanded her and her friends about their clothing, telling them that "the children of Mecca's porch (*anak Serambi Mekkah*) should behave and cover their bodies (*tutup aurat*)." For a long time she listened politely, until one day she lost her patience and told him that she "had her own values, which were her business." The man became angry and never talked to her again. Male company, however, was another matter. Yani sometimes had groups of friends staying over during the night, and on rare occasions this included men. Also, if her younger brother had friends visiting, Yani allowed them to watch TV in her house. This was not without risk. As in Jurong, there were occasional cases of neighborhood vigilantism against *khalwat* or *zina* (adultery) in Daruet and sometimes these turned violent, particularly if the people involved were "outsiders" (*pendatang*), who had come to Daruet recently or temporarily. According to my older interlocutors, such incidents happened in the past as well, but they had become more frequent after the tsunami.

In Blang Daruet, as in other tsunami-affected places, senses of loss and grief were accompanied by disruptive social and physical changes. There had been an influx of *pendatang*, including social categories that were seen as relatively risky from a public morality point of view: single people (young men and women looking for jobs, students), but also members of the *aparat* (police, military, and intelligence). Compared to the situation preceding the tsunami, it had become less clear who owned what house, who lived where, for how long, and more generally "what was going on" in the neighborhood. Although accused wrongdoers were designated as "violators of shari'a" (*pelanggar syariat*), the implementation of shari'a law was seldom the primary interpretative framework. Instead, people pointed at the changed atmosphere after the tsunami, the many newcomers, the attraction of the *kampung* for people looking for a temporary place to stay, or, more specifically, for "evil-doers" (*orang jahat*). The WH were never called in, at least not directly. Most cases were resolved internally on the basis of *adat* (see Kloos 2014b, 78–79; cf. Otto and Otto 2015). Yani, who worked at the *geuchik*'s office, often knew the ins and outs of such cases, but cared little about it. It was people's "own business." At the same time, she regarded those who were caught as being "not so smart." "*Adat* is strong here, and people should know that." She did not believe she would ever end up in such a situation herself.

Although in Yani's view the implementation of shari'a constituted a significant change, it would be a mistake to reduce questions of outward and inward piety to the domain of the law. For most Acehnese, discussions about proper religious comportment included lively debates in the private sphere. Take, for example, a discussion I observed when I accompanied Yani and her friend Tia to the house of Yani's niece, Neli. The discussion focused on the question of whether Tia should wear a headscarf in Neli's house (that is, in front of Neli's father). Tia asked Yani for advice, for she was the oldest and should know best. Yani suggested that it might be best if she did wear a *jilbab*, arguing that she was not *muhrim* (a closely related family member). Later that evening I learned that Neli's father, although known for his religious knowledge, could not care less whether his daughter's friends covered their heads in the house or not. Yani herself was not *muhrim* either (she was related by blood to Neli's mother, not to her father), and she had never worn a headscarf in their house. When I asked Yani, a couple of days later, why the problem was important and worth extended discussion, she answered that "this was a question for Tia, not a general matter." Tia was an adult, she said, and thus expected to make her own substantiated assessment. The question was whether Tia thought she would be committing a sin if she did not wear a headscarf, and, if yes, how bad this was. I asked whether she ever posed this question to herself (she never wore a headscarf in front of me when I was in her house). She nodded and said that she was "not perfect yet."

Most young Acehnese I knew pondered and discussed questions of moral decision-making that ranged far beyond shari'a legislation. Once, on Hari Raya Idulfitri (the holiday marking the end of Ramadan), Yani's father had gone to Medan to visit the family of his new wife. This made Yani sad, because she felt more than ever the loss of her mother and sisters. Normally in such a situation she would have visited the mosque, where at least there would be many people and a festive atmosphere. However, the problem was that she was having her menstrual period, which according to Islamic law made it *haram* (forbidden) to pray. It is generally thought, moreover, that during their period women should refrain from entering a mosque, as menstruation (*haid*) is regarded as contaminating (*menajiskan*) the purity (*kesucian*) of the mosque's sacred space. Caught in a dilemma, she called her father to ask his advice. He said that she could still go, if only she would remain seated at the back of the mosque during prayer and the sermon. His argument was that she was still allowed to "socialize" (*bergaul*) even when it was prohibited to pray. But in the end, she did not go. She gave more weight to the arguments of the "religious teachers" (*teungku-teungku*), who would probably say that to enter the mosque would be a sin. Also, she was afraid of people asking why she did not pray. When I asked her which of these two reasons was decisive, if any, she answered that it was the first, not to sin. "Actually, I was not sure who was right, my father or the *teungku-teungku*. So I decided to make the safest choice."

If sinning was a serious (though contentious) concern, so was the need to repent. During Ramadan, Yani enthusiastically joined the daily *tarawih* prayers, because this was a month "full of forgiveness" and "many rewards." It was important for her to value this opportunity granted to her by God, especially, she exclaimed, "because I have so many sins!" When I asked her what she repented for, she mentioned elements from the standard repertoire (gossiping, not wearing a headscarf). Then she explained that designating sins was pointless. "We commit sins all the time," she argued, "and most of the time we are not even aware of it." The answer lay in prayer. "*Salat*," she said, "is like the pole of a house. If you take it away, the house will collapse."

For the same reason, Yani thought it was important to ask forgiveness for her mother and sisters, both of whom "needed her prayers." The tsunami played an important role in the way in which she approached her moral responsibilities. Like most others, she regularly thought about its meaning. Nobody could know for sure, she said, because it was impossible to know God's ways. She did, however, believe that the disaster constituted a form of divine wisdom (*hikmah*; see Samuels 2015a). It had changed everything. It had caused the death of her mother and her sisters and the end of her family as she knew it. Yani had been very close to her mother so this was a crucial loss. At the same time, the relationship with her father changed. He became more strict after the tsunami and increasingly demanded the right to know where she went and with whom. Yani gradually distanced herself from him. "There is not much I can tell my father," she said. "He gets angry easily now." She got along adequately with her father's new wife, but did not confide in her. Her father still supported her financially, but she increasingly felt the need to become "responsible and self-supportive." She asked, rhetorically, "What kind of life is this? There is no more happiness (*kebahagiaan*). Life has become just ordinary (*biasa aja*), not very happy, not very terrible. In the family, I have no more friends." But "who knows, it may be *hikmah* that I finally grow up and become independent. After all, people say that the tsunami is a trial (*percobaan*)." These ponderings evoked an intense sadness, but beyond that, they contributed to a personal process of ethical formation, as Yani oscillated between framing personal ethics in terms of the tragedies connected to the tsunami and other, more immediate concerns. No one in Daruet who had experienced the tsunami up close considered life to be the same afterwards.[7] But in their reactions to the transformations that marked the post-disaster moment, they built on past certainties as much as on present doubts.

The next section discusses the lives of two friends, Aris and Indra. In contrast to the previous sections, it explores what the perception of a specific sin—gambling—tells us about the navigation of public morality, the law, and the significance of ideas about failure and success.

Aris, Indra, and the Morality of Failure and Success

In December 2008, I visited the grave of Syiah Kuala (Abdurrauf al-Singkili), located just north of Banda Aceh. There I met Aris, twenty-eight years old. He told me that he ran a small barber shop together with his friend, Indra, in a neighborhood some fifteen minutes from my house in Blang Daruet. Coincidentally, I was in need of a haircut, so I decided to stop by later in the afternoon. The shop, it turned out, was a makeshift shed, built of scrap wood, containing a large mirror, two barber chairs, and a small bench where people could sit and wait their turn. While Aris was cutting my hair, I asked him about his visit to the grave. Together with some friends, he would go there occasionally and join his teacher in a *dhikr* session in a shelter (*balai*) raised on the spot. This morning, his teacher had not turned up, which was the reason he was hanging around and able to talk to me. I suggested that he must be serious about religion. In response, he drew my attention to the religious songs (*qasidah*) playing on the background. "Do you hear that? I used to listen to other kinds of music. Rock, pop, jazz. And I used to play guitar. But now I like this music better." "And what about you?" I asked his friend, Indra, who looked at me through the mirror while he was helping the customer sitting next to me. "Me?" he said, "Not yet. I am like a Muslim KTP [Muslim "according to his identity card"]."[8] They laughed. Aris said, "Yes, Indra is still a bad boy (*anak nakal*). His life is full of sin (*hidup berdosa*)."

Aris and Indra grew up as friends in the same neighborhood. In the past, Aris said, he was "just like Indra." This changed in the years after the tsunami. Although he downplayed the relationship between the disaster and his personal transformation, there seemed to be little doubt about its impact. Many of his family lost their lives. His parents and siblings all survived, however, and his way of expressing his gratitude to God was by "seeking knowledge" (*mencari ilmu*) and trying to get "closer to God" (*mendekati Tuhan*). Then, one day, he suddenly felt that God had "entered him" (*Tuhan masuk Aris*). Not much later, he burned his guitar in front of his house, making his neighbors think that he had become crazy. He joined a group of religious students, who came together a few times each week in the house of a former student of the famous ulama Usman al-Fauzy from Ateuk Lung Ie (d. 1992), where they studied classical Islamic subjects. Compared to the common *dayah* curriculum, however, they focused especially on mystical practices as they joined their teacher in long sessions of *dhikr* and reciting their *silsilah*, the chain of spiritual descent from the Prophet Muhammad down to their teacher.

The barber shop became my usual place for a haircut or a shave. In this period, I came to know Aris as a pious and serious person, who never missed a prayer, talked often about religion, and occasionally took some days off to visit the graves of famous ulama in places as far away as South Aceh or Singkil. He had a girlfriend, whom he did not see very often because she lived in a *dayah* outside Banda Aceh. Apart from his work and studies, he seemed to spend most of his free time watching football in the coffee shop close to his home. His friend Indra I came to regard—unjustifiably, perhaps—as a rather more complex character. He was friendly, attentive, and charming, and wore his heart on his sleeve. Occasionally, however, he showed signs of a darker side, noticeable for example in the occasionally unpleasant and derogatory way he talked about his girlfriend, who worked in a hospital in Langsa (East Aceh), and who came to Banda Aceh every other month or so.

Indra was two years younger than Aris. He was born on the island of Simeuleue, a rather distant place some 150 kilometers off the coast of West Aceh. After a few years of staying there, living off the clove gardens worked for generations by his mother's family, his parents moved to Banda Aceh with their children. Indra cared little about his place of birth. He had gone back once, in his early twenties. He understood the language but could not really speak it. He thought of the place as far off, primitive, and boring. In the early 2000s, his parents separated, and his father left the house. By the time I got to know him, Indra lived together with his mother and older sister Ika, who had two small children of her own, and whose husband lived in Jakarta. Indra left school when he was seventeen years old and became a barber. Together, he and Aris began working in a large barbershop in Peunayoung, the central Banda Aceh district, where most shops and businesses are located. In early 2008, they decided to open a shop of their own, which they rented from a well-to-do family on whose premises it was built.

Both Indra and Aris valued their work for what it was. Indra emphasized that he did not finish his schooling and that there was little high-status work for him to do, such as working for a large business or in a government office. He said, "This work is okay. It is honest (*jujur*)." However, he also remarked, ironically, that it was "not very good for materialistic people," including himself. "Actually, the job is much better for Aris. He is not like that." Aris did, indeed, talk about his work in much more pious terms. He said that he liked his job because it was "clean" (*bersih*) and "sincere" (*ikhlas*). "It is important to be modest (*sederhana*). That is why I drive a [Honda] Mio. I used to have a greater motorcycle (*lebih hebat*, i.e., larger, more expensive) but I sold it. This lifestyle suits me (*cocok gaya hidup*)."

While Indra and Aris remained good friends, the change in Aris's religiosity did come with particular consequences. Indra regarded his friend's ostentatious piety with a mix of admiration and annoyance. Every time the *azan* sounded, the shop was closed, and Aris walked to the nearby mosque. Indra usually stayed behind, smoking a couple of cigarettes inside, with the door closed. Aris put pressure on him to pray as well, which every now and then Indra did. He respected Aris's intentions, even though it made him feel like a bad person. More problematic for him was the fact that it had become difficult to talk to Aris about personal things, such as his troubled relationship with his girlfriend. Indra suspected that his worries would not be taken seriously. "Aris will laugh and then he will say I should look for another girl. He will say I need to become more serious. And he will tell me to go to the mosque. That's it." I asked him, "Do you think Aris is being too strict with religion?" He answered, "In general, no. But in this regard, perhaps, yes!"

At the same time, Indra's lifestyle was also causing trouble. Although they shared the barber shop, Indra and Aris worked for themselves. They had their own clients, while new customers were equally divided. The rent, however, was a shared responsibility. When they opened the shop, they negotiated a two-year contract. Because Indra had no money at the time, Aris paid for it, with Indra promising that the next time would be his turn. In April 2010, the contract expired, and after some tough negotiations they agreed on an extension of one year, against a 50 percent increase in the price. Indra, however, had not saved enough money. He borrowed a part of the rent from his sister, but the main part was paid, again, by Aris, putting Indra in serious debt with his friend. This put a strain on their relationship.

Indra's financial situation was not particularly complex. Together with his sister, who worked at a travel agency, he supported his mother. For himself, he needed money to pay for coffee, food, petrol, and cigarettes. Other spending, he said, was "play" (*main-main*). This included some drugs (primarily marijuana and on a rare occasion crystal meth). The largest part, however, was spent on gambling. An old, still-current form of gambling in Aceh is to stake money on domino games or (somewhat less common) cock fights. Another popular practice is to place bets on the results of football matches. By far the most widespread form of gambling, however, is participating in lotteries using a mobile phone. People buy numbers by sending a text message. Once the numbers are drawn, a message is sent with the result. At times, mystical forces are attached to these numbers. One regular (male) interlocutor in Blang Daruet asked me, every now and then, whether I had dreamt about numbers. These might be worth a try. Indra also believed that "codes" were transmitted in dreams. According to Aris, such dreams were the work of the devil, who tried to persuade people to commit sins. When I suggested this to Indra, he said, "Maybe it is the devil. Maybe it is God."

Like most others, Indra bet small amounts (10,000 or 20,000 rupiah, a little over US$2). The problem was the frequency. Indra estimated that, in total, he might have lost some ten million rupiah in this way, while winning around three million. Besides losing money, there was the risk of being caught. Indonesia has strict laws against gambling, and in 2003 the practice became punishable by caning under shari'a law. Avoiding a court case was possible, Indra argued, but costly. "If the police catches you, they will extort you, rather than forward your case to court. . . . At checkpoints, the police will check the messages in your phone, so you always need to make sure that you delete all of them. It would probably cost me around two million to get rid of them."

His cheerful and attentive appearance notwithstanding, Indra was not a very happy man. He was insecure about his social status and worried that, at some point, he would lose himself in smoking marijuana, watching TV, and gambling away his money. He often said that his life was "boring" (using the English word). Whenever I asked him about his future aspirations, he would joke that he might follow me to Europe and make lots of money as a hairdresser for famous people. The more serious answer conformed to the standard ideal of many Acehnese men, namely a business and a family. To realize such a life, he needed starting capital (*modal*). "Forty million to build my own barber shop in front of the house and about the same to get married." Since Indra was making debts instead of saving money, achieving this became less and less probable. What was lacking, according to his own analysis, was the ability to discipline himself like Aris:

> I've gone wrong. If I had been more disciplined, worked harder, saved more money, I could have paid Aris back, or we could have built a shop of our own, or for myself. . . . The problem is just that I feel bored. I throw away my time. I don't have another goal in life, like Aris. Aris thinks about the next world. I think about this world.

Indra fantasized that, in the future, he might go through a conversion like Aris. "You know, I think that Aris is really doing the right thing. . . . To engage in religious study, to seek a regulated life."

Aris also worried about Indra. "He is not very good at management," he said (using the English term). I asked: "So what do you worry about most, his afterlife, or his future in this life?" "Both," Aris replied. I asked him for an example. He said that his greatest worry was not Indra's reluctance to pray, or his habit of smoking marijuana or skipping work days, but rather his inveterate habit of gambling. A few weeks earlier, a friend of theirs was caught. He had been observed by the police for some time and was clearly in deep trouble. "This can also happen to Indra," Aris stated. "So he should be very careful. And then I do not even speak about the money he throws away."

Indra was not the only one taking financial risks, however. In early 2010, something unexpected happened. For some weeks, Aris had been asking me to join his so-called network (*jaringan*) that was part of a new outfit called Quest-net. He explained to me that this was a highly profitable business in which people could join by buying a particular product, and subsequently become a link in an—ever-expanding—chain of buying-and-selling. He was rather vague about his own involvement, however, and I did not give it much attention. In April, he asked me to join him at a meeting. Skeptical and curious, I came along. The event took place, interestingly, in the building of the Government Health Service. It featured a slick presentation by a young man in a tight-fitting suit, who introduced himself as the "director" of the Aceh branch of Questnet, and who showed a PowerPoint presentation as well as a few fancy animation videos demonstrating the way in which the business worked. About twenty other people of mixed age and gender were present. A few hours later, we walked out again. Aris was delighted, and I was flabbergasted. I found it difficult to believe that the pious and responsible Aris I thought I knew could be so enthusiastic about what surely must be the most impudent pyramid scheme I had ever seen.

We sat down at a coffee shop to have lunch. Aris was cheerful, and I asked him incredulously, "Do you really believe that you can make a lot of money, easy and for free, without doing any work?" He replied, "Absolutely!" "And do you think about joining them?" (I had just learned that this would cost at least 700,000 rupiah [US$75]). He said, "I already have, last year!" It turned out that not only had he already become involved, but his way of paying for it was to exchange his old motorcycle for the "modest" Honda Mio. According to Aris, the investment would make him very rich. "If I earn a lot of money, I can buy my own barber shop and have people work for me. Or perhaps I won't be a barber at all and I will follow my *guru* to Surabaya and Brunei to study. Then, when I come back, I will get married. I will build a *dayah* and become a religious teacher myself." I went home that day feeling confused. I did not even care that much about the distorted story about the motorcycle. What occupied me was the thought that I had been seduced by the attractively dramatic but all too simplistic tension between a responsible devotee and a negligent libertine.

Aris and Indra were good friends. They were also opposing characters, with Aris being the more composed and Indra the more outgoing. Apart from working together, they led different lives, driven by different opinions, choices, and circumstances. At the same time, their future aspirations were not very far apart. Both hoped, one day, to have a family and a business of their own. Both fantasized about sudden wealth, and to make their dreams come true they were willing to take a gamble. The difference lay in the ethical framing. The lotteries in which Indra participated were seen as *perjudian*—"gambling"—an activity considered *haram* by most Muslims and therefore, ultimately, an expression of weakness. Aris's involvement in Questnet, despite being a form of financial risk taking too (and, to cite the shari'a regulation on gambling, possibly "harmful to others" as well), was seen by both of them as a sign of a disciplined life, one that comprised a "plan." Questnet was placed in a category of life "management," which also included active religious worship. Together, these activities meant investing in a vision of the future that combined piety, marriage, and financial success. Although Indra suspected (like me) that Questnet was a form of fraud (*tipu*), Aris's choice to take a risk reinforced the image that he was taking his life into his own hands, managing the future by joining a new and potentially profitable "business." It made Indra feel slacker than ever, convinced of the need for ethical improvement, but deeply uncertain of how to deal with the challenges.

Judged on the basis of outward signs of piety (praying, fasting, religious study, dress), Indra was among the least "religious" of my regular interlocutors. At the same time, his understanding of personal development—in terms of education, future aspirations, and the search for success—was thick with religious valences. The stress placed on life phase, including the statement that he was not "ready yet" to undergo a transformation similar to Aris, constitutes an important similarity with the stories of Rahmat and Yani. At the same time, the case of Aris and Indra shows that the ambition of ethical improvement may well be personal and processual, but not, for that reason, especially systematic, coherent, or based on standard interpretations of a good life. The pursuit of success and dealing with failure implied evolving and strongly personalized conceptions of morality.

The Knowledge of Sins: Competing Models of Ethical Improvement?

According to powerful shari'a bureaucrats, such as the first Head of the State Shari'a Agency, Alyasa Abubakar, state-directed Islam is a tool for "perfecting" the moral consciousness of individuals, and thereby society as a whole (Feener 2012, 286). As argued in the previous chapter, such totalizing views of Islam, which were reinforced by the "total reconstruction" discourses predominating in the public sphere after the tsunami (Samuels 2015a), have at their basis a "positive" ethics (Mahmood 2005, 27–29) directed at cultivating inner faith and shaping—through outward disciplining, bodily practice, and the eradication of sinful behavior—more "perfect" inner selves. However, as the cases in this chapter demonstrate, there seems to be a disjunction between the standardizing logic of "high-modern" (Feener 2015, 9) state Islam and the processes through which many ordinary Acehnese try to become better

Muslims. Let me try to deepen the analysis of this tension by elaborating on the relationship between the post-conflict, post-tsunami thrust of religious renewal (as exemplified by the implementation of shari'a) and the connections perceived by my interlocutors between religious practice and inner states of being.

In her work on Qur'anic recitation, Anna Gade (2004, 49) argues that equal value should be given to ritual practice as to power and ideology as "organizing principles" of religious change. While inspiring my approach of inner religious lives, her work also leaves unanswered important questions about the interactions between individual believers and state and religious authorities. Clearly, it remains a challenge to develop solid theoretical and methodological frameworks for linking affect and self-development to changes in public and political morality. To some extent, this is due to the slippery concept of "morality" itself. For this book, I have made use of Jarett Zigon's (2008) conceptualization of the "ethical working on the self." His work is part of a broader turn to ethics in anthropology but also—and this makes it particularly relevant for this study—of an emergent interest in (perceptions of) doubt, uncertainty, and imperfection as informing particular modes of agency (see Cooper and Pratten 2014; Engelke and Tomlison 2006; Kloos and Beekers 2018; Pelkmans 2013; Verkaaik 2014). My interest in sinfulness resonates with other investigations of moral failure and their impact on the ways in which people become aware of, and act on, their "moral way of being in the world" (Zigon 2009a, 82). However, in contrast to Zigon's (2009b, 257–63) theory of "moral breakdowns," or Cheryl Mattingly's (2014) focus on moral "perils" and "tragedies," I am not concerned with specific "moments" or "instances" in which moral consciousness is reinvigorated. The question I am exploring is rather how senses of failure contribute to ongoing processes of ethical formation (cf. Beekers and Kloos 2018).

To further explain this focus on failure, let me elaborate on a distinction, made by many of my interlocutors, between "knowing" and "not-knowing" sins. Earlier, I quoted Yani, who said that "most of the time we are not even aware of [our sins]." Irma, a middle-aged mother of three, when commenting on the obligation to wear a headscarf, explained: "It is said that for every single hair, a bundle of wood will be added to the fire in hell. And I do not even speak of all the sins which happen unnoticed." Although such statements constitute genuine warnings, apparently referring to quite inflexible notions of discipline and divine punishment, I gradually realized that there was also a different charge to such comments. Ultimately, these expressions reflected the everyday nature of sins. At the same time, the distinction between knowing and not-knowing sins connects to the notions of awareness (*kesadaran*) and responsibility (*tanggung jawab*) emphasized by Rahmat and Yani as they explained their personal moral development. It was on the basis of such ideas that they decided to "act on themselves." Importantly, knowing sins, as well as the understanding of what this knowledge effectuates, partly depends on the transition between life stages. These can be physical transitions or culturally determined rites of passage, like puberty (*akil baligh*), which marks the onset of moral responsibility, or they can be more subjective, extended processes of personal development, connected to the accumulation of knowledge, maturation, or character formation, of which it is often unclear when they start and when they end.

Why are these transitions so important? One reason is the view shared by many of my interlocutors that the more knowledgeable a person becomes, the more responsibilities he or she acquires, and the more likely (or grave) his or her sins are. A good example is the practice of learning how to perform particular rituals, such as prayer. Children learn how to pray by imitating their parents, the *teungku meunasah*, or the people they see in the mosque or prayer house. This practice of imitation does not stop when children become adults. Adults who are uncertain about the performance of prayer may still look at the imam, or people in front of them, in order to improve their own movements and utterings. There is, however, a tension in this type of interaction. People who feel that they have become more knowledgeable, or "more aware" (*lebih sadar*), may become careful, or even hesitant, about imitating others.

For example, Eri, the pious young man who was central in the previous chapter, regularly complained to me about the "poor" standard of religious learning in Daruet. He had learned to recite a large part of the Qur'an by heart, and upon his return recognized certain mistakes in the congregational prayers led by the village and mosque leadership. For the people who did not have the knowledge to hear these mistakes, he argued, this did not matter at all. But for him it created a dilemma. To participate consciously (or "knowingly") in these communal prayers would mean to sin. Thus, whenever the problem arose Eri would sit quietly at the back of the mosque and pray for himself. Or he would decide to pray at home instead. The reverse also applied. I was told by several people that allowing oneself to be imitated by others (for example by accepting the responsibility of leading the prayer) was a risk for those who did not consider themselves to be sufficiently knowledgeable to bear this responsibility.

Another example of the distinction between knowing and not-knowing sins is the experience of the fasting month. Generally, *puasa* was perceived as a "month of forgiveness," in which the "door to God" was opened. This led, typically, to reflections on acts of self-discipline through an emphasis on controlling one's passions (*nafsu*). This challenge (and of course the failure to live up to it) occasionally connected to emotions like fear (*takut*) and shame (*malu*). However, what emerged from many of my conversations was not so much the fear of sinning but rather the fear of failing to put to good use the opportunities associated with *puasa*. I once asked my seventeen-year-old neighbor, Santi, whether the thought of sinning weighed more heavily on her during *puasa*. She thought about this for a moment and decided, "No, that is not the point. Many of our sins we do not even know. . . . It is just that this is a month of seeking divine rewards." Like many of my other interlocutors, she believed that *puasa* constituted an opportunity for dealing with unknown sins. Like prayer, it was a "gift" from God, a fixed "time of blessing" (Feener 2006, 146), provided by God to deal with this problem (among others).

The distinction between knowing and not-knowing sins, and its connection to the transition between life stages, is an important factor in the legitimization of behavior. This becomes clear when we look at individuals' responses to the shari'a revival. One of the channels through which Rahmat was confronted on a regular basis with the notion of (state) shari'a were the sermons of the ulama, in the village or the market mosque. He was generally critical of these sermons. In the past, he argued, religious teachers taught villagers "what was right and what was wrong, without additional [monetary] interests (*tanpa bunga*)." Today, what they cared about most, at least according to Rahmat, was money. This does not mean that he did not care about their messages at all. He once returned from the market mosque on Friday and spoke very enthusiastically about the sermon. The preacher had talked about repentance, and about the importance of asking forgiveness from other people for past wrongdoings. "This is very important!" he stressed. "Imagine that someone dies. No regret could be shown, and no forgiveness could be given. The sin would remain (*tetap dosa*)." This was something Rahmat worried about, much more than the "law." About the implementation of shari'a, then, he was rather indifferent. When I asked his opinion, he said, "If they do this, they should do it properly." The shari'a laws, he argued, were not designed to apply to "important people (*orang besar*)." If the courts would start cutting off hands, perhaps, corrupt and hypocritical politicians might be challenged. However, when I asked him whether he supported politicians who endorsed a stricter version of shari'a, he replied, "I am already old. This is something for young people to solve."

One of those young people was Yani, and she was much more pronounced about this than Rahmat. Her life (and that of other young women) was directly affected by the new morality laws. Her decision to wear a headscarf was prompted by the activities of the shari'a police, who patrolled some of the places Yani frequented for leisure. Yani had never been caught in a raid, but some of her close friends had, and the possibility worried her. At the same time, she fundamentally disagreed with some of the regulations enforced by the WH:

> In Jakarta, women are free to wear a tank top or a short top. Here, in Aceh, this is not allowed. If people in Jakarta have the [religious] intention (*niat*) to wear a headscarf outside the house, they can, but they can wear whatever. Here it is different. . . . I think it would be better if people were not forced. It should be according to people's own wish. Actually, I did not yet have this wish to wear a headscarf. But because shari'a has been implemented and the headscarf is obliged, I wear it.

Yani detested the WH, its raids, and its lectures. She complained that they were too strict, inspecting women on "everything, including tight clothes." Using a common formula, she argued that "we [the Acehnese] are not ready yet." She preferred going to the beach without covering her whole body, but because she did not much fancy "being humiliated," she chose to comply. That said, the practice of wearing a headscarf did not cause Yani much trouble. On the contrary, she was rather positive about it, explaining that, once she got used to it, she felt "more tidy" (*rapi*), "clean" (*bersih*), and "comfortable" (*senang*), even if this did not change her opinion that expressions of piety should arise "within the heart" (*dalam hati*). Her experiences reflected the ways in which many young people appropriated shari'a-inspired norms in the context of their everyday lives.

The case of Aris and Indra shows yet another stance toward state disciplining, namely active selecting of religious norms. To a certain extent, Indra's opinions resonated with Yani's critique of the way in which the law was implemented and enforced. He questioned its effectiveness. Gambling, he explained, was a very common practice in Banda Aceh, before as well as after the implementation of shari'a law. The only difference was that, in the past, men simply filled in their lottery form in the coffee shop, and today they had to buy their numbers in secret. "It has become a public secret." The law's primary achievement, he said cynically, was that the police were given yet another means of extortion. Shari'a enforcement was counterproductive because it went directly against ordinary people's definition of social justice (*keadilan social*) as embedded in the *pancasila*, the official philosophical foundation of the Indonesian nation-state (which, like most Indonesians, he was able to recite by heart).[9] What I found particularly striking, however, in Aris's and Indra's account is that, even though *perjudian* is one of the major domains in which shari'a criminal law has been put into effect, they hardly ever referred to the practice explicitly as "sinful" (*dosa*). Certainly, they thought of it as morally suspect, a "passion" (*nafsu*) that implied weakness, but neither one of them defined gambling as a major problem jeopardizing their personal relationship with God. In this sense, their story is an example of the extent to which shari'a laws have failed to achieve their goal of "perfecting" official norms both among individual Muslims and in Acehnese society at large.

Instead of simply rejecting or adopting state and public discourses, my interlocutors actively selected and appropriated official moral discourses to make decisions, assess emotions, or justify behavior. Their experiences thus resonated strongly with the ideas about internalization theorized by Gade. At the same time, I observed that the powerful affective qualities of individual ethical improvement provided them with considerable agency regarding the judgment and adaptation of the standardized models propagated by powerful state and religious authorities. According to Lambek (2000), an important tension exists within the conceptual domain of religion between the fields of power and morality. The latter may be seen as a culturally embedded alternative to power, in the sense that everyday practice distorts, changes, or subverts power in a variety of ways. Rahmat, Yani, and Indra were not particularly enthusiastic about shari'a law, and the same might also be said about Aris. At the same time, it would be wrong to understand their reactions primarily in terms of defiance, or even discipline at large. Rather, these people selected and appropriated some elements in these discourses, while rejecting, ignoring, or rendering irrelevant other elements. The logic undergirding this routine of selection and appropriation was driven by processes of ethical improvement that they interpreted as life-long, fragmented, and in the end highly personal.

Conclusion

Looking beyond differences in gender, age, education, personal character, social status, and living environment, there was an important similarity in the ways in which my interlocutors shaped and experienced their religious lives. This was not the fact that they saw themselves as (ideally) "pious" Acehnese, but rather that they regarded their morality as a process that required, above all, personal reflection. This stance depends, at least partly, on a broadly shared cultural concern that morally reprehensible behavior—sinfulness being the primary example—does not necessarily reveal itself immediately, or at all times. As I have shown in this chapter, the manifestation of sinfulness is often connected to subjective perceptions of life stages. The moments, periods, or situations in which sins revealed themselves and prompted moral action were framed not just in terms of a need for religious disciplining, but also in terms of inner religious development, requiring senses of composure, awareness, guilt, disappointment, failure, and success. These were ethical terms, embedded in a more general conception of social and moral responsibility.

A mode of agency is vested in this domain of personal religiosity. As elsewhere, the agencies of ordinary people in Aceh are contingent on a combination of shifting identities, social and cultural capital, repertoires of power, and a wide variety of learned practices and customary behavior. Class and gender are important categories, organizing these agencies in particular (acceptable and recognizable) ways. However, the ability to practice Islam both within a socially defined set of norms and on the basis of a customized and individualized interpretation of these norms is never dependent on such categories alone. Religious agency and its inherent flexibility, drawn out in the cases in this chapter and the material presented throughout this book, reflects a perception of religious consciousness and associated action that allows for certainty and truth as much as ambivalence, doubt, and imperfection. This agency is explicitly religious in nature and must be understood, equally explicitly, in these terms.

Conclusion

When Aceh is featured in the media, in Indonesia, Europe, or the United States, the focus is often on Islamic law. Does the process of shari'a implementation in Aceh mean that Indonesia, the largest Muslim country in the world, is gradually becoming an "Islamic state"? Or is this province, historically rebellious and self-consciously religious, an exception that ultimately has little to say about the rest of the country and the region? Such reports tend to ignore debates that take place within Aceh. Various analysts and opinion makers in Aceh have been critical, arguing that the current shari'a regulations, or the ways in which these have been enforced, are discriminatory in nature, affecting women rather than men, the poor rather than the rich. Another often-heard comment is that the Acehnese have never asked for these laws, that they "already have shari'a," and do not need the help of the government to tell them how to practice their faith. A common denominator in these responses is the view that the implementation of shari'a was orchestrated by a small group of conservative local politicians and Islamic activists, in cooperation with the national government, as a tool for accelerating the resolution of the conflict. In the meantime, a good many Jakarta pundits, including a number of legal scholars from different universities, have simply argued that, "if this is what Aceh wants," there is little that anyone could, or should, do about it.

Judging from these debates, it often seems that the majority of Acehnese are only passive players in the making of their own future. This book rejects such a view. People in Aceh, I have demonstrated, rely on their own personal space for action as they negotiate the norms established "for them" by state institutions and religious authorities. The resulting interactions should be reduced neither to the domain of resistance (cf. Scott 1985) nor to the "politics of piety" (Mahmood 2005). I have also tried to stay clear from reifying the artificial dichotomy between normative Islam and "lived" experience. Instead, I have found a theoretical basis in an idea advanced by Michael Lambek (2000), namely that morality, as the domain where the good is articulated and appropriate behavior is defined, constitutes an existential alternative to the realm of power. Morality and power are closely connected concepts, but they do not share the central terms in which human existences are cast.

The complex of moral interactions involves a particular form of agency, understood as a "capacity to act" (Ahearn 2001). In this book I have employed the concept of "religious agency" as the capacity of individual Muslims to engage in religiously defined moral actions. Agency is a crucial concept, because of the way in which it expands and contracts possibilities, options, and choices. Powerful actors, be they individuals, institutions, or the state, set limits to this space, but not always as they intend. Obviously, individual agency is not the same for every person. It is contingent, depending in its scope on the context in which it is produced. However, this heterogeneity does not make it less important or more difficult to identify. The crucial point is that an exclusive focus on power relations will lead to an overly simplistic understanding of the ways in which religion informs, and is embedded in, society. Religious experiences and expressions must be taken seriously, neither reified nor discarded as an object of social or political analysis.

Although this book is not a study of politics, the state is present in all chapters. In a large part of the world, the development of the modern state has been accompanied by a gradual officialization of religious thought and practice (Bayly 2004, 480). Education is one of the most important realms in which the state has tried to control religious affairs. In the Muslim world, this was traditionally the domain of the ulama, scholars of religious law. At the same time, both the state and the institutions emanating from local traditions of organized religion have penetrated into spheres of private life, elaborating the norms that guide people in the making and the imagining of a "good" society. I have demonstrated that the boundaries between these realms—of state, organized religion, and individual agency—are not fixed or unequivocal. They mean different things to different people. They are ambiguous, easily unsettled, and often (and sometimes violently) challenged. It is important to emphasize that many of my interlocutors in Aceh were acutely aware of, and often quite articulate about, the contested nature of official norms. For them, these blurred boundaries were hardly something to be surprised about. Fendi, after the theft from the *dayah* and the arrest of his younger brother Irwan, respected his father for his moral sense yet found fault with him for not thinking strategically about the relationship between their family and local officials and religious leaders. Meli admired her son Eri's newly acquired religious knowledge, yet defended the sincerity of her own "old" beliefs against his habit of imposing scripturalist norms on the family.

Scholars of Islam have increasingly addressed questions of personal piety and ethical formation. This shift toward individual religiosity has led to important new perspectives on the nature of agency in Muslim societies. Many of these studies, however, employ a (nearly) exclusive focus on practices of (self-)discipline. As a result, personal religiosity has been studied primarily within the paradigm of pious practice (such as prayer or religious study). This book builds partially on the work of scholars who are critical of the emphasis on discipline as a central organizing principle for analysis, and who focus on ordinary Muslims' ambivalent commitment to both religious and nonreligious concerns (e.g., M. Marsden 2005; Schielke 2015). While I acknowledge this tension, I have also tried to take seriously the inner processes through which religiosities are shaped, guided by the question of how individuals try to meet prevailing norms while simultaneously and creatively building their identity as Muslims.

In recent years, a rather unhelpful contrast has emerged within the anthropology of Islam between studies of (self-)disciplinary movements and quests for ethical perfection (see, e.g., Hirschkind 2006; Mahmood 2005) and studies that are centered instead on the notion that religious subjects are fundamentally ambivalent, incoherent, or unstable (see, e.g., Marsden 2005; Marsden and Retsikas 2012; Schielke 2015; Schielke and Debevec 2012). Processes of ethical improvement, I argue, are based not only on expressions of piety but also, importantly, on self-perceived setbacks and on feelings of inability, weakness, and error. Thus, I have drawn into the analysis a notion of moral failure (cf. Beekers and Kloos 2018). Many people in Aceh identify and acknowledge the perception of moral failure as part and parcel of, rather than a hindrance to, the process of becoming a better Muslim. Senses of failure are a crucial factor, therefore, in the constitution of religious agency. Without a notion of failure, ethical improvement is impossible.

Religious agency is a historical phenomenon, which has developed in continuous dialectic with the forces of normative Islam. In this book I have focused on the state and organized religion as the two most important sociopolitical forces that lay claim to the definition of "correct" religious norms and behavior. A tension exists between these forces, deriving, as Max Weber already noted, from the fact that the legitimacy of political and religious institutions is built on different forms of authority. The competition between political and religious authorities is not a perquisite of modern Western societies. It is fundamentally entrenched in Islamic history (Ricklefs 2012, 469–70). At the same time, these forces have been mitigated and transformed as part of the processes of social and political interaction "on the ground." People in Aceh, be they rich and influential or poor and marginalized, operate a variety of means and strategies to enlarge their space for moral action. Religious agency includes the capacity of people to make active use of state and religious institutions, contesting the question of what it means to be a good Muslim. This process of space-making, taking place at different social, temporal, and geographical levels, from the imagining of Aceh and its place in the world to the formation of individual morality in the context of local communities, is the central theme of this book.

A major shift took place in Aceh in the eighteenth and nineteenth centuries. This was a period in which the power of the sultanate—an institution based, partly, on the fusing of state and religious authority—declined and in which the ulama established themselves as a new and largely autonomous class in the rural interior. Decentralization and the fragmentation of political and religious authority made it very difficult for Dutch colonial forces to subjugate the territory they thought to be controlled by the sultan. Gradually, however, the colonial encounter shaped the terms in which Aceh, as a place, a society, and a people, was framed and understood. In the early twentieth century—corresponding with the "Vertigo Years" in Europe (Blom 2008) and a time of "speed and/or belief in speed" in Indonesia (Mrázek 2002, 37)—the colonial state, in collaboration with indigenous leaders and an emerging class of civil servants from different social backgrounds, embarked on an ambitious project of building an administrative system based on the rule of law, modern institutions, economic development, and a strong belief in progress. Religious authorities were involved in this process, but sparsely and indirectly. The extreme violence of the war and the protracted nature of colonial repression and anticolonial resistance created a climate in which—contrary to other Indonesian contexts with long histories of Dutch violence and "holy war" (*jihad*)—the space for contestation and open debate about religious practices and interpretations remained limited.

In the same period, an Islamic reformist movement emerged in Aceh, which, as in other parts of Indonesia and the Muslim world, sought to uplift the Islamic community by returning to the "true" tenets of the religion and by reconciling religious lifestyles with aspects of civil society and modern technology. This movement has often been viewed as inherently anticolonial, especially in Aceh, where it correlated, partly, with the cultivation of a regionalist and ethnocentric rhetoric (crystallizing ultimately in the All Aceh Association of Ulama [Persatuan Ulama-Ulama Seluruh Aceh, PUSA]). Chapter 1 criticizes this view. Manifestations of Islamic reformism resonated closely with the ways in which the colonial government tried to shape Aceh as a definable and governable entity. As part of this process, the religious and ethnic variety that characterized Acehnese society was supplanted in public discourses by an inflexible mode of social, political, and geographic imagination. Both reform-minded religious leaders and colonial administrators privileged a "modern," scripturalist interpretation of Islam over the "traditional," mystical, and dangerously syncretic practices and ideas that were thought to be prevalent, particularly on the "isolated" West and South Coasts. PUSA played a central role in the eviction of the Dutch. But this dramatic event was hardly foreshadowed. In the political climate of the 1930s, the nativist current combined with reformist Islamic activism represented an officially approved, legitimate addition to Dutch-style modernization.

In the Japanese period, PUSA leaders were granted significant power, and in the first turbulent years of Indonesian independence they became the central players in the creation of a highly autonomous provincial government. However, in the 1950s the Indonesian central state became more assertive. The decision to incorporate Aceh in the province of North Sumatra persuaded a group of radical ulama, led by former PUSA chairman and Aceh governor Daud Beureueh, to declare a rebellion in the name of Islam. The Darul Islam, and its call for the creation of an "Islamic State of Indonesia," offered an important political alternative appealing to many. Yet, as shown in chapter 2, its impact was also limited. Focusing on local trajectories of social and religious change in the rural district of Aceh Besar, and drawing both on archival materials and the field notes of Chandra Jayawardena, this chapter argues that the influence of shari'a-minded reformers was uneven and, in part, temporary in nature. Changes of a more lasting nature occurred in the early New Order years. In this period, the village became an increasingly important site of political and religious contestation. The main catalyst for this process was the gradual intrusion into the village by the state, caused by the expansion of the administrative and bureaucratic apparatus, electoral competition, and the use of state resources by villagers protecting their own interests and space for action.

Chapter 3 follows the process of state assertion into the present, shifting the focus to the changing place of the ulama in the rural community of Jurong. More specifically, it seeks to add nuance to the dominant scholarly narrative of Acehnese resistance against the state. In Aceh, the state remains one of the most important resources available, for ordinary villagers and political and religious elites alike. This comes with important implications with regard to the ways in which religious norms are constructed and appropriated. In the second half of the twentieth century, religious scholars and lay Muslims became increasingly preoccupied with the question of what the state might be able to do for them, in both a worldly and a spiritual sense. This means that the state, besides being viewed as a force that imposes specific norms on society, should also be regarded as an arena for contestation, which can be seized upon to legitimize behavior, advance interests, avoid punishment, or adapt prevailing views and moral standards. The state, in other words, provides space for religious maneuvering as much as it allows for enforcement and punitive action. Central, in this regard, is the role of religious authorities, most prominently among them the ulama. Younger generations in particular have been increasingly prepared to view the ulama as either tied to, or as agents of, the state.

My argument about the relationship between religious authority and the state holds relevance beyond the particularities of Aceh scholarship.

Generalizing theories about religion in the modern world often assume that state interference in religious affairs diminishes ordinary Muslims' space for moral action. In the case of Aceh, this is only partly true. On the one hand, there is no question that the possibility for people to engage in very different forms of religious organization and practice, as well as a range of other kinds of behavior, has decreased because of the state's advancement or enforcement of Islamic norms (cf. Ricklefs 2012, 493–94). On the other hand, the "state-system" has been actively shaped, altered, and appropriated by the very people whose religiosities it claims to govern. This has led to a paradoxical situation: options have become fewer, yet religious agencies have not necessarily decreased. While the state functions as a disciplinary force, it has also provided people with a number of tools to adapt official norms according to their own particular interests and ideas.

In contrast to some influential studies of religious self-styling in Muslim contexts, I have not sought to focus specifically on pursuits of pious perfection. My interviews and conversations concentrated on a variety of everyday concerns, including work, education, money, family, friendship, village sociality, disappointments, and aspirations. Although I have used the shorthand of "ordinary Muslims" on many occasions, ultimately this is a study of the "ordinary lives of people" rather than the "lives of ordinary people" (Schulte Nordholt and Steijlen 2007, 4). For me, the major question was how, and when, Islam became important, as a topic of conversation, a contested category, or a framework for explaining social relations or the importance and nature of particular events. To an extent, this approach has resulted—in line with my original intentions—in a rigorous deexceptionalizing of Acehnese history and society. Although Aceh is often presented as a "special case," I find it important to emphasize that Acehnese Muslims struggle, in a way that is comparable to the experiences of Muslims elsewhere in Southeast Asia and the world, with the tensions and contradictions that exist between expressions (and the appeal) of normative, "universal," or globalizing Islam, and the norms and practices associated with other categories of moral action, such as the local customs and traditions commonly categorized as *adat*.

This tension is elaborated in chapter 4, which shifts the attention from the rural context of Jurong to the urban context of Blang Daruet. It details the relationship between Eri, a young man who featured a strong, outwardly oriented pious lifestyle inspired by the global revivalist movement, and his parents, Ikhsan and Meli. Their family, including five other children, miraculously survived the 2004 Indian Ocean tsunami, which annihilated their neighborhood and took countless lives in the city of Banda Aceh and along the coasts. In the aftermath, the disaster became an important register for moral inquiry. At the same time, it came to function as a container discourse, concealing and distorting moral concerns as much as bringing them to the fore. It is often stated that Aceh, because of the separatist conflict and the strong regional identity of the Acehnese, has shown itself immune to the influences of global Islamic revivalism. While it is true that national and transnational Islamic activist organizations and political parties have been less active in Aceh compared to other parts of Indonesia, it would be a mistake to think that political conditions isolated the region. This chapter shows that, rather than challenging their son's scripturalist admonitions on the basis of a reified notion of Acehnese culture or tradition, Ikhsan and Meli were receptive to some ideas, while actively contesting others. They did not simply adopt or discard Eri's views as a coherent way of life. Instead, they accommodated his recommendations as a part of their own personal processes of moral and religious development. This was done in quite different ways, contingent on class and gender but also—and this is the point I have stressed—on the way in which the perception of life phase required contrasting stances toward piety, purity, and the definition of correct behavior.

These observations illustrate very clearly that the tensions between globalizing movements and local particularities are not necessarily—or even very often—perceived as an impediment to individual ethical improvement. On the contrary, these tensions offer an important point of reference in the everyday reflections on personal choices and concerns, including perceptions of religious negligence and moral failure more broadly. The latter, I argue, offer a critical lens for viewing the inner workings and social mechanisms of ethical formation. Evoking, among others, the work of Anna Gade (2004), I have sought to take seriously the spiritual lives of my interlocutors as a potent religious force in their own right, driving everyday engagements with religious practice and authority. At the same time, I have warned against the risk of underemphasizing the extent to which inner investigations are guided by political conditions and ideologies, as well as the specific ways in which emotions are expressed and interpreted in social life.

This position functions as a point of departure in chapter 5, which develops a nuanced, grounded, and actor-centered approach toward the engagement with normative Islam. It uses three extensive vignettes, focused on the religious lives of Rahmat, Yani, and the youthful barbers Aris and Indra, to draw out an important pattern in the construction of religious norms in Aceh, namely the distinction between "knowing" and "not-knowing" sins. The concept of sinning has two faces. It is both objectified and dependent on a person's religious knowledge. This is the basis of the state Islamic legal system, which resorts to (state) bodies of Islamic authority to enforce and "socialize" particular laws and regulations (Feener 2013). At the same time, it is this very principle that allows people to circumvent, reinterpret, and appropriate the totalizing discourses of state shari'a. By making this claim, I do not mean to trivialize the impact of the new shari'a laws, which can be significant and highly disruptive or traumatizing for those who are punished or, more generally, feel constrained in their everyday lives. The state shari'a system is a means of exerting power, intended, as a former head of the state Shari'a Office expressed it, to make "better" people by imposing a particular interpretation of Islam. Fluctuating in intensity and unevenly enforced, it is also contingent on the struggle for political power and moral authority in Aceh's post-conflict, post-disaster context (Feener, Kloos, and Samuels 2015; Kloos 2014b). Nonetheless, I think it is exactly these intentions that explain why the project of shari'a implementation falls short of its formal goals. The aim of "amending" religious convictions and motivations and improving society by regulating outward behavior and pedagogical structures has deep roots in the history of Islamic legal thought and practice. It also runs counter to the way in which many of my interlocutors engaged, on an everyday basis, with ethical improvement, as a process that is deeply personal, context dependent, cumulative, and often unpredictable.

An urgent question, then, is what the shari'a project has done, in a general sense, to individual spaces for negotiation. Is the implementation of Islamic criminal law changing the ways in which people act, voice their opinions, or call into question dominant models of knowledge, practice, and truth? If yes, how do they respond to this in their everyday lives? As Michael Feener (2015) has argued, analyzing the "limits of the state" requires also taking into account the deeper discursive trends that, in the long term, might change people's thoughts and behavior. This is not an easy target. The implementation of Islamic law in Aceh has been an extremely complex political and legal experiment, involving a plural legal framework (which also includes secular law and the recognition of customary law), ongoing negotiations between different administrative levels, and the possibility of the civil war flaring up always lurking in the background. Compared to, for example, the situation in Malaysia, crucial questions have yet to be addressed (or, perhaps more precisely, "tested" in court), such as the status of shari'a regulations vis-à-vis the Constitution or the various human rights treaties signed by the Indonesian government. In addition, there is the challenge of distinguishing, at some basic level at least, between genuine attempts to create a justice system in line with Islamic values and the cynical attempts of populist politicians to increase their moral credentials. That said, it is quite clear that the defenders of religious pluralism and adherents of nonmainstream beliefs and practices are losing ground.

A few considerations are in place here. First of all, this is by no means a process that takes place exclusively in Aceh. There is not an essential difference between the ban placed on so-called deviant groups and behavior in Aceh and the aggressive actions taken by agents of the state against religious minorities (such as the Ahmadiyah sect) or alleged transgressors of Islamic norms elsewhere in Indonesia. As this book goes to press, a possible (nation-wide) ban on sex outside marriage is on the agenda of the Constitutional Court. This trend is not easily stopped or reversed, firstly because—throughout Indonesia—the self-styled opponents of "Islamization" are politically weak or marginal (van Bruinessen 2013b; Ricklefs 2012), and secondly because, as Michael Peletz (1997) noted two decades ago with regard to Malaysia, for those who are critical it may be more strategic to remain silent than to take the risk of being branded as "anti-shari'a" or "un-Islamic."

I have argued that Acehnese Muslims exercise individual religious agency and that this enables them (some more than others) to negotiate the changes wrought on society by state and religious authorities and institutions. One of my central suggestions, then, has been to distinguish among the various sociopolitical arenas in which these negotiations take place. It is my contention that we should at least consider the possibility that individual agency is expanding in some respects and diminishing in others. Let me elaborate on this by making the paradox alluded to above somewhat more concrete. In Aceh, public debates about the scope and intention of Islamic law are lively and ideologically diverse but also abstract and riddled with generalizations. This, it appears, is to the advantage of those who seek to advance, or expand, shari'a law, both in public discourse and in practice. But a question that seems equally important to me is whether, at another level, the increasing dominance of normative Islam might also increase people's space for negotiation. The concept of individual religious agency allows investigation of a rather counterintuitive possibility, namely that (some, or many) ordinary Muslims do not—or at least, do not necessarily—experience the objectification of Islam as very constraining. This is because, in a world of increasingly volatile lifestyles, worldviews, and religious commitments, and of complex personal assessments and (religious and nonreligious) considerations, the options and the choices that remain or appear carry relatively more "weight." Yani was one of the harshest critics of the implementation of shari'a law among my regular interlocutors. At the same time, she felt rather comfortable about the wearing of the headscarf. Most importantly, she found personal value in the general atmosphere of debating and reflecting on scriptural norms, such as the obligation to cover one's head in front of friends or acquaintances, or the question of whether or not a woman may join the festivities of *maulid* during the time of her menstrual period.

The historical and ethnographic material presented in this book brings to the fore a strong connection between individual ethical improvement—through active moral reflection and religious self-styling—and the ways in which impersonal formal and bureaucratic norms are shaped in public contexts. This connection is crucial for our understanding of religious identities. In a "world of urgency and necessity" (Wikan 1995, 266), immediate personal desires (money, status, sex, friendship, spirituality) sometimes clash, and more often are reconciled with structural, political, and economic constraints. As I have tried to show, the moral terms in which this process of negotiation is cast are both socially grounded and specific to local, often communal concerns: safety, harmony, solidarity, justice. This leads me to consider the exciting, and potentially radical, possibility that the focus on shari'a law, as the culmination of an extended process of purist reform intended both to "discipline" and to "enlighten," has become so universal, dogmatic, and reliant on abstracted models of the human condition that it has entered a phase of self-destructive dominance, comparable, as Kai Kresse (2003, 302) suggests in relation to Islamic reformism in East Africa, to the process of the French Revolution "devouring" its own "radicalized children." Future studies will have to address this problem. I hope that my approach, diachronic and focused on different spaces of action and negotiation, will turn out beneficial in this regard.

Let me conclude by stating what, in my view, is the main contribution of this book to the study of Aceh and the history and anthropology of Islam more generally. I started out in the introduction with an explanation of the standard narrative of Acehnese history and society. This narrative is based on two major frameworks, namely religious zeal and conflict. This book shows, instead, that the ways in which people in Aceh practice and experience their faith are diverse, unpredictable, and contingent on personal projects of ethical improvement. Thus, it corrects the standard image and the stereotypes of Acehnese fanaticism. This argument has implications for the more general question of religiosity as a subject of study and the categories and mechanisms through which religious differences are integrated in the moral order of society.

As Michael Peletz (1996) has argued, addressing the tensions and interactions between mainstream or "deviant" ideas and practices requires something more than identifying "alternative" moral frameworks (such as Islam and *adat*). Throughout their lives, people seize on, and become influenced by, a variety of political and religious ideologies, which are grounded in different social hierarchies and divergent frameworks of knowledge or truth-seeking practices. The interactions between different ideologies, as well as the ways in which people position themselves in relation to these ideologies, produce moral ambivalences. Unsurprisingly, then, the stories, experiences, and events discussed in this book are full of doubts, dilemmas, and (sometimes difficult or painful) reflections on the self. From this premise, I have attempted to rethink the use of social categories in the study of Islam in Southeast Asia. One of the major problems, in my view, is that many anthropologists, when approaching religious differences, tend to rely on categories that lie, essentially, outside religion "proper," such as gender, class, locality, and (to a lesser extent) kinship. The consequence is that religion is marginalized as a framework for explaining human action. When people in Aceh talk about moral responsibility, however, they act on individual religious motivations as much as the social and moral demands that are placed on them as a daughter, a neighbor, a village leader, or a corporate executive.

How, then, can we refine our understanding of the relationship between agency and the construction of religious personhood? I have cited, rather extensively, Francis Robinson's argument about the "inward turn"—reflected in the work of South Asian Muslim intellectuals around the turn of the twentieth century—and its connection to the emergence of the Islamic "modernist" movement. Readers may be surprised, therefore, that I have given only limited attention to Islamic activists and their influence in politics and society. This is not without a reason. During my fieldwork, I found that conceptions of Muslim personhood cannot be equated with the models of ethical improvement encountered among most, if not all, Islamic "revivalist" or *dakwah*-oriented organizations. Most of my interlocutors were not particularly interested in the goal of changing society according to particular political ideas or legal orientations. I concluded that it was necessary to work toward a different understanding, one that was less deterministic and more nuanced and inclusive compared to the abundant literature that deals with religious organizations, and that seeks to explain the increasing "piety" of Muslims, the urban middle classes in particular. Such a refined understanding should include expressions of ambivalence, moral failure, and indifference toward moralizing projects, as well as the apparent social acceptance (in many different contexts and situations) of religious negligence and imperfection as contributing to rather than obstructing personal projects of ethical improvement.

To arrive at such an understanding, I have made use of the analytically versatile notion of "concerns" (Barth 1993) as well as the concept of the "ethical working on the self" (Zigon 2008, 2009a, 2009b). How, and on what basis, do people reflect on their lives as moral beings? How do they engage with their pasts when they make moral decisions? How do they act, morally, upon themselves? A central line of inquiry has been the conjunction among ethics, moral failure, and life phase. Compared to the relationship between Islam and gender, or Islam and class, the role of age, life stages, and generational interaction constitutes a highly underdeveloped terrain in the study of Muslim personhood. This is not so strange. Building sociological theories on the basis of generation is a problem that has kept scholars busy for several decades (Mannheim 1952 [1923]). Studying the meanings and cultural connotations of a term like *pemuda*—"young adults"—requires a very different set of methods and questions compared to an investigation of, say, the experience of growing up in Banda Aceh in the 1980s. The fundamental difference between "generation" and "age" as the central unit of analysis complicates the study of religiosity, which is always a product of both social and personal transformations. On the one hand, it is a rather general and socially accepted phenomenon, in Aceh and in other parts of Indonesia (and I presume in many other Muslim societies as well), that old people worry more about the afterlife than their children because they feel closer to death. At the same time, it must be acknowledged that people grow up, and become socialized and educated, in a world that is very different from that of their parents. Formative events and phases coincide with religious ideas and contestations that belong to specific moments and periods. This makes it difficult, if not impossible, to compare how younger people and older people act morally upon themselves and their environment.

It might be useful, therefore, to treat life stages, like Peletz (1988, 227–30) has treated kinship, as a double-edged sword. When people become older, their position in the moral order changes. Changing roles and expectations are framed in personalized concepts of ethical formation, like those advanced by my interlocutors quoted in this study: awareness, consciousness, reflexiveness. At the same time, the moral responsibilities associated with the process of aging are difficult to fulfill, especially when, as Rahmat implied in his ambiguous opinion about the implementation of shari'a law, society seems to be changing too fast to keep up with. In such an approach, age, and the conceptions of moral personhood attached to it, does not signify a point in time but rather an aggregate of different temporalities and associated religiosities. As I have shown, most Acehnese do not regard the formation of their ethical selves as a straight path. They are generally articulate about the fact that, as they try to change themselves for the better, they have to deal with changing moral and political constellations, as well as countless setbacks, doubts, and conflicts. The particularities of Muslim personhood in Aceh should not be sought in the adherence to an externally defined piety. If Islam in Aceh is special, it is because the extended experience with normative Islam has strengthened reflections on personal faith.

NOTES

Introduction

1. According to a popular story, Sultan Iskandar Muda had his own son executed for committing adultery, thus showing his subjects that he would not discriminate among them before the eyes of God. A contemporary (1637) report of the Dutch East India Company confirms the execution, but says nothing about adultery. Instead, it says that the king "judged his son very resentfully and feared that, after his death, he would turn his realm into a bloodbath" (cited in Djajadiningrat 1911, 183).

2. The word ulama is the plural of *alim*, Arabic for "knowledgeable person." In Indonesia, it is used both as a singular and as a plural.

3. According to reformists, intercessions rituals implied—or came dangerously close to—a form of polytheism (*shirk*). A widely spread tradition that scripturalist reformists have objected against, in Southeast Asia and elsewhere, is that of visiting holy graves (*ziarah*) (see chapters 2 and 4).

4. In Southeast Asia, the standardization of the curriculum of religious schools (through the canonization of textual curricula and skills like Qur'anic recitation, interpretation, and jurisprudence) began in the nineteenth and twentieth centuries, which is much later than the Islamic center regions, where this process began well before the sixteenth century. See, in particular, van Bruinessen 1990, 2007; Zaman 2002. This fact might also explain why the clashes between so-called modernists (or *kaum muda*, the "young generation") and traditionalists (*kaum tua*, the "old generation") were particularly bitter in this part of the world (Laffan 2003; Roff 1967; Taufik Abdullah 1971).

5. As Craig Reynolds (1995, 431) explains, this was a continuation of the colonial (scholarly) views of Indonesian societies that emphasized the essential "foreignness" of *all* world religions, including Islam but also pre-Islamic traditions such as Hinduism and Buddhism.

6. See Siegel (1969, 137–98). It is worth noting that, so far, these gender patterns, and the theme of Acehnese masculinity in particular, have been discussed primarily in the context of religious renewal and armed struggle (cf. Siapno 2002).

7. In *dayah salafiyah*, the medium of instruction is Acehnese. The dress code features a wraparound skirt (*sarong*) and a head covering (*kopiah* or *peci*) in the case of male students and a long skirt in the case of female students. Students in these institutions receive their religious training by studying the *kitab* in a *balai* (shelter used for study and teaching) rather than a classroom, sitting in a circle around the leader of the *dayah* (often called Abu, Abon, or Waled, meaning "father" in Arabic) or one of the more advanced students who, like their master, are addressed with the (originally royal Malay) title of *teungku*. The term *salafiyah*—deriving from the Arabic word *salaf*, "predecessors," denoting the first three generations of Muslims—should not be mistaken with the term "Salafism," which is commonly used to denote a particular, and globally salient, puritanical movement in Islam.

8. Muhammadiyah, founded in Yogyakarta in 1912, is the largest Islamic organization in Indonesia. Nahdlatul Ulama (NU, Awakening of the Ulama) was founded in 1926, primarily as a reaction to the success of Muhammadiyah, which was regarded by conservative Javanese ulama as a threat to their own doctrines and practices. Muhammadiyah and NU reflect a rough divide between urban middle class and rural (generally lower class) lifestyles. In Aceh, most leaders and students of "traditional" dayah (*dayah salafiyah*) associate themselves—formally or informally—with the NU, while the leaders of "modern" dayah (*dayah modern*) may or may not associate themselves with Muhammadiyah.

9. With the exception of public figures, the names I use in this book to refer to my interlocutors in Aceh are pseudonyms.

Chapter 1: History and the Imagining of Pious Aceh

1. Particularly influential, in this respect, was the attack carried out by the reformist theologians Nur al-Din al-Raniri and Abdurrauf al-Singkili, both of whom held the position of Shaykh al-Islam (religious advisor to the sultan) in the mid-seventeenth century, against the doctrines of their sixteenth-century predecessors, notably Hamzah al-Fansuri and Shams al-Din al-Sumatrani. Doctrines that became the subject of controversy included the Sufi concepts of the "Unity of Being" (*wahdat al-wujud*) and the "Perfect Man" (*al-insan al-kamil*). The controversy ignited a sharp dispute about the place of monism in Malay religious life, which would reverberate in scholarly circles for centuries to come (see Azra 2004; Laffan 2011; Riddell 2001; Wormser 2012).

2. Commercially, the Dutch were primarily interested in the spice trade of the eastern archipelago. As a result, Johor quickly surpassed Malacca as the main entrepôt in the Strait. For Aceh, Johor was an important competitor because it was better able than Malacca to attract Muslim traders (Lieberman 2009, 862–63).

3. According to some indigenous sources, the reason for the abdication was a fatwa by the Sharif of Mecca (reaching Aceh by letter), which stipulated that it was un-Islamic for a woman to rule. It is impossible to determine, on the basis of the available sources, whether this fatwa was real, or merely an excuse for a particular faction of *orangkaya* to get rid of the sultana (Djajadiningrat 1911, 191).

4. The earliest description of a religious school (designated as beunasah [*meunasah*], communal hall or prayer house) can be found in the *Hikayat Pocut Muhamat* (The story of Pocut [Prince] Muhamat), an eighteenth-century epic about the war of succession that followed on the death of the first Bugis sultan, Alauddin Ahmad Syah in 1735: "The teungku had six hundred pupils (*murib*); a cheerful noise and bustle was prevailing there. Some pupils were reciting the Qur'an, others the Masail [a book for basic Islamic instruction; see Snouck Hurgronje 1893–94, 2:2, 4, 30]. Some were reading the Ayurrumiyya [an Arabic grammar written by the Moroccan scholar Ibn Ayurrum (d. 1323)], others were translating the Fatiha [the first chapter of the Qur'an]; some were reading a Malay book (*kitab jawoe*), but others were chatting animatedly. In the western house (*rangkang*) the pupils were studying grammar; in the eastern house spelling. In the house upstream they studied mysticism (*teusawoh*), the subtle wisdom of the Hikam and the Ihya. Everyone according to his capacity; some studied Arabic works, others Malay ones. The teungku exercised the superintendence, but he had a deputy (*waki*) in every house. The *waki* bent his head in order to see how the pupils were busy spelling. Dressed in white and with white head-covering, very spruce indeed" (Drewes 1979, 130–35).

5. Van Langen (1988, 56–91) provides two examples of these decrees, including transliterations and a Dutch translation.

6. For an analysis of Dutch scorched-earth tactics, see Kreike (2012). For more comprehensive accounts of the war, see Stolwijk (2016) and van 't Veer (1969).

7. A. G. H. van Sluys, "Nota Atjeh en Onderhoorigheden 1928—October 1920," p. 8, Archief van het Koninklijk Instituut voor Taal-, Land- en Volkenkunde [currently part of the Special Collections of Leiden University Library; henceforth: KITLV], Collectie R. A. Kern, H.797, inv. nr. 417. "Normalization," for van Sluys, included a relaxation of the passport system (created in 1889), a suspension of the forced labor system, and measures intended to reverse the process of outmigration caused by the war. Many people had fled from the violence, or sought better economic opportunities in Malaya, where rubber and tin mining sectors were booming. Official reports cited grievances against the regime—including ongoing violence against the population, forced labor, limitation of movement, and the burden of taxes—as the most important reason for the outflux. Report by F. A. Liefrinck, Batavia, July 31, 1909, KITLV, Collectie R. A. Kern, H.797, inv. nr. 411; R. A. Kern, "Onderzoek Atjeh-moorden," December 16, 1921, Nationaal Archief, Den Haag, Ministerie van Koloniën: Politieke Verslagen en Berichten uit de Buitengewesten, nummer toegang 2.10.52.01 [henceforth NL-HaNA, Politieke Verslagen Buitengewesten, 2.10.52.01], inv. nr. 6; "Nota Atjeh en Onderhoorigheden 1928—October 1920; Vervolg over de jaren October 1920—Juni 1922" (undated), p. 8, KITLV, Collectie R. A. Kern, H.797, inv. nr. 418.

8. The idea of the decline of the Acehnese was very strong among European observers (Snouck Hurgronje primary among them) and connected to a more general misrepresentation of indigenous economic and political patterns and institutions as archaic versions of more advanced European models (cf. Sutherland 1995). The image of Aceh as a disorderly land, where quick tempers and pig-headedness were common features, blinded European observers to the structural transformations that had characterized Acehnese society in preceding centuries. Revisions of this historiography—for example with regard to the supposed decline of Acehnese trade under Sultana Safiyyat al-Din Syah (Khan 2017)—are still in progress.

9. Between 1873 and 1875, Kruyt served aboard a warship that patrolled the waters of the North and East Coast. In May 1873, his ship dropped anchor at the dock of Idi, one of the most important pepper ports on the North Coast. The chief of Idi was seeking an alliance with the Dutch, in return for protection against the aggression of the Sultan of Aceh and his ally (and Idi's main competitor) Simpang Ulim (Kruyt 1877, 17–20).

10. The Malay term *ilmu* (derived from the Arabic *ilm*, pl. *ulum*) may be translated as "science" or "knowledge" but also—and this is the meaning Snouck Hurgronje refers to—as knowledge of the supernatural, magical skill, or "esoteric wisdom."

11. "Governor Hens to the Governor-General," April 20, 1923, NL-HaNa, Politieke Verslagen Buitengewesten, 2.10.52.01, inv. nr. 6. One SI activist, Teuku Abdul Latif, was regarded as a risk in West Sumatra and Aceh at the same time. However, Hens stated that it was "useless" to try and keep an eye on his movements, because he worked primarily with messengers.

12. O.M. Goedhart, "Memorie van Overgave van het gouvernement Atjeh (1929)," p. 8, Nationaal Archief, Den Haag, Ministerie van Koloniën: Memories van Overgave, 1849–1962, nummer toegang 2.10.39 [henceforth NL-HaNA, Koloniën/Memories van Overgave, 2.10.39], inv. nr. 158; A.Ph. van Aken, "Memorie van Overgave van het gouvernement Atjeh (1930)," p. 27, NL-HaNA, Koloniën/Memories van Overgave, 2.10.39, inv. nr. 160.

13. The Acehnese, Snouck Hurgronje argued, had never learned to live in association with "differently-minded" (D. *andersdenkenden*). Even "foreign" Muslims, such as Arabs and Indian Muslims (Kelings), were annoyed by Acehnese arrogance and complacency. Past political and diplomatic relations had failed to make the Acehnese conscious of their own "inferiority" (Snouck Hurgronje 1893–94, 1:174, 2:372–73).

14. As suddenly as this upsurge of piety emerged, it seemed to subside again, perhaps (as one report suggested) because the economic crisis temporarily delayed associational activities. "Politiek-politioneel verslag 1932," March 4, 1933, NL-HaNa, Politieke Verslagen Buitengewesten, 2.10.52.01, inv. nr. 7.

15. Van Aken, "Memorie van Overgave," p. 144.

16. Before embarking on a career as a writer and a journalist, Zentgraaff served in the Dutch military and fought in the Dutch-Acehnese War. In 1929, he was appointed editor in chief of one of the largest newspapers in the Netherlands Indies, the *Soerabaiasch Handelsblad*. Three years later he switched to the conservative *Java-Bode*, and in 1938 he published *Atjeh!* (1938), a kind of coffee table book, or "glossy" avant la lettre: populist in tone and with lots of pictures. An homage to the infamous General van Heutsz (known in The Netherlands as the "pacificator" of Aceh) and the Dutch military, *Aceh!* was both a popular and a controversial work. In his response to the book, the "ethical" writer E. du Perron wrote that Zentgraaff was "the embodiment of everything he had come to detest in 'the Indies.'" P. J. Drooglever, "Zentgraaff, Henri Carel [1874–1940]," *Biografisch Woordenboek van Nederland*, http://resources.huygens.knaw.nl/bwn1880–2000/lemmata /bwn4/zentgraaff (accessed November 10, 2016). Zentgraaff, meanwhile, regarded *Atjeh!* as his masterpiece.

17. Sitti Saniah is a student of home economics. Nja' Ahmat is a civil servant and member of the national Indies Party (Nationaal Indische Partij), who seems to have all the characteristics of Zentgraaff's "lanky youngsters": "There is a young man there, wearing a white shirt, flannel trousers, and a black velvet kopiah [cap]. On a string around his neck dangles a golden brooch, in the form of an Acehnese rencong [dagger]. He is good at talking high Malay and eloquent. Sometimes his language is mixed with Acehnese or Dutch, just for the sake of adding charm to his talk" (Zainoe'ddin 1928).

18. Van Sluys, "Nota," p. 17. For the list, see ibid., Bijlage [appendix] No. IV.

19. Ibid., p. 14.

20. For details regarding this specific case, see Mailrapport 966X/1921, Mailrapport 1049X/ 1921, Mailrapport 1259X/1921, and Verbaal V19/4/23 No. 21, NL-HaNa, Politieke Verslagen Buitengewesten, 2.10.52.0, inv. nr. 6.

21. "Besluit van de Gouverneur-Generaal van Nederlandsch-Indië," February 15, 1922, NL-HaNa, Politieke Verslagen Buitengewesten, 2.10.52.0, inv. nr. 6.

22. "Verslag betreffende den politieken toestand in het gouvernement Atjeh en Onderhoorigheden over het jaar 1927," February 9, 1928, NL-HaNa, Politieke Verslagen Buitengewesten, 2.10.52.0, inv. nr. 7.

23. "De politieke toestand gedurende het jaar 1926," February 7, 1927, NL-HaNa, Politieke Verslagen Buitengewesten, 2.10.52.01, inv. nr. 7. See also Zentgraaff 1928, 281–82.

24. For example, a 1928 political report spoke favorably of the secretary of the Acehnese branch of the Muhammadiyah, who reportedly published "a very tolerant little tract" in which, among other things, a stand was made against the "prang sabil doctrine." There were, however, also minor irritations about the growing confidence displayed by leaders of the movement, expressed in speeches and sermons, as well as an apparent reluctance to inform the authorities about prospective meetings. "Verslag betreffende den politieken toestand in het gouvernement Atjeh en Onderhoorigheden over het jaar 1928," NL-HaNa, Politieke Verslagen Buitengewesten, 2.10.52.01, inv. nr. 7. For a more extensive discussion of Muhammadiyah in Aceh and its relationship to the colonial government, see Gedacht 2015, 461–68.

25. Sumatra Thawalib established its first Acehnese branches in Tapaktuan (early 1919) and Takengon (1926). Muhammadiyah established its first branch in Banda Aceh in 1927. Muhammadiyah leaders were formally requested not to expand their activities beyond Aceh Besar and the North Coast. "De politieke toestand gedurende het jaar 1926" (cf. Sulaiman 1988).

26. There was a direct cause for this. The government was unpleasantly surprised by the establishment of a branch in Tapaktuan, believing there was an agreement to keep the expansion on hold for the time being. When, on top of this, a public *tabligh* was organized without

requesting government permission in advance, this was seen as the straw that broke the camel's back. Communication between the government and Muhammadiyah took place through mediation by the Advisor for Native Affairs, generally on request of the Governor of Aceh. "Politiek-politioneel verslag betreffende het gewest Atjeh en Onderhoorigheden gedurende het jaar 1936," NL-HaNa, Politieke Verslagen Buitengewesten, 2.10.52.01, inv. nr. 7.

27. Mohammad Isa Sulaiman (1988, 493–94) wrote about "Arabic traders" establishing reformist schools in Aceh. There has been some debate over the question of which institution may be called the first "truly" reformist *madrasah* in Aceh. Most authors regard the Madrasah Al Khairiyah, founded by Tuanku Raja Keumala in the Great Mosque complex in Banda Aceh (possibly as early as 1916) as the first of its kind. While this school did not yet include secular elements in its curriculum, it introduced modern elements in its teaching methods, including desks, chairs, and a blackboard (Hasbi Amiruddin 2003–2004, 1:93–98; Sulaiman 1988, 494–95; Hamdiah 1992, 28–29).

28. "Verslag Tablegh Akbar! Di Loeboek III Mks. Keurekon dan Pertemoean Oelama-Oelama di Koetaradja 1–2 October 1936," p. 10, Nationaal Archief, Den Haag, Collectie 540, Dr. A. J. Piekaar, 1933–1990, nummer toegang 2.21.283 [henceforth NL-HaNA, Piekaar, 2.21.283], inv. nr. 3.

29. After the Japanese occupation, Teuku Nyak Arif became the first Resident of Aceh under the Republican government.

30. "Verslag Tablegh Akbar!"

31. Ibid. Speakers included Teungku Abdullah Lam U, Teungku Hasballah Indrapuri, and Teungku Abdullah Ujong Rimba.

32. "Politiek verslag Atjeh en Onderhoorigheden over het 1ᵉ halfjaar 1939," August 25, 1939, NL-HaNA, Politieke Verslagen Buitengewesten, 2.10.52.01, inv. nr. 7.

33. Ibid. The most prestigious project of PUSA in this early phase was the Sekolah Normaal al-Islam institute in Peusangan. In addition to religious subjects, this school was intended to offer secular education in Dutch and English. At the opening, Teuku Mohamad Djohan Alamsjah, the *zelfbestuurder* of Peusangan, thanked PUSA for "accepting his advice to build the school outside the city [kotta], where the lessons would not be disrupted by all kinds of entertainment," and where, moreover, land was available in abundance for agricultural education. "Politiek-politioneel verslag betreffende het gewest Atjeh en Onderhoorigheden gedurende de maand oktober 1939," NL-HaNa, Politieke Verslagen Buitengewesten, 2.10.52.01, inv. nr. 7.

34. After traveling and teaching for a number of years in different places in Aceh, Daud Beureueh established his own school in a village near Sigli in 1930. According to Morris (1983, 80) and Reid (1979, 23), he enjoyed all of his education in traditional *dayah* in Pidie. However, according to Hasbi Amiruddin (2003–2004, 1:67–70), he also studied for a short period at the Dutch Inlandsche School in Seulimeum. Together with Teungku Abdullah Ujong Rimba, he established Jamiatul Diniyah (1930), an organization for the creation of a network of schools based on identical curricula. See "Atjeh bergerak!," *Soeara Atjeh*, March 15, 1930; "Politiek-politioneel verslag 1932."

35. "Politiek-politioneel verslag betreffende het gewest Atjeh en Onderhoorigheden gedurende de maand december 1939," NL-HaNa, Politieke Verslagen Buitengewesten, 2.10.52.01, inv. nr. 7. Ismail Yakub (1980, 351–53) wrote that he was the first to propose the idea of uniting Acehnese ulama, after an earlier initiative (called PERGUISI, Persatuan Guru-Guru Islam di Aceh; "Association of Islamic Teachers in Aceh") had failed. Of course, it is not impossible that Ismail Yakub overstated his own role.

36. *Sinar* 3, No. 7–8, April 15, 1940.

37. T.M. Hasan, "Pendjaga agama di Atjeh," Ibid.; cf. Arif 1951; Hamdiah 1992; Sulaiman 1988.

38. Gedacht 2015, 464–65; Piekaar 1949, 41. Importantly, the cooperation between different reformist organizations did not suddenly stop in 1939. When the Sigli branch of Muhammadiyah organized a meeting to commemorate *isra mikraj* (the night journey of the Prophet Muhammad), it featured Daud Beureueh as one of the main speakers. Some people held double positions. For example, PUSA leader Teungku Abdul Wahab was appointed secretary of a new Muhammadiyah branch in Seulimeum. And when Daud Beureueh's organization Jamiatul Diniyah held a reception in Lam Paseh, it invited the Consul of Muhammadiyah Aceh, Teuku Tjoet Hasan, to give a speech. With regard to more practical issues, such as the beginning of Ramadan, both organizations followed the same line. "Politiek-politioneel verslag betreffende het gewest Atjeh en Onderhoorigheden gedurende de maand september 1939"; "Politiek-politioneel verslag betreffende het gewest Atjeh en Onderhoorigheden gedurende de maand oktober 1939," NL-HaNa, Politieke Verslagen Buitengewesten, 2.10.52.01, inv. nr. 7.

39. See, e.g., an interview with Governor A. H. Philips, *Deli Courant*, October 3, 1932.

40. "Governor Van Aken of Atjeh en Onderhoorigheden to the Governor-General in Batavia," February 25, 1934, NL-HaNa, Politieke Verslagen Buitengewesten, 2.10.52.01, inv. nr. 7.

41. Van Aken, "Memorie van Overgave."

42. For Piekaar (1949, 23–24), a Dutch historian and former government secretary in Aceh, the discussion of the changing social, economic, and political "situation" ultimately boiled down to the question of why the Dutch did not or could not recognize the "potentially dangerous" character of PUSA. Reid (1979, 25) writes: "To younger Acehnese writers of the time what was happening was an exciting total transformation of their society, marked not only by modern schools and organizational life, but by newspapers, irrigation projects, and shops and businesses in Acehnese hands. 'Awareness' (*kesadaran*) and 'consciousness' (*keinsafan*) were the key words by which the younger writers described this transformation, and for many of them it was preeminently Daud Beureu'eh who deserved the title, 'Father of the self-awareness of the Acehnese people.'" Siegel (1969, 96), in his analysis of the attraction of "modernist" Islam in the 1930s and the mid-twentieth century, focused on economic relations and the marginalization in the economy of ordinary Acehnese men (in the favor of the self-enriching class of *uleebalang*), arguing that "it was in this situation that the teachings of the [reformist] ulama were first popularly accepted as the ulama had intended them."

43. In many cases, resistance was infused by messianic or millenarian motivations, centering on the idea of holy war as a motivating force (Kartodirdjo 1972). The emergence of institutions such as the *perdikan* and the *pesantren*, which were relatively independent from the authority of local rulers and the colonial state, was a central element. Peter Carey (2007) and Michael Laffan (2011, 40–46) have argued that a large part of the followers of Prince Dipanegara, the main resistance leader in the Java War, were students of such institutions.

44. "Now, in the age of movements, the family was caught up in a series of potent political metaphors that moved it from the intimate sphere of the house (*babiliak kacie'*) to the public sphere of the newspaper and auditorium (*babiliak gadang*)" (Hadler 2008, 142).

Chapter 2: The Limits of Normative Islam

1. The spatial dimension of state practice may be taken literally as much as metaphorically. As argued by Akhil Gupta (1995, 392), "any analysis of the state requires us to conceptualize a space that is constituted by the intersection of local, regional, national, and transnational phenomena."

2. The field notes can be found at http://asiapacific.anu.edu.au/blogs/acehfieldnotes/ (accessed May–June 2012). They comprise nine handwritten notebooks of about 100 pages each, which were photocopied and then transcribed in order to be published online. Jayawardena col-

lected his data in different villages, the choice for which, in his own words, was "determined by my contacts with headmen and prominent residents from who I could expect understanding and reliable co-operation." In this book, I refer to individual notebook entries by mentioning the date (where available) as well as the number of the notebook and page numbers (of the complete entry), e.g., March 15, 1971 (VII, 62–64). In direct quotations, for the sake of readability and consistency, I have replaced symbols like "&" and added italics for non-English terms. I have not, however, changed the spelling in favor of a more modern one. The quotation above comes from the draft preface of Jayawardena's unfinished manuscript.

3. "Speech by His Excellency and Honorable Head of the Department of General Affairs (Padoeka Jangmoelia Toean Somubucho)" [1942, undated], NL-HaNA, Piekaar, 2.21.283, inv.nr. 11.

4. "Hari Raya dan Hari Merdeka," *Atjeh Sinbun; Soentingan Menjamboet: Hari Raya Idilfitri dan Djandji Kemerdekaan Indonesia*, Kugatu 2604/Sjawal 1363 [September 1944], NL-HaNA, Piekaar, 2.21.283, inv.nr. 14.

5. Only Sabang, the island located just off the coast of Banda Aceh, was re-occupied by allied forces.

6. See, e.g., "Mededeelingen toestand Atjeh, November/December 1945 (by A.J. Piekaar), No II," NL-HaNa, Piekaar, 2.21.283, inv.nr. 14. See also *Mimbar Oemoem*, No. 18, November 27, 1945; *Mimbar Oemoem*, No. 24, December 4, 1945, NL-HaNA, Piekaar, 2.21.283, inv.nr. 14.

7. The fiercest of these attacks came from Teuku Teungoh Hanafiah, an *uleebalang* from Idi and government secretary during the Japanese period. In an article entitled "Mengapa Atjeh Minta Daerah Otonoom" (*Indonesia Raya*, August 11, 1950), he compared the new leaders with *badau*, a kind of fish that eats its own young. The attacks were considered sufficiently dangerous for PUSA to spread pamphlets in which they denied the accusations. Copies of the pamphlets can be found in NL-HaNA, Piekaar, 2.21.283, inv.nrs. 20 and 23.

8. The most important communist leader in Langsa was Abdul Xarim M.S., who was appointed "government coordinator" in December 1949. See Dutch government representative J. van Baal, "Enkele gegevens over Atjeh," December 31, 1949, NL-HaNA, Piekaar, 2.21.283, inv. nr. 23.

9. See, e.g., Aspinall 2006; 2009, 152; Sulaiman 1997, 235–51. In the course of 1951, local communities increasingly clashed with the Indonesian military. See, e.g., "Intimidatie van de ABRI in Atjeh?," *Aneta*, January 15, 1951; "Verklaring van de woordvoerder van het ministerie van defensie," *Aneta*, January 16, 1951; "Razias in Kutaradja," *Aneta* August 31, 1951; "Terhadap razzia di Atjeh," *Keng Po*, November 27, 1951.

10. "Ondernemers kunnen terug naar Atjeh," *Aneta*, September 15, 1951; "De teruggave van ondernemingen in Atjeh," *Aneta*, October 3, 1951; "Teruggave ondernemingen in Atjeh practisch voltooid," *Aneta*, October 30, 1951.

11. "President bezoekt getroffen gebieden in Atjeh," *Aneta*, March 15, 1953.

12. Chandra Jayawardena Notes [henceforth CJN], undated (1964, II, 42). See also CJN, January 14, 1973 (IV, 98–100).

13. The administration of justice and the imposition of punishments was contested within the Darul Islam. See, in particular, Sjamsuddin 1985, 208; cf. Bowen 2003, 95.

14. This included violence against "traitors," as well as more mundane forms of extortion and antigovernment propaganda to align village populations with the goals of the rebellion (Sjamsuddin 1985, 207–208). John Bowen (2003, 95) discussed the Darul Islam courts with his Gayo interlocutors and was told by one of them that "in serious matters, such as someone fooling around with another man's wife, the rebels would just shoot the suspects as there was no jail."

15. According to Morris (1983, 207), the Governor of North Sumatra, S.M. Amin, "in effect handed over the *pamong praja* apparatus to the *uleebalangs*." Among the prominent traditionalist ulama who aligned themselves with the government were Muhammad Hasan Krueng Kale in

Aceh Besar, Teungku Habib Muda in West Aceh, and, most notably, Teungku Muda Waly, the revered leader of Dayah Darussalam in Labuhan Haji (South Aceh), all of whom declared the rebellion to be a violation of Islam.

16. Rusdi Sufi (2008, 78) mentioned a figure of 3,000 victims in Aceh, but his source is unclear. According to Morris (1983, 246), estimates varied between 2,000 and 6,000. Jess Melvin (2013) has recently published on anti-Chinese violence in Aceh in 1965–66.

17. "Musyawarah Alim Ulama se Daerah Istimewa Aceh yang berlangsung dari tanggal 17 s/d 18 Desember 1965," December 18, 1965, in *Kumpulan Fatwa-Fatwa Majelis Ulama Propinsi Daerah Istimewa Aceh Tahun 1965 s/d 31 Maret 1970* (Banda Aceh: Sekretariat Majelis Ulama Propinsi Daerah Istimewa Aceh, 1979).

18. "Verslag betreffende den politieken toestand in het gouvernement Atjeh en Onderhoorigheden gedurende het eerste halfjaar 1930," August 18, 1930, NL-HaNa, Politieke Verslagen Buitengewesten, 2.10.52.01, inv. nr. 7; "Politiek verslag betreffende den politieken toestand in het gouvernement Atjeh en Onderhoorigheden gedurende het jaar 1930," January 23, 1931, NL-HaNa, Politieke Verslagen Buitengewesten, 2.10.52.01, inv. nr. 7.

19. CJN, March 15, 1971 (VII, 62–64). They explained that three out of seven shares of *zakat* were raised in the form of *padi*, collected initially in a large warehouse at the Indrapuri market. This system was replaced, eventually, by a more professional organization, established and managed by Syahbandar Hasjmy, the father of later governor Ali Hasjmy (1956–64).

20. See, e.g., "Verslag 1e halfjaar 1930"; "Politiek verslag betreffende den politieken toestand in het gouvernement Atjeh en Onderhoorigheden gedurende het jaar 1930," January 23, 1931, NL-HaNa, Politieke Verslagen, 2.10.52.01, inv. nr. 7. The relationship between Panglima Polem and Teuku Tjhi' Baet, the *uleebalang* of the 7 Mukim Baet, was particularly sour. The conflict escalated in 1930, when Panglima Polem unexpectedly announced that he would lead the Friday prayer in the Baet mosque. Teuku Tjhi' Baet perceived this move as an explicit infringement of his personal authority. The government forced them to reconcile. In subsequent years, T. Tjhi' Baet's ostentatious refusal to celebrate Hari Raya Idulfitri in Lam Sih became a kind of tradition, repeating itself every year until the end of the colonial period. See "Politiek verslag 1930" (cf. Piekaar 1949, 59–60). On the longer history of conflict between both families, see Snouck Hurgronje 1893–94, 1:141; van de Velde 1982, 48.

21. P. Scholten, "Memorie van Overgave van de onderafdeeling Lam Meulo" (1933), NL-HaNa, Koloniën/Memories van Overgave, 2.10.39, inv. nr. 607.

22. CJN, November 13, 1972 (I, 71). According to Snouck Hurgronje (1893–94, 1:86–87), this was the only one of the "great mosques" founded in the seventeenth century by Sultan Iskandar Muda that had survived and still functioned as a center of religious instruction.

23. Jayawardena was also told that Panglima Polem had paid off Teungku Hasballah's debts in Kedah, thus making it possible for him to leave and return to Aceh. CJN, March 15, 1973 (VII, 62–64); November 22, 1972 (II, 26–32).

24. One of Jayawardena's interlocutors cynically added that, while the "conservatives" were prepared to send their own children to Dutch schools, they could not live with the idea of an Islamic school based on a "modern" model of instruction. CJN, February 17, 1973 (VI, 53–54).

25. CJN, January 20, 1973 (V, 5–12).

26. "It is said that the males were more divided than the females. The latter were mostly in favour of the school; and instances are cited of women helping to build the school being dragged away by anti-school husbands." CJN, November 20, 1972 (II, 8–15).

27. CJN, September 18, 1972 (I, 21).

28. Sjamsuddin (1985, 176–77) relates an incident in which Teungku Hasballah was hit by a military truck. "The accident shocked the villagers, and the situation in the rural areas of Great Aceh became tense. Hence, the military authorities feared that it would provoke riots as a pro-

test. Before it was too late, the military authorities made a special effort to apologize to the ulama and publicly announced that it was a genuine accident and that the driver of the truck had been punished."

29. Chandra Jayawardena, fieldwork report, "Religious influences on social life in Atjeh" (undated); see http://asiapacific.anu.edu.au/blogs/acehfieldnotes/unpublished-material/applications -for-funding-and-reports-to-the-university/religious-influences-on-social-life-in-atjeh (accessed November 8, 2016).

30. CJN, September 19, 1972 (I, 32). It is not clear from the notes whether this is one informant's reflection or Jayawardena's summary of multiple recollections.

31. CJN, undated (1964, II, 56–59).

32. Ibid., 3–7.

33. *Ziarah* and *kenduri kematian* are as common today as they are contested (see chapter 4). For an elaborate discussion of debates about these practices in the context of Gayo history and society, see Bowen (1993, 21–32, 229–72).

34. CJN, November 22, 1972 (II, 33–35).

35. According to Snouck Hurgronje (1893–94, 1:417), "Srabi" or "Sirabi" was the much feared spirit of an adulterous woman, a daughter of a religious scholar originally named "Rabiah," who was killed by her lover and buried in Tanjong, close to Banda Aceh. According to Siegel (1969, 157–60), Nek Rabi was regarded as a particularly powerful and dangerous spirit, who occasionally took possession of midwives, particularly during difficult deliveries, and thus had to be appeased. In Pidie, a different story about the origin of Nek Rabi was told. "Nek Rabi is the spirit of a woman who lived in Kotaradja, the capital of Atjeh. One night as she was returning home from reading the Koran, someone mistook her for a thief and cut off her head. The murderer took her head to a place in Atjeh proper called Indrapuri and buried it. Her body was buried in Kotaradja. Because Nek Rabi died before her appointed time, she goes about asking for things from women while they are giving birth. She only appears, however, if something improper has been done in the ceremonies before birth, especially during the chandoeri of the seventh month. She possesses the midwife, who then speaks with the spirit's voice and who cannot continue to deliver the baby."

36. CJN, November 25, 1972 (II, 44–45).

37. CJN, November 22, 1972 (II, 33–35).

38. CJN, January 1, 1973 (IV, 33).

39. CJN, November 26, 1972 (II, 63).

40. CJN, undated (1964, II, 8–11).

41. Ibid.

42. *Pawang* may be translated as "expert" (often used in the context of knowledge of magical powers), "guide," or "steersman." Snouck Hurgronje also made note of the term, but only in reference to the owners of fishing boats, not in relation to healers or diviners (Snouck Hurgronje 1893–94, 1:302–307). I never came across this term during my own fieldwork. Both in Blang Daruet and in Jurong people spoke of *orang berobat* or *dukun*. Of these two terms, *orang berobat* was generally seen as the safest choice, while *dukun* was also used in derogatory ways, evoking associations with superstition, deceit, magic, or witchcraft.

43. CJN, undated (1964, I, 64–65).

44. Ibid.

45. CJN, December 18, 1972 (III, 55–61).

46. "Laporan Umum Pemerintah Daerah Propinsi Daerah Istimewa Atjeh kepada Bapak Presiden Republik Indonesia Jendral Soeharto," August 30, 1968.

47. See the yearly reports of the Indrapuri subdistrict government ("Lapuran tahunan daerah Ketj. Inderapuri"), 1965–68 and 1972–73. Badan Arsip dan Perpustakaan Provinsi Nanggroe Aceh

Darussalam, Daftar Pertelaan Arsip Kecamatan Indrapuri Kebupaten Daerah Tingkat II Aceh Besar Periode Tahun 1966–1983 [henceforth Arsip NAD, DPA Indrapuri], no. inv. 38/8.

48. "Seruan meramaikan Mesdjid-Menasah dan Musalla2," August 15, 1967, Arsip NAD, DPA Indrapuri, no. inv. 45/8.

49. "Rapat Musjawarah Kemukiman Gle Jeueng," April 17, 1966. Arsip NAD, DPA Indrapuri, no. inv. 25/3.

50. "Keputusan No. 171/1963," November 23, 1973, Arsip NAD, DPA Indrapuri, no. inv. 44/8.

51. "Keputusan No. 6/II/KIH/1964," April 15, 1964, Arsip NAD, DPA Indrapuri, no. inv. 44/8.

52. See, e.g., the folder entitled "Surat-surat sehubungan dengan penumpulan-pengupulan zakat fitra dalam kecamatan indrapuri tahun 1974 s/d 1976," Arsip NAD, DPA Indrapuri, no. inv. 55/9.

53. CJN, March 25, 1973 (VII, 83–87); March 11, 1973 (VII, 37–38).

54. According to Snouck Hurgronje, villages were led by a *geuchik*, who took care of worldly affairs, and an *imam meunasah*, who took care of religious affairs, both of them enjoying a similar level of authority. Within the system of the New Order, however, the role of the *geuchik* became more central. Siapno (2002, 168–69) speaks in this context of the "Javanization" of Acehnese villages. It seems that the *geuchik* came to be mostly appointed by the *camat* or the *bupati*, disregarding a 1962 regulation by Governor Ali Hasjmy, which had stipulated that village heads should be elected (or reelected) every five years.

55. "Lapuran tahunan . . . 1965," Arsip NAD, DPA Indrapuri, no. inv. 38/8.

56. CJN, February 4, 1973 (V, 94).

57. As one of Jayawardena's interlocutors put it, "in some situations the *keuchik* is in front and the *teungku* at the back," while in other situations it should be the other way around. CJN, November 22, 1972 (II, 37).

58. In order of the total number of votes: Golkar (28,467), Parmusi (26,870), Perti (18,637), PSII (11,422), and NU (6,564) (Soeyatno 1977, 74).

59. The police granted Golkar much more time and space to campaign than the other parties. In addition, various tactics of intimidation were employed by the government, including the *camat* instructing local leaders and the army to go door to door telling people to vote for Golkar. CJN, November 22, 1972 (II, 37).

60. No party branches were allowed below the district (*kebupaten*) level. However, as Soeyatno and also Jayawardena noted, party politics affected the subdistrict and the village (and vice versa) in a range of informal ways.

61. "This expressed itself in behaviour when those in authority were somewhat restrained in their use of power to restrict PSII activities—that is the local authorities. This mood continues still. The motto is 'djangan keras' [don't be harsh]. That is, don't provoke the [government] to such a point where it must act to save face. Whatever your opposition, there are some things that you can cooperate in—such as education, economic development, other projects that will help the locality—in these cooperation is possible. In return they may help with some money in political activities, even attend a general discussion." CJN, November 22, 1972 (II, 37).

62. CJN, September 19, 1972 (I, 22). In the 1987 article, Jayawardena used pseudonyms. As the original field notes were publicly available at the time of my research, and because it would be confusing to use different designations, I decided to use the real names here. In quotations from the article, I replaced the pseudonyms with the real names, placed between square brackets.

63. The term *rateb* refers to a religious practice that includes Sufi-inspired chanting (*dhikr*), poetry, body movements, and dance, often in the form of a competition between two or more groups. The practice of *rateb* has an edifying component, educating ordinary people in basic reli-

gious knowledge through a form of popular entertainment (Snouck Hurgronje 1893–94, 2:220–65). The form of *rateb meusifeut*, although not performed by opposing "teams," is similar to the more familiar *rateb seudati*, in that it follows a pattern of alternating questions and answers in certain fields of Islamic knowledge, like *fiqh* or *tauhid*, for an actively participating audience.

64. As was explained to Jayawardena, the *camat* had told the *geuchik* that "he was now too old, that new processes of administration required literacy, [and that] many people in the kampung were opposed to him." CJN, December 27, 1972 (IV, 6–7); January 22, 1973 (V, 26–28).

65. The full text of the letter to the *bupati* is copied in the field notes. "Permohonan pengembangan kampung Darang mesjid, pada statusnya semula sebagai satu kampung yang berdiri sendiri," May 7, 1972; See CJN, February 4, 1973 (V, 95–98). For the earlier appeal made to the *camat*, see CJN, January 20, 1973 (V, 5–12).

66. CJN, February 3, 1973 (V, 87–91).

67. CJN, February 17, 1973 (VL, 53–54).

68. CJN, March 14, 1973 (VII, 48).

69. CJN, February 3, 1973 (V, 84–85).

Chapter 3: Village Society and the Problem of Moral Authority

1. The Aceh-born anthropologist Irwan Abdullah once explained this to me in the following way: "In Java, if there is a problem, a village problem or a political problem, people may call a *kiai* [leader of a *pesantren*]. . . . They may do so openly or discretely, or they may choose not to go to the *kiai* at all. But in Aceh, if something happens, whether in a small village in the countryside or in the *pendopo* [the Governor's Residence], the ulama are always there, sitting side by side with officials. This is the difference" (personal communication, October 2008).

2. The word *masalah* is usually translated as "problem" or "issue." Since these words do not convey the charge and sensitivity that the use of *masalah* carried in this particular context, I have taken the liberty of translating the word as "crisis."

3. As other scholars have argued, this process was reinforced, firstly, by the emergence of a class of Muslim intellectuals who were not affiliated to the centers of traditional Islamic learning, and secondly, by mass media, which have made public debates about religious norms accessible to a majority of ordinary Muslims (Eickelman and Anderson 2003, 4–12; Riddell 2001, 294–97; cf. Farish 2002; Feener 2007; Hirschkind 2006; Hoesterey 2015; Howell 2008; Kamrava 2006; Kersten 2011; Taji-Farouki 2004).

4. As administrators, academics (mainly economists), engineers, and intellectuals, the technocrats were the embodiment of the New Order's focus on economic development and political stability. See Aspinall 2009, 52–55; Kell 1995, 29–32; McGibbon 2006, 320–29; Morris 1983, 269–302; Schlegel 1979.

5. The *ulama dayah* were reluctant, moreover, to support a socially disruptive rebellion for reasons categorized by Aspinall (2009, 204) as "legalistic." Traditionalist ulama have a general aversion, based on particular dispositions in Islamic Shafi'i jurisprudence, against rebellion. As Isa Sulaiman (2006, 130–31) explained, rebellion is thought of as a situation of chaos and "discord" (*fitnah*), which might be seen as worse than the prevalent situation. Thus, in the 1950s traditionalist scholars condemned the Darul Islam rebellion as "*bughat* (a revolt against a legal government) and as such forbidden."

6. According to Tim Kell (1995, 47–50), by entering the state bureaucracy and the "modern sector" of the economy, the ulama ceased to be "a cohesive and independent class powerful enough to confront political and ideological foes." In Rodd McGibbon's (2006, 328–29) view, by the time the New Order collapsed in 1998, they had already given up their historical role as

"agents of change." Instead, they had become a "fragmented and deeply conservative political force" (cf. Aspinall 2009, 202–208; Ishak 2001; Morris 1983).

7. The ideological basis of shari'a law in Aceh is what Feener calls the "*da'wa* paradigm," a synthesis of Islamic scripturalism, economic developmentalism, and Indonesian nationalism. The *da'wa* paradigm is an Indonesian rather than an exclusively Acehnese phenomenon. However, it has been particularly salient in Aceh, because the central state has treated the province as a kind of "laboratory" for shari'a-inspired policies and regulations. In this process, Feener (2013, 42–47) argues, the "technocrats" played a central role.

8. Partai Daulat Aceh (PDA) was founded in 2007 as a party of non-GAM ulama and *dayah* students. It has been regarded as "largely representing the religious establishment co-opted by the Indonesian government during the conflict" (ICG 2008, 2). However, in the run-up to the 2009 legislative elections it became attractive both to HUDA and to "a number of pro-GAM religious leaders and *dayah* students because of its high rhetorical commitment to the implementation of Sharia" (Salim 2009, 13). Electorally, PDA has not been particularly successful, winning about two percent of the votes and securing one representative in the provincial parliament in the elections of 2009 and 2014.

9. It is important to emphasize, though, that horizontal conflicts—although certainly occurring—were not very widespread and were actually quite rare. It seems that dissatisfaction about the distribution of aid and uneven economic opportunities and development was directed more often at the government and the so-called Badan Rehabilitasi dan Rekonstruksi Aceh-Nias (BRR), the "Agency for the Rehabilitation and Reconstruction of Aceh and Nias," which oversaw the process of post-disaster reconstruction (Annemarie Samuels, personal communication, January 21, 2016).

Chapter 4: Islamic Scripturalism and Everyday Life after the Disaster

1. The PKS has been less successful in Aceh compared to the national level, winning only 3.8 percent of the votes. One of the most visible and vocal Islamic students' movements in the province is Kesatuan Aksi Mahasiswa Islam Indonesia (KAMMI), which established a branch in 1998. KAMMI activists associate themselves with the global Islamist movement, and have campaigned fiercely for a strict implementation of shari'a law (Aspinall 2009, 193–99). For the growing influence of "salafist" streams—and the political tension that results from it—see IPAC 2016. Radically Islamist movements, such as Hizbut Tahrir Indonesia (HTI) and the Front Pembela Islam (FPI) have had difficulties establishing themselves in Aceh (Marzi Afriko 2010). On the failure of an offshoot of Jemaah Islamiyah (an extremist and violent fringe group tied to Al Qaida) to establish a training camp for aspiring *jihadis* in Aceh, see ICG 2010.

2. As Annemarie Samuels (2012b, 745–46) has shown, this was a more general feature of tsunami-affected areas in Aceh.

3. This is a common argument, both in Aceh and elsewhere in Indonesia (see, e.g., Jones 2010). Meli illustrated her point with a personal experience. Once, when visiting the hospital, she sat next to a woman with a folded up headscarf in her hand. Obviously, Meli said, this woman planned to put on the scarf once she was called for treatment. But the hospital itself was also a public place. So clearly, she was being hypocritical. A similar complaint I heard often was about the girls and young women visiting the Pizza Hut, an American fast-food restaurant accessible only to the higher ends of the middle class. Here, women would arrive in big expensive cars, occasionally with male companions, while everyone could see that they quickly put on their scarf only seconds before leaving their vehicles.

4. In English, the Indonesian word *semangat* is often translated as "spirit." I do not use this term because of the possible confusion with spirit-beings. There is a range of other possible translations, including "soul," "passion," "zeal," "vigor," "morale," and "vitality."

5. This was not an outrageous thought. In Aceh, it is commonly thought that witches seek out the body parts of dead babies for use in their magic. When babies die, their graves are guarded for a period of at least ten days to make sure that they are not opened.

6. *Berobat* means going to a doctor. In this context, it meant going to a religious specialist, or someone with the religious or mystical knowledge to neutralize the spell. At a later moment we talked more explicitly about the use of "white magic" (*ilmu putih*).

7. In Aceh, as in other parts of Indonesia, there are many different traditional healers, ranging from specialists in fractured bones to more esoteric types.

8. It is commonly said that every person has to deal with his or her mother in three worlds: the womb (*kandungan*), the world of the living (*alam dunia*), and the afterlife (*akhirat*). As a result, mothers are thought to have a greater responsibility for their children compared to fathers. Analogously, people carry a greater debt toward their mother.

9. Meli told me two stories in this context. The first was the West Sumatran story of Amad Ramanyong (more widely known in Indonesia as the story of Maling Kundang), a tale about a rebellious son who turns to stone after renouncing his own mother, thereby denying his origins as well as the existence of God. The second story was about a man who lived in the time of the Prophet Muhammad and who could not die. Although he wanted to die, his spirit (*nyawa*) refused to leave his body. When the people noticed this, they called the Prophet, who said that the man had disobeyed his mother. Only after the man had visited his mother and asked her for forgiveness was he able to depart from the world.

10. Other strange things happened. According to Meli, her mother suddenly knew things for reasons that were unexplainable. If people walked by, she knew what they were up to. She knew the character of people she had never met. When Meli's brother had visited a *dukun*, and wanted to give her blessed water to drink without saying what it was, she knew it was *air rajah* (water from an amulet) and refused to drink it.

11. When I asked her whether she had considered borrowing the money, she answered resolutely that this was not an option. Like many others, she believed that the meaning of the pilgrimage lies in the process that leads up to it as much as in the ritual itself. The act of saving is an act of sacrifice. There is also another reason why borrowing money is considered a bad idea. When people die during the hajj, they are thought to go straight to heaven. One of the exceptions is when there are unpaid debts.

12. See also, in this regard, the work of Daan Beekers (2014, 2015, 2018) on the impact of the inward turn—or what he calls a "'reflexive turn': a strong emphasis on inner conviction, dedication and self-reflection" (2014, 73)—among young observant Muslims and Christians in the Netherlands. The inward turn, it appears, is a truly global phenomenon, not limited to Muslim majority societies, or—indeed—adherents of Islam (cf. de Koning 2018; Robbins 2004).

Chapter 5: Becoming Better Muslims: Sinning, Repentance, Improvement

1. A particularly fascinating element in the drafting of the Qanun Jinayat in 2008–2009 was the active involvement of a number of prominent women's rights advocates. They withdrew from the consultations when a conservative faction hijacked the process and the provision of stoning was included (see Großmann 2015).

2. According to the Jakarta-based Institute of Criminal Justice Reform, 339 people were punished by caning in 2016 (the vast majority of whom were convicted gamblers). See http:// icjr.or.id/praktek-hukuman-cambuk-di-aceh-meningkat-evaluasi-atas-qanun-jinayat-harus -dilakukan-pemerintah/ (accessed May 21, 2017). On May 17, 2017, in the first case of its kind, two men were sentenced to 85 strokes of the cane for engaging in a sexual relationship. See http://icjr .or.id/icjr-kritik-keras-hukuman-cambuk-bagi-pasangan-lgbt-di-aceh/ (accessed May 21, 2017).

3. Controversial local bylaws include, for example, a regulation announced in 2010 by the *bupati* of West Aceh that prohibited women from wearing pants, as well as a measure announced by the mayor of Lhokseumawe that prohibits women from sitting on the back of a motorcycle with their legs astride. Both regulations prompted heated debates in local, national, and even international media.

4. Formally, members of the WH are not allowed to arrest people, but only to "reprimand" (*tegur*) and offer "advice" (*nasehat*). Most transgressions of shari'a regulations result in public lectures and the "registration" of the transgressors' names and personal details (both of which can be perceived as deeply humiliating). Arrests are made, however, by the Civil Service Police Unit (Satpol Polisi Pamong Praja), the organization with which the WH was merged in 2008. Officers of the Satpol PP regularly join the WH on their patrols (see Feener 2013, 219–49 and Otto and Otto 2015 for detailed discussions of the role and daily routines of the WH).

5. A commonly heard complaint, for example, is that the shari'a police, during their patrols and "raids" (*razia*), stop motorcycles rather than cars. Another problem is that poor people are much more likely than rich people to be subjected to corporal punishments, as they often do not have the option to pay a (large) fine instead.

6. While in Indonesia the word "youth" (*pemuda*) is used in a general sense, in this particular context it refers to the institutionalized role of male-gendered young adults (roughly between fifteen and thirty years old), who, according to local customs, are responsible for a number of village chores, such as digging graves or preparing festivities, but also for guarding the village against disruptions and bad influences from "outside." The latter may include thieves, but also public morality breaches. As Syihab, the "head" of the *pemuda* (Ketua Pemuda) in Jurong, summarized it, the *pemuda* are those "in front," taking care of the boundaries between the domain of the village and the "outside world."

7. In an article on "embodied narratives of disaster," Annemarie Samuels (2016, 810) analyzes how the tsunami was experienced as the world's "unmaking," with embodied narratives functioning as "a crucial site of disaster memory and a social way of remaking the post-disaster world."

8. That is, a "nominal" Muslim. Kartu Tanda Penduduk (KTP) is the official Indonesian identity card.

9. According to Indra, shari'a was directed primarily to "small people" (*orang kecil*). "My phone has become a piece of evidence. If they think that gambling is a problem, then they should take on the center (*pusat*) and tackle the bosses (*towkay*), not the people who play."

GLOSSARY AND ABBREVIATIONS

The terms appearing below in italics are from Indonesian/Malay, except where specifically listed as Acehnese (Ac.), Arabic (Ar.), Chinese (C.), or Dutch (D.).

adat. local custom

akhirat. the afterlife

alim (Ar. *ʿalim*). (religiously) learned person

aparat. (colloquial) the security "apparatus" (military, police, and intelligence)

asar. mid-afternoon prayer; one of the five mandatory daily prayers in Islam (Ar. *salat al-ʿasr*)

azan. call to prayer

balai. hall or pavilion; used to refer to a simple wooden structure that is used for community gatherings and religious study

bupati. district head

camat. subdistrict head

daerah istimewa. special region; used to refer to the exceptional legal status accorded to the province of Aceh in the 1950s and 1960s, and from 1999 onward

dakwah (Ar. *daʿwa*). Islamic religious propagation

Darul Islam. (DI) abode of Islam; armed insurrection against the Indonesian Republic to establish an Islamic state in the 1950s

dayah (Ac.). traditional Islamic boarding school in Aceh

desa. village

dhikr (Ar.). Sufi ritual "remembrance" of God

DI/TII. (Darul Islam/Tentara Islam Indonesia). see Darul Islam

doa (Ar. *duʿa*). invocation, or supplicatory prayer

dosa. sin

DPRA. (Dewan Perwakilan Rakyat Aceh) Aceh Provincial Legislative Assembly

DPRD. (Dewan Perwakilan Rakyat Daerah) Provincial Legislative Assembly

dukun. healer, or shaman

fatwa. legal opinion issued by a Muslim jurist

fiqh (Ar.). Islamic jurisprudence

fitnah. trial, or testing; commonly used to refer to treachery or discord

fitrah. see *zakat al-fitr*

GAM. (Gerakan Aceh Merdeka) Free Aceh Movement

gampong (Ac.). see *kampung*

geuchik (Ac.). village head

Golkar. (Golongan Karya) Functional Groups; government "party" and political apparatus during the Suharto era

gotong royong. literally "to share the burden"; used to refer to communal work or labor

hadith (Ar.). words and deeds of the Prophet Muhammad transmitted through tradition hajj (Ar.). Muslim pilgrimage to Mecca

halal. lawful, or permitted according to Islamic law

hantu. ghost, or demon

haram. unlawful, or forbidden according to Islamic law

hikmah. wisdom, often with religious connotations

HUDA. (Himpunan Ulama Dayah Aceh) Assembly of Traditionalist Ulama Aceh; established in 1999

hukum. law; often used to refer to Islamic law

IAIN. (Institut Agama Islam Negeri) State Islamic Studies Institute

ibadah. ritual practice, or worship

ilmu. literally "knowledge"; used in Indonesia to refer to religious learning, modern science, or esoteric/magical knowledge

imam. leader of congregational prayers in a mosque

imam meunasah (Ac.). village-level religious leader; also teungku meunasah

iman. faith

isya. evening prayer; one of the five mandatory daily prayers in Islam (Ar. *salat al-isha*)

jihad. literally "struggle"; used popularly in the sense of "holy war"

jilbab. Muslim women's headscarf

jinn (Ar.). spirit, or supernatural being

kadi (Ar. *qadi*). Islamic judge

kafir (Ar./Ac. *kaphe*). unbeliever, or infidel

kampung (Ac. *gampong*). village

kaphe (Ac./Ar.). see *kafir*

Kapolsek. (Kepala Polisi Sektor) Local Chief of Police

kaum muda. young generation; used to refer to reformist Muslims in the early to mid-twentieth-century Malay-Indonesian world

kaum tua. old generation; used to refer to traditionalist Muslims in the early to mid-twentieth-century Malay-Indonesian world

kebupaten. district

kecamatan. subdistrict

kedai. (coffee-)shop

kenduri. ritual meal, or feast

keramat. holy or miracle-working quality (ascribed to people, trees, objects, graves, etc.), sanctity, or shrine

khalwat. literally "seclusion"; often used in the sense of inappropriate association between marriageable men and women

khamr (Ar.). wine, or intoxicating drink

(Hari) Kiamat. Judgment Day

kiblat (Ar. *qiblah*). the directions Muslims face during prayer

kitab kuning. literally "yellow books"; used to refer to the religious texts studied in traditional institutions of Islamic learning in Southeast Asia (*pesantren, dayah*, etc.)

kolot. traditional, or orthodox

Kompeuni (Ac.). (Dutch East India) Company; used to refer to the Dutch, or the Dutch colonial government

KTP. (Kartu Tanda Penduduk) Indonesian state-issued identity card

KUA. (Kantor Urusan Agama) Office for Religious Affairs

madrasah. "modern-style" Islamic school in Indonesia

magrib. sunset prayer; one of the five mandatory daily prayers in Islam (Ar. *salat al-maghrib*)

Mahkamah Syariah. Shari'a Court

Maibkatra. (Madjelis agama Islam oentoek bantoean kemakmoeran Asia Timoer Raja di Atjeh) Islamic religious council for the advancement of Greater East Asia in Aceh (established during the Japanese occupation)

maisir (Ar.). gambling

masjid. mosque

Masyumi. (Majelis Syuro Muslimin Indonesia) Consultative Council of Indonesian Muslims); established in 1943 during the Japanese occupation; banned in 1960 by President Sukarno

maulid (Ar. *mawlid*). birthday (especially of the Prophet Muhammad)

merantau. long-term sojourn away from home for purposes of work or education

meunasah (Ac.). traditional village institution used for basic Islamic education, prayer, and other communal functions

MPU. (Majelis Permusyawaratan Ulama) Aceh's provincial-level Ulama Council

Muhammadiyah. Indonesian "modernist" Islamic mass organization, established in 1912 in Yogyakarta, Central Java

MUI. (Majelis Ulama Indonesia) Indonesian National Ulama Council

mukim. area served by a mosque; in Aceh also a territorial unit consisting of several villages

musapat (Ac.). *adat* (customary) court

musholla. prayer house or room

musyawarah. consultation, or meeting leading to a consensus

nafsu. desire, or (bodily) passion

negeri. land, or state; in early times also used to refer to a town or city

New Order. the authoritarian developmentalist state under President Suharto (1965–1998)

NGO. nongovernmental organization

NII. (Negara Islam Indonesia) Islamic State of Indonesia; proclaimed in 1949 by Kartosoewirjo in West Java

NU. (Nahdlatul Ulama) Indonesian "traditionalist" Islamic mass organization; established in 1926 in Surabaya, East Java

orangkaya. literally "rich person"; used to refer to merchant-aristocrats in the early modern Malay-Indonesian world

PA. (Partai Aceh) Aceh Party; political party established in 2007 by members of the disbanded GAM

pahala. divine rewards for good works

panglima. (military) commander

Parmusi. (Partai Muslimin Indonesia) Muslim Party of Indonesia; successor of Masyumi, established in 1970 in Malang, East Java

pawang. literally "expert," or "navigator"; often used to refer to healer-diviners

PDA. (Partai Daulat Aceh) Aceh Sovereignty Party; political party of "traditionalist" ulama established in 2007.

pemuda. literally "youth"; often used to refer to (semi-)institutionalized groups (or gangs) of young adult males

Pemuda PUSA. PUSA Youth; youth organization affiliated with PUSA

pendatang. newcomers, or immigrants

pengajian. assembly for purposes of Islamic learning

perang sabil. holy war

perdamaian. reconciliation ritual

Perti. (Persatuan Tarbijah Islamijah) Islamic Educational Association; established in 1930 in West Sumatra

pesantren. traditional Islamic boarding school

peusijeuk (Ac.). Acehnese ritual practice of "cooling down" things that are new and therefore "hot"

PKS. (Partai Keadilan Sejahtera) Justice and Prosperity Party; initially established as Partai Keadilan (Justice Party) in 1998 in Jakarta

PNS. (Pegawai Negeri Sipil) civil servant

PPP. (Partai Persatuan Pembangunan) United Development Party; Islamic political party established in 1973 as the result of a merger of four Islamic parties (NU, Parmusi, Perti, and PSII).

PSII. (Partai Sarekat Islam Indonesia) Islamic Association Party of Indonesia; political party based on the former Sarekat Islam, established as a split-off from Masyumi in 1947

puasa. to fast; often used in reference to the Islamic fasting month (Ramadan)

PUSA. (Persatuan Ulama-Ulama Seluruh Aceh) All Aceh Association of Ulama

qanun **(Ar.).** law or regulation enacted by a government; used to refer to Islamic legislation in contemporary Aceh

Qanun Jinayat. Aceh's Islamic criminal law code

Qur'an. The book of Islamic revelation

Ramadan. Islamic fasting month

Raskin. (Beras untuk Rakyat Miskin) Rice for the Poor; government program providing subsidized food to the poor

rateb **(Ac.).** Acehnese religious practice that includes Sufi-inspired chanting (*dhikr*), poetry, and/or body percussion

razia. raid by the police or the WH (Aceh's "shari'a police")

rezeki. blessing, or gift from God; often used to refer to livelihood or earnings

sagi. literally "corner"; (pre-)colonial era district of Aceh Besar

salat. Islamic prayer; required of individual Muslims five times daily (respectively *subuh*; *zuhur*; *asar*; *magrib*; *isya*)

santri (wati). (female) students from Aceh's traditional Islamic schools

sarakata. royal edict, or seal

sawah. irrigated rice field

sedekah **(Ar.** *sadaqa***).** voluntary giving, or alms

Sekdes. (Sekretaris Desa) Village Secretary

semangat. soul, spirit, or morale

serambi Mekkah. "verandah of Mecca"; used as an epithet for Aceh

seudati **(Ac.).** traditional dancing and chanting contest performed by young boys dressed as girls

shari'a **(Ar.).** literally "path," or "way"; often translated as "Islamic law" (I./Ac. *syariah*)

shirk. association with God; used to refer to a deviation from monotheism

SI. (Sarekat Islam) Islamic Association (originally Sarekat Dagang Islam, "Association of Islamic Traders"); Indonesian Islamic mass movement established in 1905 in Surakarta (Solo), Central Java

subuh. dawn prayer; one of the five mandatory daily prayers in Islam (Ar. *salat al-fajr*)

Sufism. Islamic mysticism

syariah. see shari'a

syiar **(Ar.** shi'ar**).** "symbolism" of Islam

syahid. martyr in a holy war

T. see Teuku

tabligh **(Ar.).** public religious lecture, or religious propagation

tahlil. utterance of the formula of faith, *la ilaha illa-llah* ("there is no God but God")

takdir. fate

talkin. prayer for the deceased

tarawih. recommended night prayers, typically performed during the Islamic fasting month (Ramadan) *tarbiyah* (Ar.). education, or upbringing; often referred to in association with the Islamic revivalist movement of the 1970s and 1980s

tarekat (Ar. *tariqa*). literally "path" or "way"; used to refer to a Sufi order

tasawuf. Islamic mysticism; Sufism

tauhid. Islamic doctrine that declares the oneness of God

teuha peut (Ac.). literally "four elders"; Acehnese village council

Teuku (Ac.). Acehnese *adat* title; formerly used to refer to the traditional Acehnese landed nobility (*uleebalang*)

Teungku (Ac.). Acehnese religious title; used to refer to Acehnese religious teachers (ulama)

teungku meunasah (Ac.). village-level religious leader; also *imam meunasah*

Tgk. see Teungku

TNI. (Tentara Nasional Indonesia) Indonesian National Military

towkay. (C.) boss, or business owner

UIN. (Universitas Islam Negeri) National Islamic University

ulama (Ar. ʿulama). Islamic religious teacher or scholar; in Indonesia, this plural form is also used for an individual teacher (Ar. *ʿalim*)

ulama dayah (Ac.). leader of a *dayah* (Acehnese traditional Islamic school); used to refer to "traditionalist" ulama in Aceh

uleebalang (Ac.). the traditional Acehnese landed nobility

umara. government officials

umma (Ar.). the Islamic community

Unsyiah. (Universitas Syiah Kuala) Syiah Kuala University, Banda Aceh

wakaf (Ar. *waqf*). religious endowment

wali. guardian

WH. (Wilayatul Hisbah) Aceh's "shariʿa police"

zakat. religious tithe; required of individual Muslims with sufficient financial means (also known as *zakat al-mal* [Ar.], "zakat on wealth")

zakat al-fitr (Ar.). religious tithe that is given at the end of the fasting month (Ramadan); required of individual Muslims with sufficient financial means

zelfbestuurder (D.). autonomous ruler

ziarah. visitation; often used to refer to the practice of visiting a grave for the purpose of praying for the deceased

zina. fornication, or adultery

zuhur. midday prayer; one of the five mandatory daily prayers in Islam (Ar. *salat al-zuhr*)

REFERENCES

Abrams, Philip. 1988. "Notes on the Difficulty of Studying the State (1977)." *Journal of Historical Sociology* 1(1): 58–89.

Afrianty, Dina. 2015a. "Local Women's NGOs and the Reform of Islamic law in Aceh: The Case of MISPI." In *Islam and the Limits of the State: Reconfigurations of Practice, Community and Authority in Contemporary Aceh*, edited by R. Michael Feener, David Kloos, and Annemarie Samuels, 118–40. Leiden: Brill.

———. 2015b. *Women and Sharia Law in Northern Indonesia: Local Women's NGOs and the Reform of Islamic Law in Aceh*. Abingdon and New York: Routledge.

Ahearn, Laura M. 2001. "Language and Agency." *Annual Review of Anthropology* 30: 109–37.

Alfian. 1977. "Cendekiawan dan Ulama dalam Masyarakat Aceh: Sebuah Pengamatan Permulaan," In *Segi-Segi Sosial Budaya Masyarakat Aceh: Hasil-hasil Penelitian dengan Metode "Grounded Research,"* edited by Alfian, 199–218. Jakarta: LP3ES.

Ali Panglima Polem, T. Muhammed. 1972. *Memoires van Teuku Muhammed Ali Panglima Polem*. Translated by J. H. J. Brendgen. Unpublished memoirs.

Andaya, Leonard Y. 2008. *Leaves of the Same Tree: Trade and Ethnicity in the Straits of Melaka*. Honolulu: University of Hawai'i Press.

Aretxaga, Begoña. 2003. "Maddening States." *Annual Review of Anthropology* 32: 393–410.

Arif, Abdullah. 1951. *Tindjauan Sedjarah Pergerakan di Atjeh: Bingkisan Kenang2an Kongres Besar Pusa dan P. Pusa*. Kutaradja.

Aryanti, Tutin. 2013. "A Claim to Space: Debating Female Religious Leadership in a Muhammadiyah Mosque in Indonesia." *The Muslim World* 103(3): 375–88.

Asad, Talal. 1986. The Idea of an Anthropology of Islam. Washington, D.C.: Occasional Papers Series; Georgetown University Center for Contemporary Arab Studies.

———. 1993. *Genealogies of Religion: Discipline and Reasons of Power in Christianity and Islam*. Baltimore: John Hopkins University Press.

Aspinall, Edward. 2006. "Violence and Identity Formation in Aceh under Indonesian Rule." In *Verandah of Violence: The Background to the Aceh Problem*, edited by Anthony Reid, 149–76. Singapore: NUS Press.

———. 2009. *Islam and Nation: Separatist Rebellion in Aceh, Indonesia*. Stanford: Stanford University Press.

Azra, Azyumardi. 2004. *The Origins of Islamic Reformism in Southeast Asia: Networks of Malay-Indonesian and Middle Eastern 'Ulamā' in the Seventeenth and Eighteenth century*. Canberra: Asian Studies Association of Australia.

Barker, Joshua, and Gerry van Klinken. 2009. "Reflections on the State in Indonesia." In *State of Authority: The State in Society in Indonesia*, edited by Gerry van Klinken and Joshua Barker, 17–49. Ithaca, NY: Southeast Asia Program Publications, Cornell University.

Barth, Fredrik. 1993. *Balinese Worlds*. Chicago: University of Chicago Press.

Bayly, Christopher A. 2004. *The Birth of the Modern World, 1780–1914: Global Connections and Comparisons*. Malden, MA: Blackwell.

Beatty, Andrew. 1999. *Varieties of Javanese Religion: An Anthropological Account.* Cambridge: Cambridge University Press.

———. 2009. *A Shadow Falls: In the Heart of Java.* London: Faber and Faber.

Beaulieu, M. 1705. "The Expedition of Commodore Beaulieu to the East-Indies." In *Navigantium atque Itinerantium Bibliotheca. Or, A Complete Collection of Voyages and Travels,* edited by John Harris, 717–49. Translated by John Harris. London: Printed for Thomas Bennet, John Nicholson, and Daniel Midwinter.

Beekers, Daan. 2014. "Pedagogies of Piety: Comparing Young Observant Muslims and Christians in the Netherlands." *Culture and Religion* 15(1): 72–99.

———. 2015. "Precarious Piety: Pursuits of Faith among Young Muslims and Christians in the Netherlands." PhD diss., Vrije Universiteit (VU) Amsterdam.

———. 2018. "Fitting God In: Secular Rhythms, Prayer, and Deceleration among Young Dutch Muslims and Christians." In *Straying from the Straight Path: How Senses of Failure Invigorate Lived Religion,* edited by Daan Beekers and David Kloos. New York and Oxford: Berghahn.

Beekers, Daan, and David Kloos, eds. 2018. *Straying from the Straight Path: How Senses of Failure Invigorate Lived Religion.* New York and Oxford: Berghahn.

Benda, Harry J. 1958. *The Crescent and the Rising Sun: Indonesian Islam under the Japanese Occupation, 1942–1945.* The Hague and Bandung: W. van Hoeve.

Berkey, Jonathan P. 2007. "Madrasas Medieval and Modern: Politics, Education, and the Problem of Muslim Identity." In *Schooling Islam: The Culture and Politics of Modern Muslim Education,* edited by Robert W. Hefner and Muhammad Qasim Zaman, 40–60. Princeton: Princeton University Press.

Birchok, Daniel A. 2015. "Putting Habib Abdurrahim in His Place: Genealogy, Scale, and Islamization in Seunagan, Indonesia." *Comparative Studies in Society and History* 57(2): 497–527.

———. 2016. "Women, Genealogical Inheritance, and Mystical Authority: The Female Saints of Seunagan, Indonesia." *Asian Studies Review* 40(4): 583–99.

Blackburn, Susan. 2008. "Indonesian Women and Political Islam." *Journal of Southeast Asian Studies* 39(1): 83–101.

Bloembergen, Marieke, and Remco Raben. 2009. "Wegen naar het Nieuwe Indië, 1890–1950." In *Het Koloniale Beschavingsoffensief: Wegen naar het Nieuwe Indië, 1890–1950,* edited by Marieke Bloembergen and Remco Raben, 7–24. Leiden: KITLV Press.

Blom, Philipp. 2008. *The Vertigo Years: Europe, 1900–1914.* New York: Basic Books.

Borschberg, Peter. 2010. *The Singapore and Melaka Straits: Violence, Security and Diplomacy in the 17th century.* Singapore: NUS Press.

Bowen, John R. 1989. "Salat in Indonesia: The Social Meanings of an Islamic Ritual." *Man* 24(4): 600–619.

———. 1991. *Sumatran Politics and Poetics: Gayo History, 1900–1989.* New Haven, CT and London: Yale University Press.

———. 1993. *Muslims through Discourse: Religion and Ritual in Gayo Society.* Princeton: Princeton University Press.

———. 2003. *Islam, Law, and Equality in Indonesia: An Anthropology of Public Reasoning.* Cambridge: Cambridge University Press.

———. 2013. "Contours of Sharia in Indonesia." In *Democracy and Islam in Indonesia,* edited by Mirjam Künkler and Alfred Stepan, 149–67. New York: Columbia University Press.

Brenner, Suzanne. 1996. "Reconstructing Self and Society: Javanese Muslim Women and 'The Veil.'" *American Ethnologist* 23(4): 673–97.

Brown, David. 2003. *The State and Ethnic Politics in Southeast Asia.* London: Routledge.

Bubalo, Anthony, and Greg Fealy. 2005. *Joining the Caravan? The Middle East, Islamism and Indonesia.* Alexandria, New South Wales: Longueville Media.

Buehler, Michael. 2013. "Subnational Islamization through Secular Parties: Comparing Shari'a Politics in Two Indonesian Provinces." *Comparative Politics* 46(1): 63–82.

———. 2016. *The Politics of Shari'a Law: Islamist Activists and the State in Democratizing Indonesia*. Cambridge: Cambridge University Press.

Bulliet, Richard W. 1994. *Islam: The View from the Edge*. New York: Columbia University Press.

———. 2002. "The Crisis within Islam." *The Wilson Quarterly* 26(1): 11–19.

Bush, Robin. 2008. "Regional Sharia Regulations in Indonesia: Anomaly or Symptom?" In *Expressing Islam: Religious Life and Politics in Indonesia*, edited by Greg Fealy and Sally White, 174–91. Singapore: ISEAS Press.

Calhoun, Craig. 1991. "Morality, Identity, and Historical Explanation: Charles Taylor on the Sources of the Self." *Sociological Theory* 9(2): 232–63.

Carey, Peter B.R. 2007. *The Power of Prophecy: Prince Dipanagara and the End of an Old Order in Java, 1785–1855*. Leiden: KITLV Press.

Cederroth, Sven. 1981. *The Spell of the Ancestors and the Power of Mekkah: A Sasak Community on Lombok*. Göteborg: Acta Universitatis Gothoburgensis.

———. 1991. *From Syncretism to Orthodoxy? The Struggle of Islamic Leaders in an East Javanese Village*. Copenhagen: Nordic Institute of Asian Studies.

Chaudhuri, Kirti N. 1990. *Asia before Europe: Economy and Civilisation of the Indian Ocean from the Rise of Islam to 1750*. Cambridge: Cambridge University Press.

Comaroff, Jean, and John Comaroff. 1988. "Through the Looking-Glass: Colonial Encounters of the First Kind." *Journal of Historical Sociology* 1(1): 6–32.

Cooper, Elizabeth, and David Pratten. 2014. *Ethnographies of Uncertainty in Africa*. Basingstoke, Hampshire, UK: Palgrave Macmillan.

Cooper, Frederick. 2005. *Colonialism in Question: Theory, Knowledge, History*. Berkeley: University of California Press.

Cooper, Frederick, and Ann Laura Stoler. 1997. *Tensions of Empire: Colonial Cultures in a Bourgeois World*. Berkeley: University of California Press.

Cribb, Robert. 2011. "A System of Exemptions: Historicizing State Illegality in Indonesia." In *The State and Illegality in Indonesia*, edited by Edward Aspinall and Gerry van Klinken, 31–44. Leiden: KITLV Press.

Daly, Patrick T., R. Michael Feener, and Anthony Reid, eds. 2012. *From the Ground Up: Perspectives on Post-tsunami and Post-conflict Aceh*. Singapore: ISEAS Press.

Das, Veena. 2012. "Ordinary Ethics." In *A Companion to Moral Anthropology*, edited by Didier Fassin, 133–49. Chichester, UK and Malden, MA: Wiley-Blackwell.

Debevec, Liza. 2012. "Postponing Piety: Everyday Islam in Urban Burkina Faso." In *Ordinary Lives and Grand Schemes: An Anthropology of Everyday Religion*, edited by Samuli Schielke and Liza Debevec, 33–47. New York and Oxford: Berghahn.

Deeb, Lara. 2006. *An Enchanted Modern: Gender and Public Piety in Shi'i Lebanon*. Princeton: Princeton University Press.

de Koning, Martijn. 2018. "'I'm a Weak Servant': The Question of Sincerity and the Cultivation of Weakness in the Lives of Dutch Salafi Muslims." In *Straying from the Straight Path: How Senses of Failure Invigorate Lived Religion*, edited by Daan Beekers and David Kloos. New York and Oxford: Berghahn.

Djajadiningrat, P. A. Hoesein. 1911. "Critisch Overzicht van de in Maleische Werken Vervatte Gegevens over de Geschiedenis van het Soeltanaat van Atjeh." *Bijdragen tot de Taal-, Land- en Volkenkunde van Nederlandsch-Indië* 65: 135–260.

Dobbin, Christine. 1983. *Islamic Revivalism in a Changing Peasant Economy: Central Sumatra, 1784–1847*. London: Curzon Press.

Drewes, Gerardus W. J. 1979. *Hikajat Potjut Muhamat: An Achehnese Epic*. The Hague: Nijhoff.

Drexler, Elizabeth F. 2008. *Aceh, Indonesia: Securing the Insecure State*. Philadelphia: University of Pennsylvania Press.

Eickelman, Dale F., and Jon W. Anderson. 2003. *New Media in the Muslim World: The Emerging Public Sphere*, 2nd ed. Bloomington: Indiana University Press.

Eickelman, Dale F., and James P. Piscatori. 1996. *Muslim Politics*. Princeton: Princeton University Press.

Engelke, Matthew E., and Matt Tomlison. 2006. *The Limits of Meaning: Case Studies in the Anthropology of Christianity*: New York and Oxford: Berghahn.

Evans, Peter B., Dietrich Rueschemeyer, and Theda Skocpol. 1985. *Bringing the State Back in*. Cambridge: Cambridge University Press.

Fadil, Nadia, and Mayanthi Fernando. 2015. "Rediscovering the 'Everyday' Muslim: Notes on an Anthropological Divide." *HAU: Journal of Ethnographic Theory* 5(2): 59–88.

Farish A. Noor. 2002. "New Voices of Islam." ISIM paper. Leiden: Institute for the Study of Islam in the Modern World.

Faubion, James D. 2011. *An Anthropology of Ethics*. Cambridge: Cambridge University Press.

Fealy, Greg, and Sally White, eds. 2008. *Expressing Islam: Religious Life and Politics in Indonesia*. Singapore: Institute of Southeast Asian Studies.

Federspiel, Howard M. 2001. *Islam and Ideology in the Emerging Indonesian State: The Persatuan Islam (PERSIS), 1923 to 1957*. Leiden: Brill.

Feener, R. Michael. 2006. "A Javanese Muslim Life of Learning: Professor Dr. Haji Mohamad Koesnoe." In *Muslim Voices and Lives in the Contemporary World*, edited by Frances Trix, John Walbridge, and Linda Walbridge, 137–48. New York: Palgrave Macmillan.

———. 2007. *Muslim Legal Thought in Modern Indonesia*. Cambridge: Cambridge University Press.

———. 2012. "Social Engineering through Sharī'a: Islamic Law and State-Directed Da'wa in Contemporary Aceh." *Islamic Law and Society* 19(3): 275–311.

———. 2013. *Shari'a and Social Engineering: The Implementation of Islamic Law in Contemporary Aceh, Indonesia*. Oxford: Oxford University Press.

———. 2015. "State Shari'a and Its Limits." In *Islam and the Limits of the State: Reconfigurations of Practice, Community and Authority in Contemporary Aceh*, edited by R. Michael Feener, David Kloos, and Annemarie Samuels, 1–23. Leiden: Brill.

Feener, R. Michael, David Kloos, and Annemarie Samuels, eds. 2015. *Islam and the Limits of the State: Reconfigurations of Practice, Community and Authority in Contemporary Aceh*. Leiden: Brill.

Fischer, Johan. 2008. *Proper Islamic Consumption: Shopping among the Malays in Modern Malaysia*. Copenhagen: NIAS Press.

Fogg, Kevin. 2012. "The Fate of Muslim Nationalism in Independent Indonesia." PhD diss., Yale University.

Formichi, Chiara. 2014. *Islam and the Making of the Nation: Kartosuwiryo and Political Islam in 20th Century Indonesia*. Leiden: KITLV Press.

Forrest, Thomas. 1792. *A Voyage from Calcutta to the Mergui Archipelago [etc.]*. London: sold by J. Robson, New Bond-Street; I. Owen, No. 168, Piccadilly; and Balfour, Edinburgh.

Frisk, Sylva. 2009. *Submitting to God: Women and Islam in Urban Malaysia*. Copenhagen: NIAS Press.

Gade, Anna M. 2004. *Perfection Makes Practice: Learning, Emotion, and the Recited Qur'ān in Indonesia*. Honolulu: University of Hawai'i Press.

Gedacht, Joshua. 2013. "Islamic-Imperial Encounters: Colonial Enclosure and Muslim Cosmopolitans in Island Southeast Asia, 1800–1940." PhD diss., University of Wisconsin-Madison.

———. 2015. "Holy War, Progress, and 'Modern Mohammedans' in Colonial Southeast Asia." *The Muslim World* 105(4): 446–71.

Geertz, Clifford. 2004. "What Is a State if It Is Not a Sovereign?" *Current Anthropology* 45(5): 577–93.

Gibson, Thomas. 2000. "Islam and the Spirit Cults in New Order Indonesia: Global Flows vs. Local Knowledge." *Indonesia* 69: 41–70.

Gluckman, H.M. 1971 [1940]. "Analysis of a Social Situation in Zululand." Rhodes-Livingstone Institute, paper No. 28. Manchester: Manchester University Press.

Gobée, Emile, and Cornelis Adriaanse, eds. 1957–65. *Ambtelijke Adviezen van C. Snouck Hurgronje, 1889–1936*. 3 vols. Den Haag: Martinus Nijhoff.

Gould, James W. 1956. "America's Pepperpot, 1784–1873." *Essex Institute Historical Collections* 902(92): 83–153; 203–251; 295–348.

Graadt van Roggen, C. 1934. *Een Strijd in Atjeh (Een Oogarts op Oorlogspad)*. Zeist: Stichting Steun In Medische Aangelegenheden Voor Inheemschen (SIMAVI).

Großmann, Kristina 2015. "Women's Rights Activists and the Drafting Process of the Islamic Criminal Law Code (*Qanun Jinayat*)." In *Islam and the Limits of the State: Reconfigurations of Practice, Community and Authority in Contemporary Aceh*, edited by R. Michael Feener, David Kloos, and Annemarie Samuels, 87–117. Leiden: Brill.

Guillot, Claude, and Ludvik Kalus. 2008. *Les Monuments Funéraires et l'Histoire du Sultanat de Pasai à Sumatra (XIIIe-XVIe Siècles)*. Paris: Association Archipel.

Guinness, Patrick. 2009. *Kampung, Islam and State in Urban Java*. Singapore: NUS Press.

Gupta, Akhil. 1995. "Blurred Boundaries: The Discourse of Corruption, the Culture of Politics, and the Imagined State." *American Ethnologist* 22(2): 375–402.

Hadi, Amirul. 2004. *Islam and State in Sumatra: A Study of Seventeenth-Century Aceh*. Leiden: Brill.

Hadiz, Vedi R., and Khoo Boo Teik. 2011. "Approaching Islam and Politics from Political Economy: A Comparative Study of Indonesia and Malaysia." *The Pacific Review* 24(4): 463–85.

Hadler, Jeffrey A. 2008. *Muslims and Matriarchs: Cultural Resilience in Indonesia through Jihad and Colonialism*. Ithaca, NY: Cornell University Press.

Hall, Kenneth R. 2001. "Upstream and Downstream Unification in Southeast Asia's First Islamic Polity: The Changing Sense of Community in the Fifteenth Century Hikayat Raja-Raja Pasai Court Chronicle." *Journal of the Economic and Social History of the Orient* 44(2): 198–229.

Hamdiah A. Latif. 1992. "Persatuan Ulama Seluruh Aceh (PUSA): Its Contributions to Educational Reforms in Aceh." MA thesis, McGill University.

Hansen, Gary. 1971. "Episodes in Rural Modernization: Problems in the Bimas Program." *Indonesia* 11: 63–81.

Hasan, Noorhaidi. 2017. *Public Islam in Indonesia: Piety, Politics, and Identity*. Amsterdam: Amsterdam University Press.

Hasbi Amiruddin. 2003–2004. *Biografi Ulama-Ulama Aceh Abad XX*. 2 vols. Banda Aceh: Balai Kajian Sejarah dan Nilai Traditional Banda Aceh, Bekerjasama dengan Dinas Pendidikan Provinsi Nanggroe Aceh Darussalam.

Headly, Stephen C. 2004. *Durga's Mosque: Cosmology, Conversion and Community in Central Javanese Islam*. Singapore: Institute of Southeast Asian Studies.

Hefner, Robert W. 1985. *Hindu Javanese: Tengger Tradition and Islam*. Princeton: Princeton University Press.

———. 1986. "Islamizing Java? Religion and Politics in Rural East Java." *The Journal of Asian Studies* 46(3): 533–54.

———. 1987. "The Political Economy of Islamic Conversion in Modern East Java." In *Islam and the Political Economy of Meaning: Comparative Studies of Muslim Discourse*, edited by William R. Roff, 53–78. Berkeley: University of California Press.

———. 1993. "Islam, State, and Civil Society: ICMI and the Struggle for the Indonesian Middle Class." *Indonesia* 56: 1–35.

Hefner, Robert W. 1997. "Islam in an Era of Nation-States: Politics and Religious Renewal in Muslim Southeast Asia." In *Islam in an Era of Nation-States: Politics and Religious Renewal in Muslim Southeast Asia*, edited by Robert W. Hefner and Patricia Horvatich, 3–40. Honolulu: University of Hawai'i Press.

———. 2000. *Civil Islam: Muslims and Democratization in Indonesia*. Princeton: Princeton University Press.

———. 2010. "Religious Resurgence in Contemporary Asia: Southeast Asian Perspectives on Capitalism, the State, and the New Piety." *The Journal of Asian Studies* 69(4): 1031–47.

Hefner, Robert W., and Patricia Horvatich. 1997. *Islam in an Era of Nation-States: Politics and Religious Renewal in Muslim Southeast Asia*. Honolulu: University of Hawai'i Press.

Hirschkind, Charles. 2006. *The Ethical Soundscape: Cassette Sermons and Islamic Counterpublics*. New York: Columbia University Press.

HMW (Human Rights Watch). 2010. "Policing Morality: Abuses in the Application of Sharia in Aceh, Indonesia." Report. New York: Human Rights Watch.

Ho, Engseng. 2006. *The Graves of Tarim: Genealogy and Mobility across the Indian Ocean*. Berkeley: University of California Press.

Hoesterey, James B. 2015. *Rebranding Islam: Piety, Prosperity, and a Self-help Guru*. Stanford: Stanford University Press.

Howell, Julia Day. 2001. "Sufism and the Indonesian Islamic Revival." *Journal of Asian Studies* 60(3): 701–29.

———. 2008. "Modulations of Active Piety: Professors and Televangelists as Promoters of Indonesian 'Sufisme.'" In *Expressing Islam: Religious Life and Politics in Indonesia*, edited by Greg Fealy and Sally White, 40–62. Singapore: Institute of Southeast Asian Studies.

———. 2010. "Indonesia's Salafist Sufis." *Modern Asian Studies* 44(5): 1029–51.

Hyung-Jun Kim. 1996. "Reformist Muslims in a Yogyakarta Village: The Islamic Transformation of Contemporary Socio-Religious Life." PhD diss., Australian National University.

ICG (International Crisis Group). 2006. "Islamic Law and Criminal Justice in Aceh." Asia Report No. 117. Jakarta/Brussels: International Crisis Group.

———. 2008. "Indonesia: Pre-Election Anxieties in Aceh." Asia Briefing. Jakarta/Brussels: International Crisis Group.

———. 2010. "Indonesia: Jihadi Surprise in Aceh." Asia Report No. 189. Jakarta/Brussels: International Crisis Group.

Idria, Reza. 2015a. "Cultural Resistance against Shariatism in Aceh." In *Islam, Politics and Change: The Indonesian Experience after the Fall of Suharto*, edited by Kees van Dijk and Nico J. G. Kaptein, 247–67. Leiden: Leiden University Press.

———. 2015b. "Muslim Punks and State Shari'a." In *Islam and the Limits of the State: Reconfigurations of Practice, Community and Authority in Contemporary Aceh*, edited by R Michael Feener, David Kloos, and Annemarie Samuels, 166–84. Leiden: Brill.

IPAC (Institute for Policy Analysis of Conflict). 2016. "The Anti-Salafi Campaign in Aceh." IPAC Report No. 32, October 6.

Iqtidar, Humeira. 2011. *Secularizing Islamists? Jama'at-e-Islami and Jama'at-ud-Da'wa in Urban Pakistan*. Chicago: University of Chicago Press.

Ishak, Syamsuddin. 2001. *Dari Maaf ke Panic Aceh: Sebuah Sketsa Sosiologi-Politik*. 2 vols. Jakarta: Lembaga Studi Pers dan Pembangunan.

Iskandar, Teuku. 2011. "Aceh as Crucible of Muslim-Malay literature." In *Mapping the Acehnese Past*, edited by R. Michael Feener, Patrick Daly and Anthony Reid, 39–64. Leiden: KITLV Press.

Ismail, Muhammad Gade. 1996. "Aceh's Dual Economy during the Late Colonial Period." In *Historical Foundations of a National Economy in Indonesia*, edited by Thomas J. Lindblad. Amsterdam: Koninklijke Nederlandse Akademie van Wetenschappen.

Ismail Yakub, Tgk. H. 1980. "Gambaran Pendidikan di Aceh Sesudah Perang Aceh-Belanda Sampai Sekarang." In *Bunga Rampai Tentang Aceh*, edited by Ismail Suny, 318–71. Jakarta: Bhratara Karya Aksara.

Ito, Takeshi. 1984. "The World of the Adat Aceh: A Historical Study of the Sultanate of Aceh." PhD diss., Australian National University.

Jacobs, Julius. 1894. *Het Familie- en Kamponglevan op Groot-Atjeh: Eene Bijdrage tot de Ethnographie van Noord-Sumatra*. 2 vols. Leiden: Brill.

Jamhari. 2000. "Popular Voices of Islam: Discourse on Muslim Orientations in South Central Java." PhD diss., Australian National University.

Jauhola, Marjaana. 2013. *Post-Tsunami Reconstruction in Indonesia: Negotiating Normativity through Gender Mainstreaming Initiatives in Aceh*. London: Routledge.

Jayawardena, Chandra. 1977a. "Achehnese Marriage Customs." *Indonesia* 23(1): 157–73.

———. 1977b. "Women and Kinship in Acheh Besar, Northern Sumatra." *Ethnology* 16(1): 21–38.

———. 1987. "Analysis of a Social Situation in Acheh Besar: An Exploration in Micro-History." *Social Analysis* 22(2): 30–46.

Johns, Anthony H. 1998. "The Qur'ān in the Malay World: Reflections on 'Abd al-Ra'ūf of Singkel (1615–1693)." *Journal of Islamic Studies* 9(2): 120–45.

Jones, Carla. 2010. "Materializing Piety: Gendered Anxieties about Faithful Consumption in Contemporary Urban Indonesia." *American Ethnologist* 37(4): 617–38.

Jongejans, J. 1939. *Land en Volk van Atjeh: Vroeger en Nu*. Baarn: Hollandia.

Kamrava, Mehran, ed. 2006. *New Voices of Islam: Reforming Politics and Modernity. A Reader*. London and New York: I. B. Tauris.

Kapferer, Bruce. 1987. "The Anthropology of Max Gluckman." *Social Analysis* 22(2): 3–21.

Kartodirdjo, Sartono. 1972. "Agrarian Radicalism in Java: Its Setting and Development." In *Culture and Politics in Indonesia*, edited by Claire Holt (with the assistance of Benedict R. O'G. Anderson and James T. Siegel), 71–125. Ithaca, NY: Cornell University Press.

Kathirithamby-Wells, Jeya. 1986. "Royal Authority and the Orang Kaya in the Western Archipelago, circa 1500–1800." *Journal of Southeast Asian Studies* 17(2): 256–67.

Keane, Webb. 2015. *Ethical Life: Its Natural and Social Histories*. Princeton: Princeton University Press.

Kell, Tim. 1995. *The Roots of Acehnese Rebellion, 1989–1992*. Ithaca, NY: Cornell Modern Indonesia Project.

Kersten, Carool. 2011. *Cosmopolitans and Heretics: New Muslim Intellectuals and the Study of Islam*. London: Hurst.

Khan, Sher Banu A. L. 2017. *Sovereign Women in a Muslim Kingdom: The Sultanahs of Aceh, 1641–1699*. Ithaca, NY: Cornell University Press.

Khoiruddin Nasution. 1996. "Maslahah and Its Application in Indonesian Fatwâ." *Studio Islamika* 3(4): 113–36.

Kloos, David. 2014a. "A Crazy State: Violence, Psychiatry, and Colonialism in Aceh, ca. 1910–1942." *Bijdragen tot de Taal-, Land- en Volkenkunde* 170(1): 25–65.

———. 2014b. "In the Name of *Syariah*? Vigilante Violence, Territoriality, and Moral Authority in Aceh, Indonesia." *Indonesia* 98: 59–90.

———. 2015a. "From Acting to Being: Expressions of Religious Individuality in Aceh, ca. 1600–1900." *Itinerario* 39(3): 437–61.

———. 2015b. "Images of Violence and Piety in Aceh." In *Islam, Politics and Change: The Indonesian Experience after the Fall of Suharto*, edited by Kees van Dijk and Nico J. G. Kaptein, 269–94. Leiden: Leiden University Press.

———. 2016. "The Salience of Gender: Female Islamic Authority in Aceh, Indonesia." *Asian Studies Review* 40(4): 527–44.

Kloos, David. 2018. "The Ethics of Not-Praying: Religious Negligence, Life Phase, and Social Status in Aceh, Indonesia." In *Straying from the Straight Path: How Senses of Failure Invigorate Lived Religion*, edited by Daan Beekers and David Kloos. New York and Oxford: Berghahn.

Kloos, David, and Daan Beekers. 2018. "Introduction: The Productive Potential of Moral Failure in Lived Islam and Christianity." In *Straying from the Straight Path: How Senses of Failure Invigorate Lived Religion*, edited by Daan Beekers and David Kloos. New York and Oxford: Berghahn.

Kloos, David, and Ward Berenschot. 2016. "Citizenship and Islam in Malaysia and Indonesia." In *Citizenship and Democratization in Southeast Asia*, edited by Ward Berenschot, Henk Schulte Nordholt, and Laurens Bakker, 178–207. Leiden: Brill.

Kloos, David, and Mirjam Künkler. 2016. "Studying Female Islamic Authority: From Top-Down to Bottom-Up Modes of Certification." *Asian Studies Review* 40 (4): 479–490.

Kraus, Werner. 2010. "The Shattariyya Sufi Brotherhood in Aceh." In *Aceh: History, Politics and Culture*, edited by Arndt Graf, Susanne Schröter, and Edwin Wieringa, 201–26. Singapore: Institute of Southeast Asian Studies.

Kreike, Emmanuel. 2012. "Genocide in the Kampongs? Dutch Nineteenth Century Colonial Warfare in Aceh, Sumatra." *Journal of Genocide Research* 14(3–4): 297–315.

Kresse, Kai. 2003. "'Swahili Enlightenment'? East African Reformist Discourse at the Turning Point: The Example of Sheikh Muhammad Kasim Mazrui." *Journal of Religion in Africa* 33(3): 279–309.

Kruyt, J.A. 1877. *Atjeh en de Atjehers: Twee Jaren Blokkade op Sumatra's Noord-Oost-Kust*. Leiden: Gualth. Kolff.

Künkler, Mirjam, and David Kloos, eds. 2016. "Studying Female Islamic Authority: From Top-Down to Bottom-Up Modes of Certification." Special Issue, *Asian Studies Review* 40(4).

Künkler, Mirjam, and Alfred Stepan, eds. 2013. *Democracy and Islam in Indonesia*. New York: Columbia University Press.

Laffan, Michael F. 2003. *Islamic Nationhood and Colonial Indonesia: The* Umma *below the Winds*. London: RoutledgeCurzon.

———. 2011. *The Makings of Indonesian Islam: Orientalism and the Narration of a Sufi Past*. Princeton: Princeton University Press.

Laidlaw, James. 2014. *The Subject of Virtue: An Anthropology of Ethics and Freedom*. Cambridge: Cambridge University Press.

Lambek, Michael. 2000. "The Anthropology of Religion and the Quarrel between Poetry and Philosophy." *Current Anthropology* 41(3): 309–20.

———, ed. 2010a. *Ordinary Ethics: Anthropology, Language, and Action*. New York: Fordham University Press.

———. 2010b. "Introduction." In *Ordinary Ethics: Anthropology, Language, and Action*, edited by Michael Lambek, 1–36. New York: Fordham University Press.

———. 2015. "The Ethical Condition," in *The Ethical Condition: Essays on Action, Person, and Value*, 1–39. Chicago: University of Chicago Press.

Lee Kam Hing. 1995. *The Sultanate of Aceh: Relations with the British, 1760–1824*. Oxford: Oxford University Press.

Liddle, R. William. 1996. "The Islamic Turn in Indonesia: A Political Explanation." *Journal of Asian Studies* 55(3): 613–34.

Lieberman, Victor. 2009. *Strange Parallels: Southeast Asia in Global Context, 800–1830*. Vol. 2, *Mainland Mirrors: Europe, Japan, China, South Asia, and the Islands*. Cambridge: Cambridge University Press.

Lindquist, Johan A. 2009. *The Anxieties of Mobility: Migration and Tourism in the Indonesian Borderlands*. Honolulu: University of Hawai'i Press.

Lindsey, Timothy, M. Barry Hooker, Ross Clark, and Jeremy Kingsley. 2007. "Shariʿa Revival in Aceh." In *Islamic Law in Contemporary Indonesia: Ideas and Institutions*, edited by R. Michael Feener and Mark E. Cammack, 216–54. Cambridge, MA: Harvard University Press.

Liow, Joseph C. 2009. *Piety and Politics: Islamism in Contemporary Malaysia*. New York: Oxford University Press.

Lombard, Denys. 1967. *Le Sultanat d'Atjéh au Temps d'Iskandar Muda: 1607–1636*. Paris: École Francaise d'Extrême-Orient.

MacAndrews, Colin. 1986. "Introduction." In *Central Government and Local Development in Indonesia*, edited by Colin MacAndrews, 1–5. Oxford: Oxford University Press.

MacIntyre, Alasdair C. 1988. *Whose Justice? Which Rationality?* Notre Dame: University of Notre Dame Press.

Mahdi Syihab. 2010. "Penegakan Syariat: Etnografi Aksi Razia Santri Dayah di Aceh Utara." In *Serambi Mekkah yang Berubah: Views from Within*, edited by Arskal Salim and Adlin Sila, 57–91. Tangerang: Pustaka Alvabet and Aceh Research Training Institute.

Mahmood, Saba. 2005. *Politics of Piety: The Islamic Revival and the Feminist Subject*. Princeton: Princeton University Press.

Mandaville, Peter. 2007. "Globalization and the Politics of Religious Knowledge: Pluralizing Authority in the Muslim World." *Theory, Culture & Society* 24(2): 101–115.

Mannheim, Karl. 1952 [1923]. "The Problem of Generations," in *Essays on the Sociology of Knowledge*. Translated by Paul Kecskemeti. London: Routledge & Kegan Paul.

Marsden, Magnus. 2005. *Living Islam: Muslim Religious Experience in Pakistan's North-West Frontier*. Cambridge: Cambridge University Press.

Marsden, Magnus, and Konstantinos Retsikas. 2012. "Introduction." In *Articulating Islam: Anthropological Approaches to Muslim Worlds*, edited by Magnus Marsden and Konstantinos Retsikas, 1–31. Dordrecht: Springer Science & Business Media.

Marsden, William. 1811 [1783]. *The History of Sumatra*. London: J. M'Creedy.

Marzi Afriko. 2010. "Syariat Islam dan Radikalisme Massa: Melacak Jejak Awal Kehadiran FPI di Aceh." In *Serambi Mekkah yang Berubah: Views from Within*, edited by Arskal Salim and Adlin Sila, 19–56. Tangerang: Pustaka Alvabet Bekerja Sama Dengan Aceh Research Training Institute.

Mattingly, Cheryl. 2014. "The Moral Perils of a Superstrong Black Mother." *Ethos* 42(1): 119–38.

McGibbon, Rodd. 2006. "Local Leadership and the Aceh Conflict." In *Verandah of Violence: Background to the Aceh Problem*, edited by Anthony Reid, 315–59. Singapore: NUS Press.

Meeker, Michael E. 2002. *A Nation of Empire: The Ottoman Legacy of Turkish Modernity*. Berkeley: University of California Press.

Melvin, Jess. 2013. "Why Not Genocide? Anti-Chinese Violence in Aceh, 1965–1966." *Journal of Current Southeast Asian Affairs* 32(3): 63–91.

Miller, Michelle A., and R. Michael Feener. 2012. "Emergency and Islamic Law in Aceh." In *Emergency Powers in Asia: Exploring the Limits of Legality*, edited by Victor V. Ramraj and Arun K. Thiruvengadam, 213–36. Cambridge: Cambridge University Press.

Millie, Julian. 2009. *Splashed by the Saint: Ritual Reading and Islamic Sanctity in West Java*. Leiden: KITLV Press.

———. 2012. "Oratorical Innovation and Audience Heterogeneity in Islamic West Java." *Indonesia* 93(1): 123–45.

Montana, Suwedi. 1997. "Nouvelles Données sur les Royaumes de Lamuri et Barat." *Archipel* 53(1): 85–95.

Morris, Eric E. 1983. "Islam and Politics in Aceh: A Study of Center-Periphery Relations in Indonesia." PhD diss., Cornell University.

Mrázek, Rudolf. 2002. *Engineers of Happy Land: Technology and Nationalism in a Colony*. Princeton: Princeton University Press.

Nakamura, Mitsuo. 2012. *The Crescent Arises over the Banyan Tree: A Study of the Muhammadiyah Movement in a Central Javanese Town, c. 1910–2010.* 2nd ed. Singapore: Institute of Southeast Asian Studies.

Newman, Sarah. 2009. "Patrolling Sexuality." *Inside Indonesia* 96 (April–June). Available at http://www.insideindonesia.org/patrolling-sexuality.

Nur Ichwan, Moch. 2007. "The Politics of Shari'atization: Central Governmental and Regional Discourses of Shari'a Implementation in Aceh." In *Islamic Law in Contemporary Indonesia: Ideas and Institutions,* edited by R. Michael Feener and Mark E. Cammack, 193–215. Cambridge, MA: Harvard University Press.

———. 2011. "Official Ulema and the Politics of Re-Islamization: The Majelis Permusyawaratan Ulama, Shari'atization and Contested Authority in Post-New Order Aceh." *Journal of Islamic Studies* 22(2): 183–214.

———. 2013. "Towards a Puritanical Moderate Islam: The Majelis Ulama Indonesia and the Politics of Religious Orthodoxy." In *Contemporary Developments in Indonesian Islam: Explaining the "Conservative Turn,"* edited by Martin van Bruinessen, 60–104. Singapore: Institute of Southeast Asian Studies (ISEAS).

———. 2015. "Neo-Sufism, Shariatism, and Ulama Politics: Abuya Shaykh Amran Waly and the Tauhid-Tasawuf Movement in Aceh." In *Islam, Politics and Change: The Indonesian Experience after the Fall of Suharto,* edited by Kees van Dijk and Nico J. G. Kaptein, 221–46. Leiden: Leiden University Press.

Nurlaelawati, Euis. 2010. *Modernization, Tradition and Identity: The Kompilasi Hukum Islam and Legal Practice in the Indonesian Religious Courts.* Amsterdam: Amsterdam University Press.

Nuru'd-din ar-Raniri. 1966. *Bustanu's-Salatin: Bab II, Fasal 13.* Delivered and introduced by T. Iskandar. Kuala Lumpur: Dewan Bahasa dan Pustaka, Kementerian Pelajaran Malaysia.

Olle, John. 2009. "The Majelis Ulama Indonesia Versus 'Heresy': The Resurgence of Authoritatian Islam." In *State of Authority: The State in Society in Indonesia,* edited by Gerry van Klinken and Joshua Barker, 95–116. Ithaca, NY: Southeast Asia Program Publications, Cornell University.

Ortner, Sherry B.. 1996. "The Problem of 'Women' as an Analytic Category," in *Making Gender: The Politics and Erotics of Culture,* 116–38. Boston: Beacon Press.

———. 2006. *Anthropology and Social Theory: Culture, Power, and the Acting Subject.* Durham and London: Duke University Press.

Otto, Benjamin, and Jan Michiel Otto. 2015. "Shari'a Police in Banda Aceh: Enforcement of Islam-Based Regulations and People's Perceptions." In *Islam and the Limits of the State: Reconfigurations of Practice, Community and Authority in Contemporary Aceh,* edited by R. Michael Feener, David Kloos, and Annemarie Samuels, 185–213. Leiden: Brill.

Parsons, Nicholas, and Marcus Mietzner. 2009. "Sharia By-laws in Indonesia: A Legal and Political Analysis." *Australian Journal of Asian Law* 11(2): 190–217.

Peacock, Andrew C. S., and Annabel Teh Gallop. 2015. "Introduction. Islam, Trade and Politics across the Indian Ocean: Imagination and Reality." In *From Anatolia to Aceh: Ottomans, Turks and Southeast Asia,* edited by Andrew C. S. Peacock and Annabel Teh Gallop, 1–23. Oxford: Oxford University Press.

Peletz, Michael G. 1988. *A Share of the Harvest: Kinship, Property, and Social History among the Malays of Rembau.* Berkeley: University of California Press.

———. 1996. *Reason and Passion: Representations of Gender in a Malay Society.* Berkeley: University of California Press.

———. 1997. "'Ordinary Muslims' and Muslim Resurgents in Contemporary Malaysia: Notes on an Ambivalent Relationship." In *Islam in an Era of Nation-States: Politics and Religious Renewal in Muslim Southeast Asia,* edited by Robert W. Hefner and Patricia Horvatich, 231–73. Honolulu: University of Hawai'i Press.

———. 2002. *Islamic Modern: Religious Courts and Cultural Politics in Malaysia*. Princeton: Princeton University Press.

———. 2011. "Islamization in Malaysia: Piety and Consumption, Politics and Law." *South East Asia Research* 19(1): 125–48.

———. 2013. "Malaysia's Syariah Judiciary as Global Assemblage: Islamization, Corporatization, and Other Transformations in Context." *Comparative Studies in Society and History* 55(3): 603–33.

Pelkmans, Mathijs, ed. 2013. *Ethnographies of Doubt: Faith and Uncertainty in Contemporary Societies*. London: I. B. Tauris.

Piekaar, Arie J. 1949. *Atjeh en de Oorlog met Japan*. 's Gravenhage: W. van Hoeve.

Pires, Tomé. 1967 [1515]. *The Suma Oriental of Tomé Pires: An Account of the East, from the Red Sea to Japan* [etc.]. Translated and edited by Armando Cortesão. Nendeln: Kraus Reprint.

Prakash, Om. 1998. "The Trading World of India and Southeast Asia in the Early Modern Period." *Archipel* 56(1): 31–42.

Pranowo, Bambang. 1991 "Creating Islamic Tradition in Rural Java." PhD diss., Monash University.

Reid, Anthony. 1969. *The Contest for North Sumatra: Atjeh, the Netherlands, and Britain, 1858–1898*. Kuala Lumpur: University of Malaya Press.

———. 1979. *The Blood of the People: Revolution and the End of Traditional Rule in Northern Sumatra*. Kuala Lumpur: Oxford University Press.

———. 1988. *Southeast Asia in the Age of Commerce*. Vol. 1: *The Lands below the Winds*. New Haven, CT: Yale University Press.

———. 1993. *Southeast Asia in the Age of Commerce, 1450–1680*. Vol. 2: *Expansion and Crisis*. New Haven, CT and London: Yale University Press.

———. 2005. *An Indonesian Frontier: Acehnese and Other Histories of Sumatra*. Leiden: KITLV Press.

———, ed. 2006a. *Verandah of Violence: The Background to the Aceh Problem*. Singapore: NUS Press.

———. 2006b. "The Pre-Modern Sultanate's View of Its Place in the World." In *Verandah of Violence: The Background to the Aceh Problem*, edited by Anthony Reid, 52–71. Singapore: NUS Press.

Reynolds, Craig J. 1995. "A New Look at Old Southeast Asia." *Journal of Asian Studies* 54(2): 419–46.

Ricklefs, Merle C. 2006. *Mystic Synthesis in Java: A History of Islamization from the Fourteenth to the Early Nineteenth Centuries*. Norwalk, CT: EastBridge.

———. 2007. *Polarising Javanese Society: Islamic and Other Visions, c. 1830–1930*. Singapore: NUS Press.

———. 2012. *Islamisation and Its Opponents in Java: A Political, Social, Cultural, and Religious History, c. 1930 to the Present*. Honolulu: University of Hawai'i Press.

Riddell, Peter G. 2001. *Islam and the Malay-Indonesian World: Transmission and Responses*. Honolulu: University of Hawai'i Press.

———. 2006. "Aceh in the Sixteenth and Seventeenth Centuries: 'Serambi Mekkah' and Identity." In *Verandah of Violence: The Background to the Aceh Problem*, edited by Anthony Reid, 38–51. Singapore: NUS Press.

Robbins, Joel. 2004. *Becoming Sinners: Christianity and Moral Torment in a Papua New Guinea Society*. Berkeley: University of California Press.

Robinson, Francis. 1997. "Religious Change and the Self in Muslim South Asia since 1800." *South Asia* 20(1): 1–15.

———. 2004. "Other-Worldly and This-Worldly Islam and the Islamic Revival. A Memorial Lecture for Wilfred Cantwell Smith. Delivered at the Royal Asiatic Society on 10 April 2003." *Journal of the Royal Asiatic Society of Great Britain and Ireland* 14(1): 47–58.

Robinson, Francis. 2008. "Islamic Reform and Modernities in South Asia." *Modern Asian Studies* 42(2–3): 259–81.

———. 2009. "Crisis of Authority: Crisis of Islam?" *Journal of the Royal Asiatic Society of Great Britain and Ireland* 19(3): 339–54.

Robinson, Geoffrey. 1998. "Rawan Is as Rawan Does: The Origins of Disorder in New Order Aceh." *Indonesia* 66: 127–57.

Robinson, Kathryn. 2006. "Idioms of Vernacular Humanism: The West and the East." *Anthropological Forum* 16(3): 241–55.

———. 2008. *Gender, Islam and Democracy in Indonesia.* London and New York: Routledge.

Roff, William R. 1967. *The Origins of Malay Nationalism.* New Haven, CT: Yale University Press.

Roy, Olivier. 2004. *Globalized Islam: The Search for a New Ummah.* New York: Columbia University Press.

Rudnyckyj, Daromir. 2010. *Spiritual Economies: Islam, Globalization, and the Afterlife of Development.* Ithaca, NY: Cornell University Press.

Rusdi Sufi. 2008. *Peristiwa PKI di Aceh: Sejarah Kelam Konflik Ideologis di Serambi Mekkah.* Banda Aceh: CV. Boebon Jaya.

Salim, Arskal. 2008. *Challenging the Secular State: The Islamization of Law in Modern Indonesia.* Honolulu: University of Hawai'i Press.

———. 2009. "Politics, Criminal Justice and Islamisation in Aceh." Background paper. Melbourne: Centre for Islamic Law and Society, Melbourne University.

Salim, Arskal, and Azyumardi Azra. 2003. *Shari'a and Politics in Modern Indonesia.* Singapore: ISEAS Press.

Samedi, Pujo, Michael G. Peletz, Edwin Wieringa, and Andrew Beatty. 2010. "Debate. Andrew Beatty, A Shadow Falls: In the Heart of Java." *Bijdragen tot de Taal-, Land- en Volkenkunde* 166(2–3): 315–30.

Samuels, Annemarie. 2012a. "After the Tsunami: The Remaking of Everyday Life in Banda Aceh, Indonesia." PhD diss., Leiden University.

———. 2012b. "Moving from Great Love: Gendered Mobilities in a Post-Tsunami Relocation Neighborhood in Aceh, Indonesia." *International Journal of Urban and Regional Research* 36(4): 742–56.

———. 2015a. "*Hikmah* and Narratives of Change: How Different Temporalities Shape the Present and the Future in Post-Tsunami Aceh." In *Islam and the Limits of the State: Reconfigurations of Practice, Community and Authority in Contemporary Aceh*, edited by R. Michael Feener, David Kloos, and Annemarie Samuels, 24–55. Leiden: Brill.

———. 2015b. "Narratives of Uncertainty: The Affective Force of Child-Trafficking Rumors in Postdisaster Aceh, Indonesia." *American Anthropologist* 117(2): 229–41.

———. 2016. "Embodied Narratives of Disaster: The Expression of Bodily Experience in Aceh, Indonesia." *Journal of the Royal Anthropological Institute* 22(4): 809–825.

Schielke, Samuli. 2009a. "Ambivalent Commitments: Troubles of Morality, Religiosity and Aspiration among Young Egyptians." *Journal of Religion in Africa* 39(2): 158–85.

———. 2009b. "Being Good in Ramadan: Ambivalence, Fragmentation, and the Moral Self in the Lives of Young Egyptians." *Journal of the Royal Anthropological Institute* 15 (Issue Supplement S1): S24–S40.

———. 2010. "Second Thoughts about the Anthropology of Islam, or How to Make Sense of Grand Schemes in Everyday Life." Berlin: Zentrum Moderner Orient Working Papers.

———. 2015. *Egypt in the Future Tense: Hope, Frustration, and Ambivalence before and after 2011.* Bloomington: Indiana University Press.

Schielke, Samuli, and Liza Debevec. 2012. "Introduction." In *Ordinary Lives and Grand Schemes: An Anthropology of Everyday Religion*, edited by Samuli Schielke and Liza Debevec, 1–16. New York and Oxford: Berghahn.

Schlegel, Stuart A. 1979. "Technocrats in a Muslim Society: Symbolic Community in Aceh." In *What Is Modern Indonesian Culture?*, edited by Gloria Davis. Athens: Ohio University Center for International Studies.

Schulte Nordholt, Henk. 2011a. "Indonesia in the 1950s: Nation, Modernity, and the Postcolonial State." *Bijdragen tot de Taal-, Land- en Volkenkunde* 167(4): 386–404.

———. 2011b. "Modernity and Cultural Citizenship in the Netherlands Indies: An Illustrated Hypothesis." *Journal of Southeast Asian Studies* 42(3): 435–57.

Schulte Nordholt, Henk, and Fridus Steijlen. 2007. "Don't Forget to Remember Me: An Audiovisual Archive of Everyday Life in Indonesia in the 21st Century." Indonesian Studies Working Papers, University of Sydney, No. 1.

Scott, James C. 1985. *Weapons of the Weak: Everyday Forms of Peasant Resistance.* New Haven: Yale University Press.

Shiraishi, Takashi. 1990. *An Age in Motion: Popular Radicalism in Java, 1912–1926.* Ithaca: Cornell University Press.

Shulman, David D., and Guy G. Stroumsa, eds. 2002. *Self and Self-Transformation in the History of Religions.* New York: Oxford University Press.

Siapno, Jaqueline A. 2002. *Gender, Islam, Nationalism, and the State in Aceh: The Paradox of Power, Co-optation and Resistance.* London: Routledge.

Sidel, John T. 2006. *Riots, Pogroms, Jihad: Religious Violence in Indonesia.* Ithaca: Cornell University Press.

Sidwell, Paul J. 2005. "Acehnese and the Aceh-Chamic Language Family." In *Chamic and Beyond: Studies in Mainland Austronesian Languages*, edited by Anthony Paul Grant and Paul J. Sidwell, 211–46. Canberra: Pacific Linguistics, in association with the Research School of Pacific and Asian Studies, The Australian National University.

Siegel, James T. 1969. *The Rope of God.* Berkeley: University of California Press.

———. 1979. *Shadow and Sound: The Historical Thought of a Sumatran People.* Chicago: University of Chicago Press.

———. 1997. *Fetish, Recognition, Revolution.* Princeton: Princeton University Press.

Simon, Gregory M. 2014. *Caged in on the Outside: Moral Subjectivity, Selfhood, and Islam in Minangkabau, Indonesia.* Honolulu: University of Hawai'i Press.

Sirry, Mun'im. 2013. "Fatwas and their Controversy: The Case of the Council of Indonesian Ulama (MUI)." *Journal of Southeast Asian Studies* 44(1): 100–117.

Sjamsuddin, Nazaruddin. 1985. *The Republican Revolt: A Study of the Acehnese Rebellion.* Singapore: Institute of Southeast Asian Studies.

Sloane, Patricia. 1999. *Islam, Modernity, and Entrepreneurship among the Malays.* New York: St. Martin's Press.

Smith-Hefner, Nancy. 2005. "The New Muslim Romance: Changing Patterns of Courtship and Marriage among Educated Javanese Youth." *Journal of Southeast Asian Studies* 36(3): 441–59.

———. 2007. "Muslim Women and the Veil in Post-Soeharto Java." *Journal of Asian Studies* 66(2): 389–420.

Snouck Hurgronje, Christiaan. 1893–94. *De Atjèhers.* 2 vols. Batavia: Landsdrukkerij.

Soares, Benjamin, and Filippo Osella. 2009. "Islam, Politics, Anthropology." *Journal of the Royal Anthropological Institute* 15 (Issue Supplement S1): S1–S23.

Soeyatno. 1977. "Sejarah Sosial Masyarakat Pedesaan Sibreh." In *Segi-Segi Sosial Budaya Masyarakat Aceh: Hasil-hasil Penelitian dengan Metode "Grounded Research,"* edited by Alfian, 51–77. Jakarta: LP3ES.

Spyer, Patricia. 1996. "Serial Conversion/Conversion to Seriality: Religion, State, and Number in Aru, Eastern Indonesia." In *Conversion to Modernities: The Globalization of Christianity*, edited by Peter van der Veer, 171–98. New York and London: Routledge.

Srimulyani, Eka. 2012. *Women from Traditional Islamic Educational Institutions in Indonesia: Negotiating Public Spaces.* Amsterdam: Amsterdam University Press.

———. 2015. *"Teungku Inong Dayah*: Female Religious Leaders in Contemporary Aceh." In *Islam and the Limits of the State: Reconfigurations of Practice, Community and Authority in Contemporary Aceh,* edited by R. Michael Feener, David Kloos, and Annemarie Samuels, 141–65. Leiden: Brill.

Starrett, Gregory. 1998. *Putting Islam to Work: Education, Politics, and Religious Transformation in Egypt.* Berkeley: University of California Press.

Stoler, Ann L. 2009. *Along the Archival Grain: Epistemic Anxieties and Colonial Common Sense.* Princeton: Princeton University Press.

Stolwijk, Anton. 2016. *Atjeh: Het Verhaal van de Bloedigste Strijd uit de Nederlandse Koloniale Geschiedenis.* Amsterdam: Prometheus.

Subrahmanyam, Sanjay. 2009. "Pulverized in Aceh: On Luis Monteiro Coutinho and his 'Martyrdom.'" *Archipel* 78(1): 19–60.

———. 2012. *The Portuguese Empire in Asia, 1500–1700: A Political and Economic History.* 2nd ed. Oxford: Wiley-Blackwell.

Sulaiman, M. Isa. 1985. "Les Ulèebalang, les Ulémas, et les Ensignants de Madrasah: La Lutte pour le Pouvoir Local en Aceh de 1942 à 1951." PhD diss., L'École des Hautes Études en Sciences Sociales.

———. 1988. "Madrasah dan Pembentukan Elite Modernis di Aceh." In *Bunga Rampai Temu Budaya Nusantara PKA-3,* edited by Ismuha, 488–509. Banda Aceh: Seksi Seminar.

———. 1997. *Sejarah Aceh: Sebuah Gugutan terhadap Tradisi.* Jakarta: Pustaka Sinar Harapan.

———. 2006. "From Autonomy to Periphery: A Critical Evaluation of the Acehnese Nationalist Movement." In *Verandah of Violence: Background to the Aceh Problem,* edited by Anthony Reid, 121–48. Singapore: NUS Press.

Suryadi. 2001. "Shaikh Daud of Sunur: Conflict between Reformists and the Shaṭṭārīyah Sufi Order in Rantau Pariaman in the First Half of the Nineteenth Century." *Studia Islamika* 8(3): 57–124.

Sutherland, Heather. 1979. *The Making of a Bureaucratic Elite: The Colonial Transformation of the Javanese Priyayi.* Singapore: Heinemann.

———. 1995. "Believing Is Seeing: Perspectives on Political Power and Economic Activity in the Malay World 1700–1940." *Journal of Southeast Asian Studies* 26(1): 133–46.

———. 2011. "Whose Makassar? Claiming Space in a Segmented City." *Comparative Studies in Society and History* 53(4): 791–826.

Sviri, Sara. 2002. "The Self and Its Transformation in Sūfīsm." In *Self and Self-Transformation in the History of Religions,* edited by David D. Shulman and Guy G. Stroumsa, 195–215. New York: Oxford University Press.

Taji-Farouki, Suha. 2004. *Modern Muslim Intellectuals and the Qur'an.* Oxford: Oxford University Press.

Tarling, Nicholas. 2001. *Imperialism in Southeast Asia: "A Fleeting, Passing Phase."* London: Routledge.

Taufik Abdullah. 1971. *Schools and Politics: The Kaum Muda Movement in West Sumatra (1927–1933).* Ithaca, NY: Cornell Modern Indonesia Project.

Taylor, Charles. 1989. *Sources of the Self: The Making of the Modern Identity.* Cambridge, MA: Harvard University Press.

Taylor, Jean G. 2011. "Aceh Histories in the KITLV Images Archive." In *Mapping the Acehnese Past,* edited by R. Michael Feener, Patrick Daly, and Anthony Reid, 199–239. Leiden: KITLV Press.

van Bruinessen, Martin. 1990. "Kitab Kuning: Books in Arabic Script Used in the Pesantren Milieu." *Bijdragen tot de Taal-, Land- en Volkenkunde* 146(2): 226–69.

———. 2007. "Pesantren and Kitab Kuning: Continuity and Change in a Tradition of Religious Learning." In *Texts from the Islands: Oral and Written Traditions of Indonesia and the Malay World*, edited by W. Marschall. Bern: Institute of Ethnology, University of Bern.

———, ed. 2013a. *Contemporary Developments in Indonesian Islam: Explaining the "Conservative Turn."* Singapore: Institute of Southeast Asian Studies.

———. 2013b. "Postscript: The Survival of Liberal and Progressive Muslim Thought in Indonesia." In *Contemporary Developments in Indonesian Islam: Explaining the "Conservative Turn,"* edited by Martin van Bruinessen, 224–31. Singapore: ISEAS.

van Bruinessen, Martin, and Julia Day Howell. 2007. *Sufism and the "Modern" in Islam*. London: I. B. Tauris.

van de Velde, J. J. 1982. *Brieven uit Sumatra, 1928–1949*. Franeker: Wever.

van Dijk, Kees. 1981. *Rebellion under the Banner of Islam: The Darul Islam in Indonesia*. Leiden: KITLV Press.

van Doorn-Harder, Pieternella A. 2006. *Women Shaping Islam: Indonesian Women Reading the Qur'an*. Urbana: University of Illinois Press.

van Klinken, Gerry. 2009. "Decolonization and the Making of Middle Indonesia." *Urban Geography* 30(8): 879–97.

———. 2014. "Introduction: Democracy, Markets and the Assertive Middle." In *In Search of Middle Indonesia: Middle Classes in Provincial Towns*, edited by Gerry van Klinken and Ward Berenschot, 1–32. Leiden: Brill.

van Langen, Karel F.H. 1988. *De Inrichting van het Atjehsche Staatsbestuur onder het Sultanaat*. 's Gravenhage: Nijhoff.

van 't Veer, Paul. 1969. *De Atjeh-oorlog*. Amsterdam: De Arbeiderspers.

Verkaaik, Oskar. 2014. "The Art of Imperfection: Contemporary Synagogues in Germany and the Netherlands." *Journal of the Royal Anthropological Institute* 20(3): 486–504.

Vickers, Adrian. 2005. *A Modern History of Indonesia*. Cambridge: Cambridge University Press.

Voll, John O. 1994. *Islam: Continuity and Change in the Modern World*. New York: Syracuse University Press.

Walker, Andrew. 2012. *Thailand's Political Peasants: Power in the Modern Rural Economy*. Madison: University of Wisconsin Press.

Weber, Max. 1946. *From Max Weber: Essays in Sociology*. Translated, edited, and with an introduction by H. H. Gerth and C. Wright Mills. Oxford: Oxford University Press.

Wikan, Unni. 1995. "The Self in a World of Urgency and Necessity." *Ethos* 23(3): 259–85.

Wormser, Paul. 2012. *Le Bustan al-Salatin de Nuruddin ar-Raniri: Réflections sur le Rôle Culturel d'un Étranger dans le Monde Malais au XVIIe siècle*. Paris: Association Archipel.

Zainoe'ddin, H.M. 1928. *Djeumpa Atjéh*. Weltevreden: Balai Pustaka.

Zaman, Muhammad Q. 2002. *The Ulama in Contemporary Islam: Custodians of Change*. Princeton: Princeton University Press.

Zentgraaff, Henri C. 1928. *Sumatraansche Indrukken*. Offprints of a series of articles by "Z" in *Soerabaiasch Handelsblad*. Soerabaja: Soerabaiasch Handelsblad.

———. 1938. *Atjeh!* Batavia: De Unie.

Zigon, Jarrett. 2008. *Morality: An Anthropological Perspective*. Oxford: Berg.

———. 2009a. "Morality and Personal Experience: The Moral Conceptions of a Muscovite Man." *Ethos* 37(1): 78–101.

———. 2009b. "Within a Range of Possibilities: Morality and Ethics in Social Life." *Ethnos* 74(2): 251–76.

INDEX

Numbers in *italics* refer to illustrations.

A NOTE ON THE TYPE

This book has been composed in Adobe Text and Gotham. Adobe Text, designed by Robert Slimbach for Adobe, bridges the gap between fifteenth- and sixteenth-century calligraphic and eighteenth-century Modern styles. Gotham, inspired by New York street signs, was designed by Tobias Frere-Jones for Hoefler & Co.

Princeton Studies in Muslim Politics

Diane Singerman, *Avenues of Participation: Family, Politics, and Networks in Urban Quarters of Cairo*

Tone Bringa, *Being Muslim the Bosnian Way: Identity and Community in a Central Bosnian Village*

Dale F. Eickelman and James Piscatori, *Muslim Politics*

Bruce B. Lawrence, *Shattering the Myth: Islam beyond Violence*

Ziba Mir-Hosseini, *Islam and Gender: The Religious Debate in Contemporary Iran*

Robert W. Hefner, *Civil Islam: Muslims and Democratization in Indonesia*

Muhammad Qasim Zaman, *The Ulama in Contemporary Islam: Custodians of Change*

Michael G. Peletz, *Islamic Modern: Religious Courts and Cultural Politics in Malaysia*

Oskar Verkaaik, *Migrants and Militants: Fun and Urban Violence in Pakistan*

Laetitia Bucaille, *Growing Up Palestinian: Israeli Occupation and the Intifada Generation*

Robert W. Hefner, ed., *Remaking Muslim Politics: Pluralism, Contestation, Democratization*

Lara Deeb, *An Enchanted Modern: Gender and Public Piety in Shiʻi Lebanon*

Roxanne L. Euben, *Journeys to the Other Shore: Muslim and Western Travelers in Search of Knowledge*

Robert W. Hefner and Muhammad Qasim Zaman, eds., *Schooling Islam: The Culture and Politics of Modern Muslim Education*

Loren D. Lybarger, *Identity and Religion in Palestine: The Struggle between Islamism and Secularism in the Occupied Territories*

Augustus Norton, *Hezbollah: A Short History*

Bruce K. Rutherford, *Egypt after Mubarak: Liberalism, Islam, and Democracy in the Arab World*

Emile Nakhleh, *A Necessary Engagement: Reinventing America's Relations with the Muslim World*

Roxanne L. Euben and Muhammad Qasim Zaman, eds., *Princeton Readings in Islamist Thought: Texts and Contexts from al-Banna to Bin Laden*

Irfan Ahmad, *Islamism and Democracy in India: The Transformation of Jamaat-e-Islami*

Kristen Ghodsee, *Muslim Lives in Eastern Europe: Gender, Ethnicity, and the Transformation of Islam in Postsocialist Bulgaria*

John R. Bowen, *Can Islam Be French? Pluralism and Pragmatism in a Secularist State*

Thomas Barfield, *Afghanistan: A Cultural and Political History*

Sara Roy, *Hamas and Civil Society in Gaza: Engaging the Islamist Social Sector*

Michael Laffan, *The Makings of Indonesian Islam: Orientalism and the Narration of a Sufi Past*

Jonathan Laurence, *The Emancipation of Europe's Muslims: The State's Role in Minority Integration*

Jenny White, *Muslim Nationalism and the New Turks*

Lara Deeb and Mona Harb, *Leisurely Islam: Negotiating Geography and Morality in Shi'ite South Beirut*

Ësra Özyürek, *Being German, Becoming Muslim: Race, Religion, and Conversion in the New Europe*

Ellen McLarney, *Soft Force: Women in Egypt's Islamic Awakening*

Avi Max Spiegel, *Young Islam: The New Politics of Religion in Morocco and the Arab World*

Nadav Samin, *Of Sand or Soil: Genealogy and Tribal Belonging in Saudi Arabia*

Bernard Rougier, *The Sunni Tragedy in the Middle East: North Lebanon from al-Qaeda to ISIS*

Lihi Ben Shitrit, *Righteous Transgressions: Women's Activism on the Israeli and Palestinian Right*

John R. Bowen, *On British Islam: Religion, Law, and Everyday Practice in Shari'a Councils*

Gilles Kepel, with Antoine Jardin, *Terror in France: The Rise of Jihad in the West*

Alexander Thurston, Boko Haram: *The History of an African Jihadist Movement*

David Kloos, *Becoming Better Muslims: Religious Authority and Ethical Improvement in Aceh, Indonesia*